DR. PRITCHARD

THE POISONING ADULTERER

First Published by La-Di-Dah Publishing
This Edition 2017

Copyright ©W.M. Rhodes 2017
The moral rights of the author have been asserted.

Printed and Bound in The United Kingdom.

ISBN Print— 978-0-9957752-6-8
ISBN eBook— 978-0-9957752-4-4

DR. PRITCHARD

THE POISONING ADULTERER

Based on a True Story

W.M. Rhodes

TABLE OF CONTENTS

ACKNOWLEDGEMENTS

To my husband Paul, and all my family. All the team that helped to bring this book to publication. Thank you to my friend John Pearson for reading the drafts and for his encouragement.

A Special and well-deserved thank you to the talented artist Gareth Jenkinson for drawing the cover of the formidable Dr Edward William Pritchard.

W. M. Rhodes Filey 2017.

'Murder most foul, as in the best it is;
But this most foul, strange, and unnatural.'
Shakespeare.

DEDICATION

In memory of Mary Jane Pritchard, Jane Taylor, Elizabeth McGirn, the Pritchard children, and all victims of serious crime worldwide.

Many of which go undetected.

R.I.P.

INTRODUCTION

Dr Edward William Pritchard was born in 1825, in Southsea, Hampshire, he was the son of a navy captain and came from a family with distinguished naval connections.

On the surface, the doctor was well mannered and respectable. He was a kind and loving husband who adored his wife and family. Beneath that pleasant exterior, however, lurked a darkness that few would have guessed existed. He was a loathsome, arrogant man, a serial adulterer, and a sociopathic liar who would go down in history as one of Britain's most evil killers.

But, was the doctor innocent of such sinister crimes? What was his motive for murder? In a case that gripped the nation, reports suggest the possibility of even more victims.

Based on historical records, and written creatively, this account closely examines the Pritchard's lives and the circumstances surrounding the deaths of the sinister doctor's victims.

* * *

PART ONE

CHAPTER ONE
FILEY-JUNE 1854

Doctor Edward William Pritchard studied his reflection in the ornate gilt mirror. Except for his receding hairline, he liked what he saw, no wonder the ladies found him handsome and were instantly attracted to his charismatic good looks and his irresistible charm. His features were sharp and striking; his aquiline nose resembled the beak of an eagle giving him an aura of mystery, nobility, and courage. His deep-set eyes complimented his arched forehead perfectly and sparkled with a fleck of amber and green.

He took a bottle of Bloom of Circassia hair oil from the fireside table and shook it. The brown oil, a mixture of bear's grease and beef marrow was reputed to have talismanic properties. After pouring a few drops into his palm, he rubbed his hands together, and pulled a strand of hair, twisting and teasing it into place with his fingers until it concealed the crown of his bald head. He shook the bottle of oil once more and combed the mixture through his mutton-chop sideburns, the curling ends of his moustache and his long dark-brown beard.

He looked back at himself in the mirror. 'Perfect,' he whispered.

Edward reached into his waistcoat for his pocket watch. He checked the time and ran his long fingers over the intricate detail of the timepiece, an attractive gold skull and compass, presented to him on his discharge from the Navy.

On the wall, next to the picture of him standing beside an aborigine in the Pitcairn Islands and a portrait of Queen Victoria, hung his venal medical diploma, a recent purchase he had made at The University of Erlangen, Germany.

Lizzie, the maid, knocked on the door twice before she entered. 'Good morning, sir,' she said in her fine Scottish accent and bent down to stoke the fire. The doctor crept up behind her and pinched her plump bottom.

'I have three hours to spare before I officiate at the opening of the Crescent Hotel, soon to be the most fashionable hotel on the Yorkshire Coast.' He grinned at the blushing maid. 'How shall we spend the time, my dear?'

Lizzie McGirn giggled, 'Oh, sir, I am sure we can think of something.' She gave the doctor an ardent gaze, as her nimble fingers unbuttoned his waistcoat. 'We mustn't be too long; we don't want that sour-faced wife of yours catching us at it!'

The doctor grabbed her around the waist, put his hands inside her crinoline petticoat and pulled down her lace-trimmed pantaloons. He turned her to face him and drew his lips to hers. He untied the front of his breeches and roughly hurled Lizzie across the chaise longue.

'Now be a good girl!' His hot hands reached under her and pulled her close to him; one hand now pressed firmly in the small of her back as he straddled her from behind.

Lizzie's red curly hair cascaded over her rosy face; she smiled with satisfaction as her master finished his deed with a satisfied grunt.

The servants' bell rang from Mrs Mary Jane Pritchard's chambers. The doctor looked at Lizzie. A moment of understanding passed between them. Lizzie checked her clothing, opened the door, and left.

* * *

Edwin Taylor and his wife Constance stood outside their new hotel and admired its splendour. 'What a magnificent building!' Edwin said, as he put his arm around his wife's slender waist, and kissed her on the cheek.

'Edwin, you are smart. You have done such a marvellous job of organising the hotel. The interior is just fabulous.'

'Well, all thanks to John Wilkes Unett. Without his vision of what he called 'new Filey,' we wouldn't have these elegant buildings in this beautiful Crescent.'

'I can hardly believe that tonight is the opening night and already it's successful. You must look at this evening's attendance list. There are aristocracy and nobility from all over the country. The Honourable Admiral Cary and Major and Mrs Mitford have booked in for three extra days,' Constance said, proudly.

'Yes, a sign of things to come, my dear. Times are changing. People want to get away from the hustle and bustle of the city. They want time to relax and enjoy themselves. And who can blame them, just look around you,' Edwin said as he pointed out towards the magnificent gardens in front of the building. 'There is everything here. They can stroll around these beautiful pleasure gardens, or walk on the sands or the Brigg.'

'Absolutely,' his wife agreed. 'Very true, let us not forget we also have a spa well, where people can take in the benefits of the healing waters.'

'Spa waters!' Edwin grimaced. 'You'd not catch me drinking that! I fail to see how drinking something that tastes so bad can be good for you!' he said screwing his face up in disgust.

'Well, it doesn't suit everybody. Perhaps you would prefer to try one of the new bathing machines,' Constance said with pride, linking her arm through her husband's. 'We are the first hoteliers on this coast to own such things, and our guests can now experience a paddle in the sea if they wish. The ladies will love that.'

'Yes, it's bound to catch on here – it's all the rage in the south.'

Constance laughed, 'You never know, I may even have a go myself!'

'Oh, darling, I forgot to mention that the chap from the Filey Post called around earlier. They are going to do a piece in their paper on the opening. A full list of our distinguished guests will appear in the publication in a few days, as it will each week from now on.'

'Splendid, Edwin. I should imagine that there will be many a jealous hotelier in Scarborough and the surrounding areas when they see just who is staying at our prestigious hotel.'

'That is for certain. Taylors Hotel will be the jewel of the coast as will the town of Filey,' Edwin declared with satisfaction, as he looked at all the beautiful carriages parked along the full curve of the Crescent.

'Yes, Edwin, I could not agree more.' Constance looked at the cars, then turned her eyes across the German Ocean and admired the extensive views over the bay of this 'new' up and coming sea-bathing spa town. 'We best join our guests,' she said as she took her husband by the arm and proudly led him through the revolving door and into their new hotel.

* * *

Mary Jane Pritchard admired the Italian-style architecture of the new hotel; the classic interior equally as stunning with damask draperies and contrasting wall coverings, dazzling crystal chandeliers, and the elegant furniture throughout. The guests were dressed impeccably, especially the ladies who were without a doubt a vision of elegance and grace. Many wore low-cut dresses with Princess fronts made from glistening silk and ivory satin, lavishly trimmed with frills, ruched lace, and ribbons. She looked shyly down at her dress, a simple affair of dark green silk with an embroidered bodice, which she had painstakingly stitched herself just for the occasion. Knowing how important appearance was to her husband, she'd tried to look her best. Edward had complimented her and said that she looked a 'vision of loveliness', which made her happy, but she couldn't help feeling uncomfortable with her thick petticoat, layers of underclothes, hooped skirt and the tight corset which she wore under the whalebone bodice. She decided that fashion and displaying an aura of stylishness and sophistication with an illusion of ease and comfort came with a price and not one of convenience.

Mary Jane wished she had the same confidence Edward had; she envied the way he could talk in a proficient and intelligent level on almost any subject with anyone he encountered. In comparison, she often felt inferior to him. Sometimes she didn't understand why he had chosen her. He could have had his pick of any woman in the land. Mary Jane reminisced about the ladies' ball in Portsmouth where she had first met him. Her Uncle David Cowan had insisted she join him. David was an ex-naval surgeon, a widower who loved to party. He asked her parents' permission to take his niece out on the town and hopefully find her an appropriate partner. With apprehension, they and Mary Jane agreed, she hadn't attended many parties having led a sheltered life in Edinburgh. There had been a couple of outings with men, but nothing serious. Sometimes she resigned herself to think she would be an old maid. Her parents hoped that Portsmouth might broaden her horizons and that as this was the town of the Navy headquarters, it may prove to be a perfect place to find a suitable suitor.

A week ago, Edward had returned from a voyage to Africa aboard H.M.S. Hecate. Following a couple of days in Portsmouth, he had reluctantly met up with his elder brother, Dr Francis Bowen Pritchard, who suggested they go to the ball at the Assembly Rooms held by the ladies of the town in honour of naval officers. He had accepted, despite trying not to socialise with his elder sibling too often, as Edward found Francis too much like his father for his liking: loud, arrogant and rude. Edward also didn't like the fact that again, like his father, his brother had reached the rank of Captain and a medical officer in the Royal Navy, something Edward had always aspired to.

Mary Jane had noticed Edward as soon as he entered the room, she had been sitting quietly with her uncle when Edward came over to her table and introduced himself as Dr Edward William Pritchard, a physician in the Royal Navy. His credentials were impressive as he explained his family background of an impressive line of Captains and Commanders in the Navy. Mary Jane had never seen a man as handsome; her parents would approve of this soft-spoken, yet confident, well-mannered man. He had an aura around him and a commanding presence. When he asked her to dance Mary Jane thought him a perfect gentleman; like the heroes, she had read about in her favourite gothic novels. To her amazement, they were inseparable all evening, dancing, and she found herself relaxed and comfortable engaging in stimulating conversation.

The following day Edward called at Mary Jane's uncle's house. David Cowan had been a 'big fish' in the Navy and an important character. Edward believed that the means to success would be through his friends, and the little spinster niece had sparked his curiosity. A plain dull girl, nothing like his usual type, quite the opposite in fact; nothing about her attracted him to her physically, but on the other hand, she did have a slender pleasing figure. On reflection, he supposed that she could be a valuable asset. Edward turned over the idea of a union with this girl; he supposed that she did have wifely qualities. A shy, innocent girl with a gentle character. More importantly, she had the right connections and would make an entirely respectable doctor's wife. In his usual style, Edward flattered Mary Jane with grandiloquent compliments. No doubt she would be easy to dominate, and would soon be under his spell.

Mary Jane thought it most unusual for a man to make ceremonial calls unless he had intentions. At first, she had been apprehensive, Edward could have his choice of any woman, they doted on him with his long flowing beard, sparkling eyes and full red lips, so she found his interest in her difficult to understand.

In the autumn of 1850 after a short courtship, Edward proposed, and they were married a few months later with the full approval of her family.

* * *

From the other side of the room, Edward engaged in deep in conversation with Captain Mitford. Mary Jane could not hear what they were talking about, but it must have been interesting as the Captain appeared to be heavily engrossed in Edward's conversation. As she looked at her husband, she felt a fluttering in her stomach. He looked so handsome dressed immaculately in crisp white pleated shirt and narrow trousers, which made him look much taller. He had spent time choosing a striped plum waistcoat which accentuated the rest of his attire. To her, nobody compared to Edward, with his boyish good looks he stood out as the best-looking man at the party by far. Mary Jane's reverie came back down to earth as the chairman's gavel banged down loudly on the table.

'Order, order!' the chairman roared in a deep rasping voice as the gentry around the table quietened.

Edward rose to his feet and grasping the opportunity; he bellowed, 'I propose a toast to the Army, the Navy, and the brave men combating this Crimean War.' He raised a glass to the audience while furtively catching the eye of his host, the beautiful Constance Taylor who stared at him attentively. He had to admit he enjoyed the attention, knowing that his wife's eyes were on him, but thought it best not to linger too much on his host's gaze – although intrigued at her obvious flirtation.

'Hear, hear,' the crowd chorused.

Not wanting to miss a chance to boast about his accomplishments, Edward announced, 'I am proud to say I have once borne this commission and served amongst its rank. Those who live across the water will soon testify to the power of the British Isles and will succumb to the force of our artillery.'

The crowd rose from their chairs and gave the doctor a standing ovation. Vice-chairman Carter brought the group to order with the thump of his gavel on the oak table. 'The Mayor of Scarborough cannot attend this evening. He sent his apologies by letter.' A grumbling of 'typical' murmured through the crowd.

Edward remained on his feet. 'Let us stand, and raise our glasses to the success of the Taylor's Crescent Hotel.'

* * *

CHAPTER TWO
VILLAGE LIFE AND FAMILY SCANDAL

A typical intermittently cloudy spring day in May, Mary Jane sat on a bench in her garden in Warburton House, Hunmanby and watched her four-year-old daughter Jane Frances, whom they had nicknamed Fanny, and two-year-old son Charles Edward as they played on the lawn. Edward had taken over the position of General Practitioner from Doctor Thomas Haggard and his son Francis, and with a deposit loaned from her parents, they had bought Warburton House – a large house in the centre of the village. Mary Jane felt happy there. She watched in delight as her children innocently pulled the daisies from the grass screeching with joy as they pulled off the flower petals one by one before throwing them up in the air. Mary Jane smiled. Her children were so precious to her. Her first-born 'Fanny' with her blonde ringlets, blue eyes, peachy cheeks and perfect temperament was 'such an adorable child' everybody said. Her mind wandered, as she thought of her middle daughter, Zillah Catherine, who had died from a fever aged just three months. Would Zillah have looked like her and Jane Francis? Or darker like Charles and Edward? Unfortunately, she would never know. Following her child's death, Mary Jane had been inconsolable for quite some time and still longed to hold Zillah in her arms, to smell her scent. To watch her grow; she wanted for the things she knew she would no longer be able to do.

Now five months pregnant again Mary Jane knew she had to take things easy, the thought of losing another child inconceivable. The peace of her garden provided the solace. Many a day she sat and watched the garden change with the seasons. Now the beginning of spring and daffodils began to burst through the softened ground displaying their delicate pale-yellow trumpets as they swayed softly in the wind like a parade of young chorus girls. Small creatures and insects crawled with confidence, no longer confined to their winter resting place. Mary Jane felt so much better in spring, like the garden, she came alive. Watching nature cheered her soul, such a simple, yet a fascinating sight.

The people of the village tarnished this idyll. Mary Jane found them strange. Meddlesome. It seemed that the social infraction of many of the women in the community depended upon the need to spread village gossip, with no regard to whether the rumours were true or not. This idle chin-wagging tested Mary Jane's patience to the extreme; she understood that chatter had both a positive and adverse effect, which could sometimes unite fractions but went some way in destroying the harmony of the village. In this isolated village knowing your business topped many people's priorities. The people here were far nosier than the people of Scotland or those from the south. What infuriated her most was the way they stopped talking, looked away, or covered their mouths with their handkerchiefs, whenever she walked into a shop or walked through the village. They were also full of strange superstitions that Mary Jane refused to follow. 'Don't wash your hair on a Saturday, don't comb your hair on a Sunday, don't sit out in the sun!' She felt most uncomfortable at the church on a Sunday with Edward and the children. She began to think that she and her family were on show in a cattle market or a raffle. One day, she could have sworn she heard Edward's name mentioned in an underrate way, but as always, the person concerned stopped talking as soon as she realised that the wife of her subject matter had overheard her.

Mary Jane had been brought up to believe that uttered words may cause harm by themselves and that she should never engage in the uncontrolled use of a loose tongue, whether the conversation proved genuine or not. It just wasn't done.

Like her, Edward wasn't keen on the village people, 'inbreeds' he called them; 'prick one and they all bleed!' was his favourite saying. Still, they were his patients, so he had to conform, and they were both grateful to her parents for securing this opening for Edward.

Thanks to their help and investment, Mary Jane and the children were more settled. The future looked good for her expanding family now. She thought back to when they had first married and had to live separately. Edward had just started on his medical career and needed more experience; he did not have the means to leave the Navy and provide a home for his wife. He'd no choice but to continue to cruise as a Naval Surgeon with H.M.S. Hecate. Mary Jane did not mind. They had both agreed that it would not be forever, she just counted the days until her handsome husband would return so that they could settle down permanently and start a family.

From an early age, Edward's family had expected him to follow in the family tradition and train as a doctor. Edward didn't mind. If he had the guts, he would have liked to have pursued a career as an actor. Edward preferred to spend his time at the theatre whenever the chance arose. Sometimes he would watch the same production over and over. He even memorised the leading actor's lines and became so engrossed in the performance. He never forgot his father's reaction when he discussed the possibility of him going on the stage and treading the boards. 'A bloody actor; don't be bloody ridiculous. Real men don't want to prance about on the stage. I've never heard anything so preposterous in my life!' his father had bellowed at him, so that had been the end of that. Besides, his brother had already succeeded in passing his medical exams, and Edward had no choice but to follow his lead.

His father had many contacts and at the age of fifteen arranged for him to take an apprenticeship with surgeons Edward John and Charles Henry Scott. Unfortunately, and much to Edward's disappointment the doctors were not impressed by the standard of Edward's work and left Edward astonished when they terminated his internship with no permanent position offered. Unperturbed, Edward ignored their rebuttal and told his father a different story and appraised himself as a diligent student. He dreaded the day when his father found out the truth, which would be inevitable.

Not wanting to lose face, he applied for as many openings as he could. On applications, he claimed to have studied at King's College London for three years. His grandfather's old comrade John Pascoe had put a word in for him, so he had been fortunate enough to be admitted into the College of Surgeons, and like the rest of his family, he achieved his wish and was accepted as an assistant surgeon in the Royal Navy. He lived in fear that one day this fabrication of the truth would come to light, which, if it did, would have seen the end of his career and his reputation. So far, he had sustained this secret from his family, the Navy, and the medical authorities.

Since moving to Yorkshire, life for Edward and Mary Jane had improved. Edward had opened a second surgery on North Street in Filey. He had also accepted an appointment as medical officer to the local workhouse, or The No 3 District Bridlington Union, its official name. Mary Jane couldn't be prouder of her husband's achievements. She just wished that she could stop this niggling cloud of doubt that had been hovering around her the past couple of months, but why she felt this way she didn't understand

* * *

A few weeks ago, Edward, had been flabbergasted to receive a letter from his father together with a newspaper cutting from the Hampshire Advertiser dated Friday 8th April 1856. At first, he thought that there must have been a death in the family, as he had not received any correspondence from his family since leaving the family home in Southsea when he'd gone to join the Navy. His father had not gone into any detail and had merely said. 'I hope you and the family are well. Please read the enclosed. Obviously, I am sure you will understand the need for the household to stand firm through this, your brother needs moral support, he is distraught.'

Edward read the newspaper article, not believing the words printed on the paper. His brother, 'the brother that could do no wrong', the brother Edward had been passed over for all his life. The illustrious Captain Francis Bowen Pritchard, a staff surgeon in the Royal Navy, was the subject of a Court Marshall. There was to be a trial in under a month's time in Portsmouth on a charge of cruelty to the sick. 'Cruelty to the sick,' Edward repeated with astonishment. A serious charge indeed. Edward thought of his father – he must be furious with his favourite son's name splattered all over the papers. Edward laughed uncontrollably imagining his father's face as he read the paper. Edward imagined him shouting abuse at the reporter's words, his face purple, his eyes bulging, the veins on his forehead would be protruding, as he sweated profusely with pure rage. It was ironic; there was Edward the proverbial 'black sheep' tending to the needs of the sick and the weak, and his distinguished 'intelligent' older brother who allegedly beat the poor folk senseless. His father's son without a doubt! The Hon Rear Admiral Richard S Dundas would chair the Court Marshall aboard the H.M.S. Victory. Perhaps, he should go and give his brother the support he needed. 'Yes, why not,' he said, chortling to himself.

* * *

CHAPTER THREE
SOMETHING'S NOT QUITE RIGHT

Friday was market day in Filey. Mary Jane felt nauseous as she observed the colourful stalls, she just couldn't keep her food down now, no sooner had she eaten something she threw it all back up. Concerned that she could be contracting the dreaded enteric fever. Mary Jane didn't want anything to affect this baby. Edward had tried his best to reassure her.

'It is understandable, darling, and hardly surprising in your condition. Perhaps you have caught a slight fever; you are of a delicate disposition. I prescribe bed rest. Would it be a good idea if your mother came to stay for a short while, a visit from her may lift your spirits?'

Mary Jane's depressed mood lifted. How thoughtful of Edward, he knew how much she missed her family, she couldn't wait to see her mother again.

The town square was awash with the cries of street-sellers, organ grinders, and the clopping of horses' hooves, which echoed throughout the small seaside town. Impish boys cocked their heads to one side, as they observed the crowd, their grubby pockets bulging with the russet apples they'd pinched off the fruit stall; undetected, they'd crawled beneath a stall's canvas tarpaulin to eat their pickings.

Mary Jane untied the drawstring of her purse, took out a silk handkerchief, and mopped her brow. The layers of her crinoline dress rustled in the chilly February breeze. She raised the folds of the fabric just above her kid-leather boots, conscious not to show her ankles as she crossed the bustling road. She felt restless and eager to return home to get some rest.

Through an elegant lace-covered window of the Crescent Hotel, Constance Taylor observed Mary Jane furtively, watching her every move. Constance turned to her husband Edwin, who was absorbed in organising the guest list for the annual Society Ball.

'Edwin, what are your thoughts on Doctor Pritchard and his wife?'

'Why do you ask, my dear?' Edwin looked up through his gunmetal half-moon spectacles.

'No reason, dear, I wondered on your opinion of them, that's all.'

'They both seem all right to me.' Edwin exclaimed. 'Edward is a charming fellow and a competent doctor; he's a medical officer at the Bridlington Union. I hear he is doing a marvellous job helping the unfortunate tykes in the poor house.'

'He considers himself important,' said Constance disgruntled, 'he has taken up writing a local journal now… A visitor's guide to Filey… I ask you. What does he know about such matters? He's from the south!'

Edwin removed his spectacles and arched his dark bushy eyebrows. 'You disapprove, my dear?'

'Well, I ask you, he has even written medical articles for the Lancet!' she replied, with an air of moral superiority.

'Well, my dear, he is a doctor, and therefore knowledgeable on such matters!'

'Well, yes, I suppose he is, but there is something not quite right about him. Something I cannot put into words.'

'His wife is most agreeable and comes from a well-respected family. Scottish, father's a silk merchant. I understand.'

Constance ignored her husband's vacant stare as she walked across the room and picked up her embroidery from the chair.

She thought it best not to discuss the conversation she had overheard in her dressing room when she'd eavesdropped on the servants gossiping about the clandestine relationship between the doctor and Lizzie his servant girl. Lizzie had told the others of her fabulous moments of passion with her experienced lover. Rumours often escalated from the lofty servants' quarters, imagined and distorted into malicious gossip, but, as Constance thought of the doctor, she nibbled down hard on her lower lip and her nerves tingled with desire as a ripple of longing tore through her limbs.

* * *

CHAPTER FOUR
AN ULTERIOR MOTIVE

Edward sat beside the open grate in the small unventilated infirmary. The embers glowed orange before they died and disintegrated into a crumbling grey cloud of dust. How he hated being a doctor for the Bridlington Union! He looked around the cramped room with its single lavatory and water closet which served thirty men. For the last week, there had been no water, and no trap in the toilet, so the foul stench soon became putrid and offensive. Not for the first time, he asked himself why he worked in a place like this. He thought of his brother and his upcoming trial. Surely, a man of his standing would not be found guilty of such an offence. A shock, yes, but if the people he'd allegedly been abusing were anything like this lot, then he could quite understand him losing his patience with them.

He despised the clanging of the workhouse gates. He couldn't abide the deafening thud of the lump-hammers as the destitute poor smashed granite rocks for the railways. Neither could he get used to the offensive decaying smell that oozed out of every orifice of their untreated flesh and their festering wounds. They sickened him. He loathed the constant howling and wailing of the feeble-minded, the uselessness of the blind, and the immobility of the crippled. He wanted more from his life. He deserved it. After all, the Pritchard name counted for more than wasting his time in a place like this.

Like many others of his social standing, Edward believed that the poor had no place in the higher echelons of Victorian Society. They should be grateful for a place to sleep and general medical relief, and food for their ragamuffin offspring. They were such improvident people, squandering their money on drink and gambling. 'Fools,' he said, shaking his head in annoyance. He thought of his father – Captain John White Pritchard a mean, nasty man with a bombastic streak to him. He came from a family of Navy captains, and could not differentiate between work and home. Captain Pritchard would lose his temper at any little thing, usually directed at Edward. Edward still bared the scars of the beatings he had received by him as a child; he shivered at the thought of him taking off his leather belt with the big silver buckle, or flexing the beech cane he loved so dearly. It would not have been so bad if Edward remembered why he had received the beatings in the first place.

Unlike his 'bright' older brother Francis and his quieter younger siblings, Edward had not found his schooling easy, but he had persevered and managed to scrape a decent education. Both his parents were strict, and they had ruled the house as they would an army and demanded that as parents they should be obeyed. Edward decided many years ago that he would never treat his children in the same regimented manner his parents had handled him. Neither of his parents had much time for Edward or their other children; they preferred to spend their time and money on their first-born son. Edward could not remember ever receiving any affection from his parents, particularly his mother, a cold and distant woman. He so tried to please them, but, for most his childhood, his parents ignored him. A burden to his family, Edward blended into the background

As he watched the tired grey faces of the penurious people around him, he couldn't understand why these people could not buckle down and sort themselves out. These paupers had no self-respect; the way they lived their lives disgusted him.

Edward detested the sight of them, but thankfully, he would not be around the impecunious paupers much longer. He would show his parents just how smart he could be. Thanks to Constance Taylor, who had persuaded her husband to rent him two small vacant rooms to use as consulting rooms at a property Edwin owned nearby, at a peppercorn rent. This arrangement suited him and the coquettish Constance well.

* * *

In the past six months, Constance had been suffering from recurring melancholia; she decided that she should consult Doctor Pritchard. With the hotel doing so well she did not get to spend time with her husband Edwin as often as she liked, she missed his company, perhaps she needed to take up a hobby of some kind, anything to snap her from this depressed mood.

'Constance, a pleasure to see you,' said the doctor as Lizzie ushered Mrs Taylor into the surgery. 'Please come in.' He waved his hands towards a leather chair as he gestured for Constance to sit across from him near the fireplace.

'Thank you, doctor.'

'That will be all, Lizzie.' He dismissed the maid with an official nod of his head. Lizzie narrowed her eyes and glared at him as she closed the door behind her. He turned to his patient.

'Please, my dear, call me Edward.'

Constance bowed her head in acknowledgement as she sat down elegantly. The sharp smell of medicinal alcohol filled the air, making Constance feel a little giddy, her heart fluttered as her body temperature soared. Why did she feel this way, after all, she knew of the doctor's reputation with the ladies? Still, for some reason, the doctor dazzled her, and her nerves tingled.

'Constance, you look rather hot, shall I fetch smelling salts?' the doctor said tantalisingly, aware of the effect his attention had on his patient.

'Please move closer.' He deliberately brushed past her ensuring that his arm touched her shoulder as he moved Constance's chair towards him.

Edward bent his head forward so that his breath blew softly against Constance's cheek and in a small raspy voice, he said, 'I have been waiting for us to be alone together.' A sly, dry smile spread across his face.

Constance blushed and looked away; she could smell the delicate aroma of the doctor's hair as his fingertips softly caressed her temple. His arms were strong as he steadied her in the chair.

'Constance, I suspect that your medical problems are psychotic. Still, I think it best to undertake a thorough examination to confirm my findings. Please go behind the screen and get undressed.'

With apprehension, Constance did not go behind the screen. Instead, she sat seductively in the chair, and looked the doctor in the eye as she unbuttoned her blouse; her nimble fingers trembled, as she fixed her attention on the handsome doctor's face. Edward removed the pins from her chignon, allowing her hair to fall around her smooth shoulders.

He could see the nervous tension in her expression and took his chance. His hands cupped Constance's voluptuous breasts as he expertly stroked her pale, smooth flesh with tender strokes of his fingertips; he bent down and brushed her neck with his lips. Constance turned her head to meet his, their eyes locked, their noses touched. Instinctively, she parted her lips, and the excitement stirred in the pit of her stomach as Edward's tongue explored her mouth with a passionate kiss.

Edward knew what to do. Two months ago, he'd put money in investments that had failed to come to fruition, and he had become embroiled in a shady share broking business. If he wasn't careful, he stood to lose everything; his reputation would be ruined and in tatters. He knew that Constance could be easily 'persuaded' to ask her husband to lend him a 'small sum' to tide him over, confident that Constance would not want her husband to know of her afternoon infidelity. Edward smirked to himself, as his confidence returned. Without hesitation, he regained his composure and removed his hands from her fervent body.

'Constance, I need to ask you a favour. I am embarrassed to ask, you understand, but I am a little low on funds, and I need a short-term loan. I would be obliged if you could ask your husband to 'lend' me two hundred pounds.

'Well… I, err…' She hesitated. 'I could ask I suppose. Short-term you say,' Constance said, taken aback by his sudden request.

'Yes, just for a few months. And please don't worry; I will say no more of our little indiscretion!'

'Our indiscretion. Edward, you wouldn't. It would ruin me!'

Edward looked into her eyes and patted her hand as if reassuring a child.

'No, of course not, my dear. After all, we would not want your husband to have grounds for divorce for adultery, would we?'

Embarrassed at her behaviour, Constance realised that this awful man had taken advantage of her and ultimately manipulated her. Her usually pale complexion flushed and turned ruby-red, she felt cheap and ashamed. Humiliated, she buttoned up her blouse as the doctor spoke.

'For the record, my diagnosis is that you are suffering from female hysteria most common in ladies of your age. My wife and her dear mother are resting with similar symptoms. I will prescribe you a tonic of Batley's Sedative Solution; this will make acts of shall we say 'violence' less likely. Which, my beautiful Constance, could well be the case in your delicate condition!'

Constance felt her temper rise. Why had she allowed this rascal to take advantage of her? Now she had no choice but to do as he requested and convinced Edwin to lend him money. Annoyed, she snatched the script from his outstretched hand. Her eyes bulged as her anger raged: 'You are a charlatan and no doubt a quack!' she yelled as she gathered her belongings and stormed from the room, not bothering to wait for the maid to see her out.

* * *

CHAPTER FIVE
MAY 1856 THE COURT MARSHALL

The Court Marshall of Edward's brother Francis opened on 2nd May 1856. Edward travelled to Portsmouth a few days before the trial. For the first time since his childhood, he stayed at his childhood home. The house never changed and was just as he remembered it with its pointed pitched roof and gothic style lancet windows. The gorgons above the front door still to this day instilled terror into Edward. The pictures of his family's ancestors hung in the hall; the family resemblances were evident. The house smelled damp, old and musty. The chair coverings were frayed and not in their best condition.

He didn't see much of his mother, now old and infirm, she stayed in her room most of the time. He did go and see her, but she barely recognised him, and the conversation soon became awkward and strained, so he did not see much point in spending a lot of time with her. After all, she had done the same to him as a child. On the other hand, he saw more of his father than he would have liked. The man continued to be a constant reminder of why he had wanted to leave home at such an early age. An obnoxious and domineering man who followed Edward everywhere, pacing up and down the house, shouting some obscenity or another, usually directed at the 'plebeians' in the Navy. 'Blithering idiots, how dare they accuse my son, of such a thing – cruelty to the sick. I mean, I ask you. I'm a Commander; I fought at the battle of Trafalgar. No, they don't know just who they are dealing with!'

Edward soon became tired of hearing his father's constant chanting and his terrible, vile temper. It reminded him of being a child sitting in his father's study accused of something he hadn't done. He had spent many an hour sat in silence, staring at the plain white wall, while he waited for his father's flap-gold face to stop bellowing abuse, and the dreaded moment when he would take off his leather belt and whip him with it.

He had slept in his old room, and that seemed somewhat strange. Nothing in there had changed much. It even had the little peephole in the interconnecting door where he used to spy on his sister, Emma-Louisa as she got undressed for bed. He loved teasing his sister, 'show me yours, and I'll show you mine.' She enjoyed playing that game did Emma-Louisa. In fact, if he remembered correctly Emma-Louisa was the first person to touch his penis. She hadn't wanted to, but she soon gave in to Edward's demands. Something to do with threatening to tear the head off her favourite doll. He could still picture the look of fear and disgust as she wiped the sticky white liquid from her hands onto her dress. She got used to it after that.

'Emma-Louisa, you've broken it!' Edward had teased laughing his head off.

The day of the trial finally came. Edward and his father sat together in the public gallery, amongst some relatives of the victims and general spectators. Francis entered the dock. He looked terrible, and in Edward's opinion, he had aged rapidly since the last time he had seen him. Both brothers had a liking for beards, but this is where the resemblance ended. Edward, the more attractive sibling, had a far more distinguished and cultured look to that of his elder brother, whose thin, wispy grey beard let him down. Edward moved a strand of hair across his forehead, grateful that he still had some hair, and was not entirely bald like his brother. Francis took after his mother's side, whereas Edward and his younger brother Charles resembled their father. Edward studied Francis's face and his overall demeanour. His complexion was ruddy and his cheeks puffy around his shapeless chin. His eyes had deep hollows around them, and he had wrinkles on his forehead. His nose, Edward thought, had changed considerably and was now bulbous with pimples. A drinker Edward diagnosed. By the looks of him, a heavy drinker too. He had seen it all before with the people in the workhouse, and with his association with the Temperance Society.

Edward watched his brother's face turn the colour of clay, as the judge read out the charges.

'Captain Francis Bowen Pritchard, you are a surgeon of her Majesty's steamship Rattler, and you are accused of the following. That between the years of 1850 and 1856 you did not perform your duty aboard ship proficiently, and that you did not treat the men in your care with sufficient kindness or medical attention when they were in a bad state of health. How do you plead?'

Francis looked the judge in the eye and stood as straight as he could. 'Not guilty, your honour,' he answered awkwardly with all the impressiveness of tone he could command.

Edward's eyes widened as he realised the extent of the offences. He listened attentively as the judge deliberated on the details of the serious charges and the names of the fifteen men involved – all of whom were now deceased. There were also some lesser accusations of cruelty. Edward could not believe what he heard. Fifteen! Disgraceful; his brother had inherited his father's mean streak, and Edward knew that Francis must be guilty of all charges He couldn't see him worming his way out of this one. He laughed to himself for once in his life thankful that his elder brother had overshadowed him. At least he had learned to be more compassionate towards his patients.

After calling a high number of witnesses for the prosecution, all of them telling their tales of drunkenness and neglect, Francis Bowen Pritchard made his defence. He had been briefed on what to say and did not dramatise events too much, relying instead on his expert witnesses to support his statement.

At precisely twelve o'clock the court vacated for deliberation and did not reopen until five the same day.

'May the accused please stand!' Francis took to his feet; and looked the judge in the eye.

'The court believes the first charge against Captain Francis Bowen Pritchard has not been proved.'

Not been proved! Edward sat stiffly in his chair and gasped as his mouth fell open in shock. He could not believe it. Typical. For him it was a kick in the teeth, and brought back memories of his childhood, taking the rap for something his 'bright' brother had done. Edward was so incensed he almost didn't hear the ruling on the second charge.

'Guilty!' Ha, at last, the favourite son had been cornered. His father jumped out of his seat and true to his character couldn't resist banging his hands on the back of the chair in front of him and shouting abuse at the commanding officer. Heads turned to look at the old man causing such a commotion.

'Poppycock. These charges are bloody ridiculous; my son is not guilty!'

'Order, order; this court is still in session!'

The court fell silent as the judge delivered the punishment. Once again, Francis had been let off easy. The reprimand he received in comparison to his crime would be that his name would appear at the bottom of the list of surgeons who served the Royal Navy, and he would forfeit all claims to an increase in pay to which he would otherwise be entitled, between September 1851 and May 1856. Edward could almost see the colour return to his brother's face. With light relief, he looked over at Edward and smiled. The same smile of satisfaction he always gave him when he knew he had got away with something. The punishment would not bother him. He retired soon anyway, and the money would not be an issue to him. He had married well. His wife Annabella had plenty of money. The one satisfaction that Edward could gain from the situation was that the trial and his brother's guilt would be reported in the press, and would tarnish his previously unblemished reputation. Edward prayed that the news of his brother's guilt would not travel to Yorkshire. He knew what the gossip would be like there, and he would hate to be tarred with the same brush and be labelled 'guilty' just by association.

* * *

CHAPTER SIX
1859-THE ROOT OF ALL EVIL

Edward sat at the desk in his private office at Prospect House, Filey, a residence he had rented for the summer. The post had been delivered earlier in the day. He studied the parchment envelope; the postmark said, Glasgow. He could tell by the official red wax seal of Lewis & Lewis, Esq, that it must be important. He put his reading glasses on, took a mother-of-pearl letter opener from his drawer, and sliced the letter open. It read:

Glasgow
26th July 1859
Lewis & Lewis, Solicitors

Dear Doctor Edward Pritchard,

We act on behalf of our client, Clydesdale Bank. The Bank is concerned that your overdraft exceeds the agreed principle sum of one hundred and thirty-one pounds, twelve shillings and four pence. We would be obliged if you could remit this amount in full to the Bank forthwith.

Yours faithfully

Edward was not amused. He wiped beads of sweat from his forehead with the back of his hand and shook his head in disbelief. Annoyed, he screwed the letter into a tight ball and threw it on the floor.

'Nonsense,' he exclaimed. 'How dare they, who do they think they are? I am a man of means. I am a doctor – a Freemason Master of the Royal Lodge no less!' His face flushed red with anger; he took a bottle of the finest malt from his cabinet and poured himself a glass.

'Bloody scoundrels,' he shouted venomously. He stood and looked through the window. He contemplated his position as he watched the elegant ladies with their chaperones strolling through the beautifully laid out gardens. An abundance of coloured parasols twirled in the July sunshine. Small children sat on the grass picking daisies to make chains as they looped the flowers together. A well-dressed man sat on the bench and looked across at Carr-Naze and the rugged rocks of Filey Brigg, his straw boater dipped over one eye, protecting his view from the intense rays. They were just ordinary people getting on with their day; Edward wished he could be one of them. How nice it must be to be 'ordinary' without a care in the world.

After a moment Edward retrieved the crumpled letter from the floor, it felt flimsy in his hands, yet there was nothing insubstantial about its wording. No, this time he had tested the bank's patience, long enough, there was no going back now, he was well in the thick of it.

'What am I to do?' he asked himself, as he reached for the bottle of malt, and refilled his glass. Reflecting on his situation, he took stock of his position, affirming that his social standing had much improved over the last four years since he moved to Yorkshire. His practices were also doing well, but with a wife, three young sons, a daughter, and a household to provide for, his finances were perpetually unstable.

He had given his time freely in the town with talks and lessons in literacy for the benefit of the uneducated farmers and fishermen at the town's Mechanics Institute. It proved an excellent way for him to promote the book he had just written: *A Visitors Guide to Filey*. It supported the town and highlighted the medicinal advantages of holidaying in a spa resort. He continued to be surprised at how well he got on with these people, despite him having very little in common with them.

Edward would always be grateful to his wife's family for their continuing generosity. Mary Jane's father, David, a wealthy retired silk merchant had settled five thousand pounds in trust for his daughter's expenses when she married Edward. Her father would not be amused if he knew that his son-in-law, a medical doctor, had spent the lot and was now deep in debt.

'Damn the blasted stock market!' he bellowed. He twirled the deep amber liquid around his glass and then poured himself another. Edward needed to think of a plan to resolve his unfortunate financial situation. Constance Taylor could no longer be considered reliable, not without raising her husband's suspicions. As the golden liquid burned his throat, he glanced at the stack of newspapers on his bookcase. The first headline read of the execution of Doctor William Palmer, known as the Rugeley murderer. Intrigued, Edward read the article in full, his curiosity fuelled.

At that moment, an idea came to him: Constance's mother, Betty, who lived alone in Hunmanby was one of his patients. Betty and her husband William had been a speaker at the Temperance Society. William had died four months before, and his widow was still in mourning. Edward tipped his head back and finished his drink. He opened his medicine cabinet and took out a small brown bottle and a clear glass phial. He put them in his pocket, grabbed his coat, and hurried to the stable to saddle his horse.

* * *

CHAPTER SEVEN
THE DEMISE OF TEMPERANCE BETTY

Betty Chandler sat in the parlour talking to her beloved cat when the doorbell chimed; she had not been expecting visitors. It was most unusual for someone to call on her unannounced. With curiosity, Betty placed her tapestry on the table at the side of her chair and moved towards the window. With trepidation, she peered through the curtains.

'I wonder who is calling on us at this hour,' she said to the cat who had jumped onto the windowsill to look.

Betty was surprised to see Doctor Pritchard standing there.

'It's the doctor, Sooty. I wonder what he wants?' The cat soared from the windowsill and sat on the rug in front of the grate.

'Two minutes, doctor,' Betty said in her thick croaky voice as she hobbled to the front door. Her eyes were dark and dulled with age, and her back ached with months of wearing the dark black crepe mourning veil, which had not helped.

'Doctor, what a surprise. Please come in. Can I take your hat and coat?' Betty was pleased to have company. In the last three months since her husband had died, she had not seen many people, just her daughter Constance, and the congregation at church on Sunday.

The room was sparse, except for black banners on the wall – a typical display of mourning. Edward watched the black cat as its glass-like eyes followed him around the room with hatred and suspicion. Edward loathed cats, especially black ones. 'Vermin,' he said under his breath as he stood on the cat's tail, making it look like an accident. The cat yelled, sprang up, and fled out of the open door.

'What brings you here at this hour, doctor? It's not Constance, is it?'

'No, no, my dear, Constance is in fine fettle, maybe a little worried about you and she suggested that I come out and see you, and as I was passing, I thought I'd call in. Constance said you are rather weak and frail and that you are not entirely yourself! I have the perfect tonic that will nourish and strengthen you. It is ideal for both the body and the brain; it has done wonders for my wife and her mother!'

Betty watched the doctor pour a generous measure of tonic into a glass he had picked up from the dresser. She couldn't understand why Constance had mentioned her ailments to him, from what her daughter had told her she did not much care for the doctor; still, how thoughtful of her, Betty needed perking up.

'Don't you worry yourself, Betty my dear, you will be back to your old self in no time. Your husband would be proud of the way you have handled his affairs since he passed. Such a generous man and much missed at the Temperance Society. He did so much to encourage the impoverished working class, helping them to see the error of their ways and stop the demon drink from ruining their families. William helped many of them keep sober and prove their self-respect!'

Betty did not much care for the thick dark syrup, it tasted bitter, but if the doctor thought it best, then she had better gulp it down fast. The doctor took the glass from her wrinkled parchment hand and poured her a generous second measure. Watchful not to let Betty see the glass phial that contained a mixture of antimony aconite and brandy as he took it from his pocket, opened it, and emptied its contents into the glass.

Edward could see that Betty's eyes were drooping. He needed to work fast.

'Betty, your husband bequeathed the sum of one hundred pounds to the Temperance Society. He wanted to spread the principles of total abstinence to the working class, and to encourage others to denounce the demon drink, and advocate the benefit of teetotalism, and clean living throughout this province,' Edward said with sincerity.

Betty stirred with a jolt. At first, she didn't quite hear what the doctor said. Her memory returned. William had left an envelope containing two-hundred and fifty pounds, which was his entire life savings. Over the years, they had scrimped and saved and fought against indulgence. The Temperance Society had been their passion. William and Betty had one daughter – Constance – and she and her husband were wealthy and did not need money. Constance did not even realise that they had any savings. With trepidation, she stood and steadied herself as the doctor held her arm and guided her into the drawing room. Betty hesitated as she lifted the lid of the small tin chest where William had kept his valuables.

For a few minutes, she let her fingers caress the initials on the top that her late husband had etched before his death. Was she doing the right thing? Would her William approve? With apprehension, she looked at the doctor, then back at the envelope. William would do anything to help the cause. Before his death, he had signed the pledge and joined The Band of Hope, to try to save working-class children from the parents of drinkers by teaching them the importance and principles of sobriety. Happy with her decision, she nodded to herself, took out the envelope, and gave it to the doctor.

'I know my William would want his savings to be used to help spread the word of the power of temperance within the community. I am sure that you, doctor, will make sure that it is.'

'Betty, of course, I will. Yours and William's generosity holds no bounds.' He took the envelope from her weak hand and put it in his waistcoat pocket. 'You know that this bequest will help so many people to get back to the right way. God's way.' Taking out his pocket watch, he said. 'My good lord, where does time go? I am sorry, my dear, I must leave.' He guided Betty to her bed-chamber where he helped her to lie down on the bed, covering her clothed body with an embroidered eiderdown. Betty did not stir. With speed, Edward retrieved the glass from the dresser and put it in his pocket. In the kitchen, he found a similar glass and left the empty bottle of Brandy and Batley's Sedative Solution next to it. The black cat's eyes looked fiercely at him as he climbed on his horse and rode away.

* * *

The following morning, Constance felt horrified when Doctor Pritchard called on her with the news that her mother had died, she had visited her mother a few days before, and despite having a cold, her mother had been in good health. 'Dead, she cannot be dead, I saw her such a short while ago, and she seemed fine!' Constance wept, as the doctor took her elbow and guided her to a chair she pulled away from his grip, even the touch of his hand made her wrench.

'Constance my dear, you have had a shock, perhaps you need to lie down? Have you been taking the tonic I prescribed, or shall I fetch your smelling salts?'

Constance had a nagging suspicion in the pit of her stomach. Ignoring the doctor's remarks, she lifted her head and looked Edward in the eye.

'Tell me, doctor, how did my mother die?'

Edward sensed the accusation in Constance's voice. Not wanting to fuel any misgivings he said, 'Your mother had secrets, my dear.'

Constance narrowed her eyes and shook her head in disbelief. 'What are you implying? She had no secrets!'

The doctor averted his eyes to avoid Constance's stare. 'Well, one cannot always tell. More than likely she hid her secret for many years!'

'Hid what?' Constance said as she became impatient and waved her arms as if conducting a symphony.

'Overindulgence, my dear. Your mother was an addict.'

Constance gasped and screeched the words, 'An addict – I don't think so. An overindulgence of what?'

'Drink and opium spirit. I am afraid her body could not stand the strain, the overindulgence weakened her heart.'

'My mother did not drink; she hated drink!'

'Sad, I know. I can understand your denial and your frustration, and the memory of your sick father; God rest his soul. Such a fine man and him being a prominent member of the Temperance Society, and a fully signed up member of The Band of Hope. Your mother's failure of fortitude will not be taken well by the members and most certainly not by the hierarchy!'

Constance bowed her head, she knew her mother was frail and lonely since her father died, but drink, no; as her daughter, she would have known.

The doctor curled his whiskers in deep apprehension; he knew he must be firm so as not to raise suspicion.

'My dear, I am sure you understand that as your mother's doctor my prerogative is to determine the cause of death… for the death certificate. Sadly, though, the verdict of over-consumption of alcohol will not bode well!' He looked Constance straight in the eye.

At once Constance realised her dilemma, she did not want her mother's good name tarnished, not worth it in this 'gossip' fuelled village, so with hesitation, she asked him. 'Have you signed the death certificate? I don't want a scandal.'

The doctor moved closer to her, his distinguished whiskers brushed against her cheek, as his warm hands moved down her cleavage and firmly cupped her pale, cold breasts.

'Well I could but — I am not too sure — perhaps if we could forget about the money owing to your husband, then I think we can think of something to get around the formalities, just like last time.'

Constance unwillingly nodded her head. Edward signed the death certificate and handed it to her, his fingers caressing her hand.

Suddenly, the door slammed open, and Edwin stormed into the room, his face contorted with rage. It twitched, as the veins in his forehead protruded and throbbed at his temple. His blue eyes turned dark as he glared at his wife with suspicion, acid practically dripping from the corners of his mouth. 'What does he mean just like last time?' Turning to the doctor, he yelled. 'Take your filthy hands off my wife!'

'Edwin, Edwin, it's not my fault; it's his. He's blackmailing me!' Constance burst into tears. 'My m…

mother is dead, and he wants money – your money!' she stuttered. 'He wouldn't sign the death certificate until I agreed. He said he would tell you we were having an illicit affair!'

Edwin had heard enough, darted across the room and grabbed the doctor by his lapels. He opened the front door and threw him down the stairs.

'Get out of my hotel — then pack your things and get out of this town or you will live to regret it! This is not the first warning of your philandering ways. This town will not stand for your type! You are a scoundrel and a liar and nothing but a medical Munchausen! Now go or I will tell your wife of your debauchery, and the medical authorities: The Brethren, and the Church. You're finished. Now get out!'

Edward was bruised and shaken, knowing that he had met his match he resisted the urge to retaliate. Instead, he adjusted his collar, shook his head, and avoided eye contact with his accuser.

'It will be my pleasure…' Edward said pompously. 'I have had all I want here; this town is far too boring and insular for the likes of me!'

A couple of the town's busybodies who were walking by witnessed the incident. Edward, shrugged the situation off as he stood and dusted himself down, and with his usual charm said, 'Sorry, ladies, a complete accident, just a slight misunderstanding – one of the privileges of my professional status!'

* * *

Edward was seething. A medical Munchausen indeed! The nerve of the man. Leave town? What would he tell his wife?

How would he explain it to his family, to his in-laws? He thought about this on his way home. Whipping his horse vigorously in anger, taking out his frustrations on the poor defenceless animal, he dug his stirrups into the animal's flesh as he rode her at speed.

Edward tied his horse up outside his house and grumbled as he stormed through the front door.

'Stable that bloody horse, will you, Lizzie. I have seen a tortoise move faster than that useless creature.'

Lizzie realised that something serious must have happened to her master for him to be in such a foul mood. He had apparently left somewhere in a hurry as his face was red and blotchy, and his hair and beard damp by the incoming sea-fret. The maid didn't want to antagonise him further; she could tell by the sinister look on his face that would not be a good idea. Instead, she tried to console him and reached up to touch his face and kiss him on the lips.

'Get your filthy hands off me!' He pulled away from Lizzie's affections.

'Well, I'm sorry I'm sure; what has got into you?' she rebuffed.

'What's got into me... that's an understatement! Everything that's what! I think it is time that we all left this small-minded town and moved to Scotland, at least there the people are normal.' He stormed out of the door and climbed the stairs to bed, leaving a bewildered Lizzie behind him.

* * *

CHAPTER EIGHT
A GOOD FRIEND

Edward did not sleep well. He got up early and skipped breakfast; he really could not face anybody today. He needed to take his mind off everything so on impulse; he decided to take a ride into Bridlington and call on his friend, Charles. He had met Charles at a lecture he had given at the Mechanics Institute in the town last year. Charles had enjoyed Edward's account of his daring adventures with the Navy. Edward could tell that Charles had a soft spot for him. He respected him. Edward had a good idea why, as he remembered how attentive Charles had been when he recalled his colourful exploits.

'I have plucked eaglets from the eyries in the deserts of Arabia, I have hunted the Nubian Lion in the prairies of North America.'

Immediately, Edward realised that to make a good friend of Charles would stand him in good stead. Charles came from a wealthy family, old money, the class of people able to maintain their wealth over multiple generations. Charles had become engaged to the daughter of a family friend. A harmonious union, which would keep the family in the position to which they had become accustomed, and hopefully the couple would produce an heir for the future to carry on the good family name. But what his didactic family did not know was that Charles harboured a secret. Edward knew that Charles had an uncontrollable weakness for good-looking men. This 'secret' Edward intended to exploit for all it's worth, and that would not come cheap.

Charles's wedding was set for the following year and expected to be a grand and lavish affair. Before the big day, Charles had planned a business trip to Egypt and the Holy Land. He would need a medical assistant to join him on his travels. Edward was just the man he needed.

'Edward, I have a proposition for you. How would you like to accompany me on my overseas journey and be my medic?' Charles asked as he looked at Edward with affection.

'Overseas? Well, yes, it is very sudden, but I suppose I could consider it. If, of course, the terms are favourable. I would obviously have to deliberate with my wife and family,' Edward said, realising that this perfect opportunity would get him out of the tight spot he had created.

Edward smiled. He looked at Charles's bony fingers, as Charles nervously began twisting and turning his emerald encrusted gold ring around suggestively.

'Of course, you must discuss this proposition with your family. It is a fantastic opportunity for someone in your position, and is bound to enhance your career.' Charles reached over to Edward and softly whispered in his ear. 'I will feel so much safer with you at my side, and I would like nothing better than to lie awake with you for endless hours and listen to the fascinating tales of your life and your various exploits, to the sound of the sea crashing against my cabin.'

Edward nodded his head, and proclaimed, 'Please make the arrangements, but my wife and children must be taken care of.' Charles had fallen straight into his hands, as he knew full well he would. If he managed Charles correctly, he could be his meal ticket for life. 'I would be foolish not to accept such a generous opportunity. I would need a monetary advance… Shall we say two hundred and fifty pounds, to put the wheels in motion, you understand.'

'Of course, my good man.' Charles moved his chair closer, placing his hand on Edward's thigh. 'Good man! I will make the necessary arrangements; you must come and meet me for lunch tomorrow, where you will meet my good friend Lavinia, she will prepare you for what your duties will be. We should be away for nine to twelve months. Shall we discuss the practicalities?'

* * *

The past few years had been hard for Mary Jane. Edward had returned from his overseas position two months ago, and she was already pregnant again; she had missed him. Mary Jane wanted another little girl, someone to clothe in beautiful dresses and ribbons and bows. Her eldest child, Jane Francis (Fanny) was settled with a new resident governess named Helen McDonald, who stayed at the house Wednesday until Friday to give Fanny one to one tuition. The young teacher had worked wonders with Fanny, and as a result, her studies had flourished. The boys were growing so much and were becoming rather boisterous. They had calmed down a little since their father returned. They needed the discipline of their father, someone to respect and look up to.

While Mary Jane had enjoyed her time living in Yorkshire, she wanted to be nearer to her family, and the children's education would be better for them in Scotland, she worried for her three boys. Her eldest son Charles did not get on at all with the local Yorkshire children, 'they are just not my type mother' he had said. As his mother, she agreed with him, 'I know, darling, they cannot help it. They do not know any better!' She had tried to reassure him knowing what Charles meant. His younger brothers Horatio and William felt the same way.

Living in the country, the schooling in Yorkshire had been elementary. A 'Ragged' school they called it, due to the tattered clothes which some of the poorer village pupils wore. The school was strict; the teacher, Miss Tempest, was a thirty-seven-year-old ugly spinster with mean eyes, a pointed chin, and thin lips. Miss Tempest came from a military family, and it showed through her teaching – running her classroom with the military precision of a naval commanding officer. Her children were petrified of speaking out of turn in class, in danger of being put on the punishment log, given detention, or worse whipped with the dreaded cane. Once Horatio had come home in tears with three red welts on the back of his legs, punishment for 'shoddy work' the tight-lipped teacher had declared.

Both she and Edward hadn't wanted their children educated in Hunmanby or Filey – far too narrow-minded for them – Mary Jane wanted them to have a broader aspect of life than that which a small Yorkshire village could offer. The age gap in the school varied and was so vast that her youngest son was expected to do the same lessons as pupils four years older than he. No wonder they deemed his work unsatisfactory. It didn't seem fair to Mary Jane; her children were her babies, and she wanted more for them.

After a few months on the market, Warburton House sold. It would have gone sooner if Edward hadn't insisted that the valuer had priced it too low, and insisted on putting a higher price on it, refusing to take any less. Eventually, he had no choice but to renegotiate the sale price. Now, with the house sold, they could move on with their lives in Glasgow. Temporarily, they rented a house at 11, Berkley Terrace. Luckily, Lizzie, the maid had agreed to stay in employment, and accompany them to Glasgow. Mary Jane found her such a comfort and the children loved her dearly.

* * *

Edward had watched the young governess for a few weeks. Understandably, she found him attractive, although she had not precisely reciprocated any feelings towards him. It was just the way she looked at him. He could sense it. Time for a change anyway. Lizzie was willing but lately had become slightly bolshie and tedious. He needed a new challenge, more excitement. This evening the young governess was sleeping over alone in one of the servants' rooms. Edward intended to consummate their relationship on a more intimate level. He could tell she was waiting for him to make the first move.

Once his wife was sound asleep, he crept upstairs to the attics where the servants slept, checking carefully that no one had seen him. He quietly turned the knob on the door where he knew the young governess was sleeping and entered the room. Helen MacDonald was sound asleep; her innocence showed on her beautiful face as it rested on the white cotton pillow. Her eyelids firmly closed and her breathing deep and relaxed, all the muscles in her face and body were entirely at peace, like a baby in its first throes of slumber. For a brief second Edward felt a pang of guilt: should he walk away, let the young girl sleep? Still, he couldn't help himself; he gently stroked the sleeping girl's hair. Such beautiful hair, the colour of precious gold and so soft and silky to the touch. Not a twitch, not a spasm, barely any movement of her breasts rising and falling with each intake of air such was the depth of her oblivion. He had to see them, if not touch them. With two careful fingers, he lifted the collar of Helen's nightdress; there they were alert, so small and white, with tips like rosebuds. Edward was brought back to reality as Helen opened her eyes wide and let out a scream. Startled Edward grabbed the pillow and put it firmly over Helen's face to stifle her cries. 'Hush my dear; I am not here to harm you.'

Helen regained her composure and grabbed the startled doctor by his collar with a sturdy grip.

'My father warned me about you! Now get out of my room right now, or I will tell him and my brothers that you attempted to rape me! I will no longer work for you in this house or any other house. I pity your wife and children, they all deserve better. Now get out!'

Meekly, Edward walked out of the door, and as he turned to go down the back stairs, he saw the door of Lizzie's room close. Lizzie had heard him. That's all he needed.

The next morning Helen MacDonald left the Pritchard household claiming that her father was unwell and needed her. Edward knew different, he was relieved that at least Helen had not breathed a word to his wife, but her quick departure had cost him a pretty penny.

* * *

CHAPTER TEN
A DEADLY FIRE-11 BERKLEY TERRACE, GLASGOW. 6TH MAY 1863

Edward jumped at the sound of a rat-a-tat-tat on the door. 'Enter,' he said. He locked the malt whisky away, just as Lizzie entered the room.

'Ave, you got a minute, sir?'

Edward looked at the gilded carriage clock on the mantelpiece. Lizzie lifted his spirits, yet today her expression seemed almost solemn. Her complexion was blotchy, and her plump breasts strained against her clean starched apron. Edward loosened his cravat as he felt his natural desire to ravish her.

'I have plenty of time, my dear,' he slurred as the effects of the malt whisky took its hold. He grabbed Lizzie around her waist and drew his lips to hers as he gyrated himself against her.

Lizzie pulled away, put her hand on his chest and stopped him from unbuttoning his waistcoat. 'Not today, Edward!' she said, 'sex is the last thing on my mind right now!'

He watched her with surprised indignation as she took his hand and placed it on her swollen belly.

'I'm with child. Your child.'

Edward sat back down in his seat; his mind drifted as he considered his plight. He knew what he must do. Under no circumstances could he risk his reputation on the mistakes he had made with this, this servant! His demeanour changed, and he put his arm around her shoulder.

'Lizzie… Lizzie do not fret. I cannot have a child out of wedlock – a bastard child. What would that do to my standing in the community? Tomorrow, my dear, we will sort this out. Do not vex – I guarantee that you will not feel a thing, trust me!'

Lizzie was not happy, but she knew there was nothing she could do, she had agreed to travel to Glasgow with the doctor. Yorkshire agreed with her, the sea air and simplicity of life suited her, but Scotland was her home and in her blood. Besides the doctor had promised her that one day they would be together, so back to Scotland, she had gone.

Insulted with Edward's response, her fiery temper got the better of her, and she snapped and yelled at him.

'Don't you try to get one over on me, I know you. I want money, or I'm spilling the beans. Don't think I don't know why that stuck up governess left so quickly. Her father wasn't ill at all. I saw you creeping into her room at night. That was what did it! And it's time you told that docile wife of yours, what's going on between us, cos if you don't tell her then I will!'

Edward pacified her saying that once Mary Jane had the new baby, then he would come clean and confess his relationship with Lizzie and that they would be together and start a family of their own, but now was not the right time. 'We have years ahead of us, Lizzie; we will have lots more children together.'

Reluctantly, Lizzie agreed, and the following day she lay on the couch in the doctor's surgery. Despite this being the same couch, she had frolicked on many times before with her zealous master, this time it felt different. A cold shudder trickled down her spine as she glanced around the room as if seeing it for the first time. Her stomach turned to ice as terror encompassed her in a vice-like grip, horrified at the collection of knives and needles.

Edward opened his medical bag and took out a brown bottle containing chloroform. He poured a generous amount of the liquid on a piece of rag and swiftly placed it over Lizzie's mouth and nose. 'This will stifle any pain and make you quite insensible,' he said.

Lizzie drifted in and out of consciousness. Edward put the rag into Lizzie's mouth to stifle her screams. He checked her pulse; happy that Lizzie was unconscious, then covered her with a blanket, took a book from his reading desk and ripped out a few pages. Carefully placing the remains of the book on the floor, he then put the torn pages on top of the blanket around Lizzie's body. He took a bottle of gin from the drawer of the desk and took a swig before he straddled his sleeping lover, removed the rag, and poured the Gin into her mouth, intentionally spilling it onto the blanket and the torn pages of the book. Taking a box of matches from his pocket, he hesitated, too late to turn back now, he said to himself. As the smell of sulphur wafted through the air, he dropped the match, and the fire ignited at once.

Edward wiped his hands on the rag and stuffed it into his pocket. He looked around the room, satisfied that the insurance company would take him at his word and not find the situation suspicious. He would explain that Lizzie liked a drink and was in the habit of reading a book in bed. She often found herself too intoxicated to turn off the gas; she could not keep away from the demon Gin and had passed out on the sofa bed in his surgery, and she must have started the fire by accident.

He took a final look at Lizzie and was shocked; she was awake! A pale red-white glow spread across her ashen face as the flames soared around her tearing up her torso. Her eyes flickered as they bulged from their sockets and froze in a glassy state of horror. Her screams were to no avail – she could not move.

Edward ensured that nobody had seen him, then, after locking the door to the surgery, he left the building and glanced back as the fire was now beyond his control. The windows blackened, popped and cracked as he hurried down the deserted street, the nauseating odour of burning flesh filling his nostrils. Edward knew that the twisted, tortured look of terror on Lizzie's face would haunt him forever.

* * *

A few hours later Edward was awakened by his son Charles, banging on his door, 'Papa; the police are here — the surgery, it's on fire.'

'Fire at the surgery, good gracious. I will be straight there!' Edward put his clothes on as fast as he could and accompanied the waiting policeman.

'Lizzie!' he shouted as he battered on the door. 'Liz…zee are you there…' He coughed the words out, overcome with smoke, which irritated his throat. He pulled the rag from his pocket and covered his mouth.

Sergeant Dunbar could smell something strange, but he could not figure out what. Did he smell it before the doctor took the cloth out of his pocket, he wasn't sure, perhaps it could have been the smoke. The sergeant wasn't happy; something was not quite right here.

'Is there anybody else in this house, doctor? Your wife, where is she?'

'My wife is in Edinburgh visiting her family. Lizzie is the only person here. It has to be her in the surgery, she often goes in there to read, and sometimes she falls asleep, it's the gin you see, she likes a tipple does Lizzie!'

The sergeant was puzzled to find the door locked from the outside. Determined to get into the room to try to help the girl he pushed hard on the door with his broad shoulders; at the second heave, the door sprung open to a sickening sight. All that was left of Lizzie was a charred mass of flesh and bones. Edward felt sick to his stomach at the sight of her. Covering his nose with his hand, the stench of scorched flesh overpowered him. Amongst the dense and suffocating smoke, Edward took the key from his pocket ensuring nobody saw him. Lizzie was lying on her back as he had left her, her left arm dangled lifelessly towards the floor like a stick of black pudding in a butcher's shop window. The flesh had burned off her breast, and Lizzie's ribs were visible. In comparison, Lizzie's legs were uninjured as her stockings and the blanket that had covered her had protected them, but her toes were black and charred.

Even the floor under the bed had burned through exposing the joists of the floor below. Edward did the sign of the cross on his temple and across his shoulders, and then bent down and picked up the blackened remains of an empty bottle of gin, raising his eyes in a knowing glance towards Sergeant Dunbar.

The sergeant was not happy. That poor girl. The state of her – burnt beyond recognition; the stench of the girl's charred flesh would stay with him a lifetime. Her sort never learned. All the years that he had been in the force he had seen so many families ruined by the curse of the Gin bottle. For the sake of a few pence folk thought they could escape from cold, hunger and boredom through an empty bottle of the spirit. Still, his instincts told him that there was something amiss here. He sensed that the doctor would claim for loss of property and valuables to his insurance company. The sergeant was due to retire next week, but before he did, he would ensure that his successor and the procurator fiscal knew about that locked door and how the key had mysteriously turned up in the doctor's hand. Most suspicious in his opinion. Hopefully, they would one day get to the bottom of it all.

* * *

CHAPTER ELEVEN
SUSPICIONS- SEPTEMBER 1863

Ever since the fire Edward had not been himself. He was always agitated and ill-tempered. Mary Jane could understand him being upset over Lizzy's death, they all were. Perhaps he had taken her death so much to heart, as he was the one at home the day she died. Maybe he felt helpless, wishing he could have done more to save her? She had tried her best to console him and reassure him that her death was not his fault. That there was nothing, he could have done. Lizzie was partial to the demon drink; the so-called 'mother's ruin' and that was the real cause of her death. Unfortunately, all her sympathy fell on deaf ears. Mary Jane thought it best to let him sort it out in his way. Her mother had put her mind at rest. 'Edward is the sensitive type, and we all grieve in different ways' she reassured her. Still, the children had noticed their papa's change of mood, it worried them. Mary Jane did not like to see the children upset.

There was no doubt about it; Edward's nerves were frayed to the core. He had trouble sleeping, and his business was beginning to suffer, his patients were losing confidence in a doctor who looked like death itself, and who couldn't concentrate or keep his eyes open. He had been foolish. Greedy. After the fire, he had the idea that he could solve some of his financial worries and hatched a plan to claim for some expensive jewellery, saying it was in the same room as

Lizzie when she died. Trouble was he hadn't known when to stop; and submitted a claim to the Caledonian Insurance Company for £700. The insurance company were sceptical and refused to reimburse him for all the loss. 'Not a trace of any jewellery was ever found' the letter had said. A fraudulent claim was declared.

'Scoundrels!' How dare they try to tarnish my reputation in such an unfounded and blatant manner,' Edward said out loud, twisting the hair of his long beard nervously.

He was also sick of his wife's nagging. 'Edward, there is nothing you could have done… Edward, nothing can bring Lizzie back. Edward… Edward…' He just wanted her to shut up and stop talking about the blasted fire, and for her not to mention Lizzie's name again. He realised that she was concerned about him, but, if only she would leave him be.

He decided the best thing to do with the insurance company was to write a letter of complaint. He was relying on the insurance payment. His bank was on his back again.

After weeks of discussion, the company had at last decided.

While Edward strenuously disagreed with the insurance company's report, he had agreed to drop the claim for the jewellery but failed to see how they could repudiate his right for damage to property. After a degree of consultation, they agreed to this and paid out one-third of Edward's original claim under the terms of the policy. 'I should bloody well think so!' Edward said with relief. After all, a verdict of misadventure had been recorded by the court. It wasn't as if he had got away with murder!

* * *

CHAPTER TWELVE
MARY MCLEOD-WHITSUNDAY 1864.
22 ROYAL CRESCENT, GLASGOW

Fifteen-year-old Mary McLeod was fed up with fetching and carrying after her drunken skunk of a father. How she hated the lecherous old sod with his wandering hands. Fortunately, Mary had a sharp left hook and had managed to fight off the dirty scumbag's advances up to now, but she'd had enough.

Mary had no siblings, so cooking (when she had any money for food) and skivvying was left up to her. Her sick mother had died a few years earlier, downtrodden and deprived, that old bugger had sucked the life from her. If her ma had known what the dirty sod was up to now, she'd have killed him. Dead at thirty-five was her mam. There was no way Mary wanted the same life. He didn't even work, the lazy sod! Too drunk most of the time – nobody would employ him. No, she'd had it. He could rot in the workhouse for all she cared.

Gathering a few possessions together, she wrapped them as neatly as she could in a pillowcase, not wanting the old bugger to come home from the pub and stop her. Mary took her last walk down the rickety old stairs and onto the dirty unpaved streets of the Gorbals, hitching up her one good dress as she tried to avoid the privy pails, and not get caked in mud and sewage that flowed openly in the foul-smelling, rat-infested street.

Her neighbour Nancy was draping a wet sheet over the iron railings. 'Do us a favour, Nance, tell that miserable bastard of a father of mine that I'll not be coming back!'

Nance said nothing, just nodded her head and continued hanging out her washing.

As she walked into Glasgow's Royal Crescent, Mary took a deep breath of clean, fresh air and looked up at the giant Corinthian white pilasters of number twenty-two. It was a beautiful house. The wages weren't much, but at least she'd have a roof over her head and food in her belly. The family had not lived there long, but they seemed respectable. There were four children of various ages and a young baby; there would be plenty to do. The master of the house was a doctor so they must be decent, caring folk.

Edward studied the girl, she was a pretty little thing, just how he liked them, dark-haired and petite. Mary had the most striking green eyes he had ever seen; her nose turned up at the end giving her a cute elfin mischievous look. Tiny brown freckles scattered across her cheeks. What Edward liked most about this new girl was her slender figure and small waist. His wife Mary Jane, who, after the birth of their daughter Elizabeth five months ago, now reminded Edward of one of the rhinos he had hunted in Namibia. Well, she had the same sized backside.

Mary liked to get up early to get on top of her chores; she had a routine. The first thing she did was to open the shutters to the breakfast room window. Then she took up the hearth rug and swept the room. Her next task was to clean and light the fire, so the room was warm and ready for the family when they gathered for breakfast. Mary opened her housemaid's box taking out a folded piece of rough cloth which she laid on the carpet next to the stove; she then cleaned the ashes from the grate, sifting the bigger ones into the cinder-pail ready to be reused in the kitchen. Mary took out her black-lead and brushes and vigorously polished the hearth. She was an expert at fire making; she'd had no choice – it was the only way she could keep her mum warm when she'd been dying in her cot in the squalid one-room tenement they'd all shared. She arranged the cinders at the bottom; then she stripped bits of newspaper followed by pieces of dry wood. The secret of a good fire was to lay the coals to the back of the grate and leave air in the middle, so the smoke went up the chimney and did not engulf the room.

'Perfect,' the doctor said. He had spent the last five minutes watching Mary as she bent down, the roundness of her buttocks visible through her starched white apron as she swayed back and forth cleaning out the fire. Edward felt instantly aroused.

Mary was far from stupid; she knew that the doctor had a soft spot for her; she had seen the way he looked at her. If she played her cards right, she could be his mistress. Mary sniggered to herself imagining the looks of that miserable old cook Catherine Lattimer; that should wipe the sneering grin from her ugly face. They would have to treat her differently then and not like she was a nobody, a drunkard's daughter from the Gorbals.

'Sorry, sir, I didn't see you there.' Mary lied, as she jumped to her feet and straightened her apron.

'No need to apologise, my dear. I did not mean to startle you. Mary, can I ask you a question?'

'Course you can, sir, you can ask me anything,' Mary answered, feeling the blush come to her cheeks.

'Can you read?'

'Ready, sir, well, yes a little… my mam taught me a bit before she got ill, I've not had any need to read books, though, just newspapers now and again.'

'Time to learn, my dear, the world is changing, – all women should be able to read proficiently. I shall teach you. Come to my study at 3 pm; we will start the lesson then.'

'Won't Mrs Pritchard mind,' Mary asked.

'She won't know; she has once again taken the children to visit her mother in Edinburgh. We have the house to ourselves!' Edward answered. A glimmer of excitement and expectation flickered in his eyes.

Mary hesitated for a few seconds, as she made her way up the back stairs to the doctor's study. Although she knew what she was about to engage in, she couldn't help feeling nervous. Twisting her hands together, she plucked up the courage to knock on the door.

'Come in, my dear.'

Mary took a deep breath and entered the room. The doctor sat behind a dark mahogany desk, a pile of newspapers in front of him. He got up from his chair as Mary entered the room. With a confident stride, he walked towards her; his eyes firmly fixed on hers. Suddenly they were side by side. Mary felt a shiver go down her spine.

The air in the room became tense; the doctor had a strange gleam in his eye. This tiny elfin girl did something to him; she was very different from the rest. His libido was on fire. Gently his hand came up, and he caressed Mary's cheek. He whispered in her ear, 'Your skin is as soft as the finest silk. I want to touch it all over.'

Mary may have been young, but she was an expert in the ways of the world. Coming where she came from and with a father like hers, Mary had no choice but to learn fast. No way would she settle for second best. She knew exactly how to play this philandering doctor.

Petulantly, Mary slapped Edward across the face so hard he stumbled backwards. She ran at him like a cat pulling his hair and tugging on his beard.

'I will tell my father on you.'

Edward knew Mary's father and knew that he would give two hoots about his daughter. This girl was wild like an alley cat. He was captivated. He grabbed her by her wrists and kissed her forcefully on the lips.

'What of your wife?'

'My wife will know nothing about our little rendezvous. From now on, this will be a regular role for you. You are my girl, and I am your master. Let us not forget that I am teaching you to read!'

They gazed at each other intensely. Slowly, Edward moved closer until his face was inches away from hers. Mary could feel the warmth of his breath on her cheek. His long beard tickled her face gently. He moved his hand to Mary's chest caressing her breast through her dress. A rush of heat stirred in Mary's loins and spread throughout her limbs. Edward leant forward and gently moved a stray hair from her face. In an instant, his mouth was on hers, his tongue probing the inside of her mouth deeply in a long passionate kiss.

His fingers were hot and trembled with excitement as he unbuttoned the back of Mary's dress. Mary's pale breasts sprung free. Edward squeezed them both in turn, then bent down to kiss each one. With his lips on her breast, he tenderly nibbled her nipple. Mary was excited and purred softly like a happy kitten. There was an aching in her groin, a sensation Mary had not felt before, she liked it. With one eye watching Mary's face Edward bit down hard on her nipple. Mary gasped as she fought back the tears. She did not want to show that secretly she was enjoying the pain.

'Mary my darling, please do not cry!' Edward said, kissing the tears from her face. 'I did not want to hurt you. I just want to give you pleasure.' Gently, he kissed the tears from her cheeks. With strong arms, he pulled her up from her feet and before she knew it Mary was sprawled out on the floor. Her long, black, maid's dress had risen, showing her stays. Edward knelt beside her, and with one hand, he ripped her drawers off. His hands were warm as he caressed her thigh, his fingers reaching up inside the dark triangle of black hair. He pushed her legs apart as wide as they would go.

Mary was utterly helpless and could not move, and her breathing became harsh as Edward pinned her down with his left arm firmly across her chest. Wriggling her body, she tried to manoeuvre into a more comfortable position, but he was too strong. Edward undid the front of his breeches unleashing his generous erect member. Skilfully, he pinned Mary's legs down with his, placed his member at her core, and roughly entered her.

Edward gasped with pleasure, as he roughly grabbed Mary's hips pushing himself in and out of her slender body. Mary winced as the pain was so intense it tore through her as Edward pummelled her. In the past, she had previously had the odd fumble with a stable lad but had never gone this far before. She decided it was best to go with the rhythm; then the pain became easier. At times, it felt like she was being ripped in half as Edward plunged deeper and deeper into her, pumping so hard until he was exhausted. Finally, he grunted and spilt his seed inside her.

Edward looked up at Mary's face. Happy that she was smiling; he smiled back, acutely aware that he had taken her virginity.

* * *

CHAPTER THIRTEEN
UNETHICAL MEANS

Mary Jane worried about her husband and money. Outwardly, they seemed to be comfortably well off, but Mary knew that if it weren't for her father helping them out, then it would be a different story. A shudder ran down her spine as she thought of her family. Where would they all be without her parents? Edward was trying his best; he had just had a degree of ill fortune. With a bit of luck, things would turn around for the better soon.

For months now, Edward had regularly sent letters to various eminent men seeking suitable employment, but for some reason, his fellow doctors treated him with suspicion and contempt. Mary Jane could not understand it. Her poor Edward wasn't sleeping too well and often woke in the middle of the night shouting out her name in excitement as if something was troubling him. 'Mary. Oh, Mary.' Last night Edward had woken her with his rantings —and she was unable to get back to sleep, what with worrying about Edward and the children (who were a handful at the best of times), Mary Jane felt tired and weary; the stress of everyday life was taking its toll.

* * *

Edward sat in his study and opened his mail. 'More parasites demanding money!' He muttered as he opened the envelopes.

Surely, amongst all these requirements, there must be some good news? He desperately wanted to be known amongst the Scottish medical circles and was hoping to join the Faculty of Physicians and Surgeons. Last week he had sent his application together with testimonials from famous English doctors. Taking great pride with his statement, he wrote:

I have had opportunities in almost every part of the world. I have gained the required practical experience, and I am acutely aware of the perplexities of modern surgery and modern medicine.

He sifted his way through the various envelopes but soon realised his aspirations were not reciprocated. His mood darkened. Through pursed lips, he bawled, 'Damn it! All I need is someone to propose me; now why is that proving so difficult for God's sake? After all, I do have a decent diploma, and I am of excellent character. It seems that these Scottish doctors disagree, the blithering idiots!'

Well, he would show them. He had been a big fish in the Yorkshire Brethren, and he would gain the same recognition here. Edward decided it was time to make his name known in Glasgow public life and he intended to resort to all manner of means to obtain it. The first thing to do was to have some carte-de-visite cards printed. 'Yes, that's what I will do. I will hand them out to everyone; I will ask the shops to stock them, my face must surely brighten their drab front windows, and my face will be recognised by all on these miserable Scottish streets.' He then wrote a letter to the secretary of Glasgow's Medical Examiners, suggesting that they do a testimonial on Dr Edward William Pritchard and he enclosed a £5 note. He didn't sign the letter. Hoping that they would take the hint and help him on his way. He did the same to his Freemason Lodge. In the meantime, he needed to increase his income and find more patients.

* * *

Dr James Paterson was visiting a friend at the Bridge of Allan when he was asked to attend to the child of one of his friend's neighbours. The sick child, a boy named Thomas was four years old; weak and sickly from birth, he was gripped with croup through the night. Unfortunately, Doctor Paterson did not have the time as he was awaiting his carriage back to Glasgow. Thomas's family were frantic desperately trying many renowned physicians with no luck. Eventually, Isabelle, Thomas's sixteen-year-old sister received a recommendation of Dr Pritchard. Pritchard attended the child examining Thomas, whose face was flushed and vivid red. The poor boy's breathing was quick and arduous, and a strange frog-like croak came from his nose.

The doctor quickly took charge and suggested that Thomas be submerged in a bath of warm water, where then he must be bled. The poor boy's parents, Mr and Mrs Dumas were beside themselves with worry, Thomas, their son, was their pride and joy; after five girls they were delighted to have a boy in the family. At last an heir to take over the family name and their prosperous family business.

Thomas's condition did not change, in fact, after the doctor had applied a laxative clyster, and rubbed his shoulders to improve circulation he became worse. Three hours later Thomas had a terrible coughing fit and could not catch his breath. He died twenty minutes later. Mr and Mrs Dumas were at their wit's end but were grateful to Dr Pritchard and all he had done to try to save their son's life. Thomas's sisters were equally upset but hoped that the doctor would call upon them again. Of that, the family could be assured.

Mrs Dumas and her daughters welcomed the doctor's weekly visits. However, when Isabelle suffered a slight fever, the doctor insisted on coming more regularly, and before too long he was visiting the family at least three times a day. With his charisma and perfect manners Edward had charmed himself into a nice earner for himself, within four months he had netted a tidy sum of one hundred and fifty pounds. Edward couldn't believe his luck, and Mr Dumas couldn't quite understand how much money he had paid the doctor. Evidently, he didn't need to visit the girls three times a day? Mr Dumas had had enough and told Edward that they would no longer be requiring his services, but despite telling him several times, Edward took no notice. Eventually, they issued him with a constraint and desist letter. However, unperturbed, Edward had offered his services to one of the Dumas's neighbours, who again was a man of means.

Mr Frazer, a wool merchant, didn't have much wrong with him except through the pressure of working too hard he had suffered from exhaustion. Edward looked around the opulent surroundings of the Frazer house, and he soon realised that this was a superb money-making opportunity for him. He wrote out a script for him and told the grateful Mr Frazer that he would collect the prescription himself. Little did the unsuspecting businessman realise that the doctor was adding a drop of tartarised antimony to the medicine. Mr Frazer was incapacitated and bedridden for a year until he decided to stop taking the medication prescribed by Pritchard. The man had almost bled him dry with his daily visits and prescription charges. He was back on his feet within two weeks and told Pritchard in no uncertain terms that he no longer required his services.

Edward proclaimed it a miracle and a great triumph that Frazer had recovered from his illness and told everyone who would listen how he had cured the man and how it was down to his medical expertise.

Edward continued acquiring patients using underhand methods. He would eavesdrop on people's conversations, and if he heard that someone was unwell, he would visit them uninvited, saying that a friend had asked him to call. He would offer a diagnosis, leave a prescription, and say he would call again. Sometimes he was met with a rebuff; he didn't care. Instead, he would send them a professional account for his services. It became a regular source of his income.

* * *

Edward's antics had caught the eye of Doctor William Bell a well-known and much-respected doctor at The Bridge of Allen. In his thirty-two years in medicine, he had never come across anyone like Pritchard. He was appalled at the way this so-called physician was acquiring clients. It just wasn't done. He invited Edward to his house to discuss the matter. After much deliberation, Edward went to the meeting, but he took an instant dislike to the pompous idiot. Who did he think he was lecturing him on ethics and telling him how to run his practice.

Doctor Bell tried to explain that it just wasn't moral for a man of medicine to acquire clients in such a backhanded manner. He watched Pritchard's facial expression change to anger as he told him in no uncertain terms that he had no choice but to report him to the medical authorities, who wouldn't be impressed with the doctor's dishonest methods and would stop Edward practising in the area. Edward could not believe what he was hearing. Report him! That would be the end of his career; he would be humiliated and would never work again. His family and his reputation would be in tatters.

Edward could feel the panic as his heart raced, the heat run through his veins. He wanted to grab hold of this doctor who could ruin his life and throttle the living daylights out of him. His temper was about to boil over to the point where Edward needed all his strength to resist putting his hands around his neck and squeezing him until the idiot turned limp. Still, he needed to stay calm, and compose himself. Instead, he pretended to agree with the doctor and thanked him for pointing out the error of his ways. With mock repentance, he apologised profusely and asked Dr Bell if he could get a glass of water.

'Yes, help yourself, in fact, you can fetch me one as well, there's a water pitcher in the kitchen.'

Doctor Bell could see the man was upset; his little talk had apparently hit a nerve. He hoped so. The sick of Glasgow didn't need this calibre of a man tending to their needs. They deserved better.

Edward came back into the room and handed a glass of water for Dr Bell. The old man took the water willingly, what the unsuspecting doctor didn't know was that Edward had added one drop of aconite to his glass of water, enough to keep the doctor quiet permanently. He watched the fool as he quenched his thirst. Within minutes the experienced physician's face turned to pure terror when he realised what Pritchard had done to him. He staggered from his chair, clutching his stomach, the pain became excruciating, and he vomited everywhere narrowly avoiding Edward.

With a menacing look, Edward jumped up and grabbed the man by his lapels and almost spat the words into his face,

'Don't worry, old fellow your demise will not cause suspicion. It will be attributed to a disease from the lead of your new water tank from the Loch Katrine reservoir! Just like those other cases reported in the newspapers. Before you go, just remember, nobody, questions my medical practices and lives to tell the tale!'

William Bell could do nothing about it. His face crumpled in horror as his pulse faded and his face took on a deadly pallor and a final vacant, glassy stare.

Edward took the glasses, washed them, and put them in the same place he got them from, and as quietly as he had come, he left the house.

* * *

CHAPTER FOURTEEN
A PRETTY LIAR

Edward prepared for his lecture in the opulent building of Glasgow's Athenaeum Assembly. His public standing was almost beginning to improve, and following his enthusiastic attendance to many of the talks given in the rooms, the society had made him a director. He was thrilled to be such a vital part of this distinguished literary and scientific club. It was such a privileged position bearing in mind that the famous author Charles Dickens had addressed a meeting there a few weeks earlier. Tonight, it was his turn to deliver a lecture. He looked forward to it. Some of the members of the Faculty of Physicians and Surgeons would be in the audience. He would show them their mistake in not offering him a position in their institution when they had the chance. He was also now Master of the Royal Arch Chapter, and this evening one of his Freemason Associates would be introducing his lecture. He had taken great care to ensure this speech put him firmly ahead and he would demonstrate to these so-called professional people just how knowledgeable and engaging he was. That would show them.

The meeting room was full, as Edward took his seat on the stage. He had taken extra care with his appearance and dressed impeccably in his recently acquired red flannel waistcoat, just like the one General Garibaldi wore. His hands gently stroked his long beard as he smiled imperceptibly at the distinguished audience. As his fellow Freemason took to the stage to introduce him, Edward was confident that these learned people would be most impressed with his connections and fascinated by the tales of his overseas exploits.

'Gentleman, please raise your glasses to tonight's speaker, Doctor Edward Pritchard, a distinguished physiologist, eminent surgeon, and a friend of General Garibaldi.'

Edward stood and placed his handwritten notes down on the table in front of him.

'Good evening. For those of you who don't know me, my name is Doctor Edward William Pritchard. I am a surgeon, a physiologist, writer, and a director of this institution. I come from a family of Navy commanders; my brother is presently the Governor General of Ceylon. As my learned colleague said in his very kind introduction, I am also a good friend of the great Italian Liberator General Garibaldi, who I met on my travels abroad. Garibaldi kindly gave me this walking stick which he inscribed.' Edward took the walking stick from his side and placed it on the table in front of him for all to see.

'Tosh! He's never even met Garibaldi let alone friended him!' a member of the audience scoffed. 'The man is nothing more than a plausible liar!' another doctor whispered to the man at his side. 'I have seen Pritchard with the same stick many times before… it had no inscription then!' In response, his colleague answered, 'I heard on good authority that when he was in Yorkshire, he was known as the prettiest liar, amongst other things!' The man shook his head in disbelief.

Ignoring the criticism, Edward continued retelling his exploits. 'Another one of my adventures that I must tell you about is on a voyage to South America. I and some of the crew went inland where we came upon what we thought was a hotel, but what turned out to be a gaming house. Unused to gambling, I tried my hand and soon found myself filling my pockets with a lot of gold doubloons. I left the gaming room as quietly as I could and returned to my ship. However, during the evening I fell over the rail doubloons and all. Before I knew it, I sank to the bottom of the sea. I had to think fast, and realised the reason I was falling quickly was that I had pockets full of gold. I drew out a knife and cut a slit the pockets, after that the doubloons all fell out. I was anxious not to lose all the money, so again from my pocket, I took a white cambric handkerchief, gathered up the coins and left them as a point of contact for sea divers. By this time, I felt faint and with lots of strength ascended to the surface. I then remembered I had a flask of brandy in my inside jacket pocket. I took a swig and revitalised myself. I soon found my ship, and luckily there was a rope hanging over the side. I was soon safely back on board without being missed.'

The room was silent, many shaking their heads in disbelief.

Edward heard the whispers, but he was undeterred and continued to recite his adventures.

'Gentleman, I understand that you find some of my exploits incredible, but let me tell you that I have plucked eaglets from the eyries in the deserts of Arabia, I have hunted the Nubian Lion in the prairies of North America.' Edward reeled off his usual spiel.

Once again turning to his friend the man in the audience declared, 'Trouble with liars, my dear fellow, is that you need to have a bloody good memory, which is something that this scoundrel does not have! The last time I heard him give this same speech, it was rhino he had speared, and he said that he'd wrestled with crocodiles in Africa. The man is preposterous!' Disgusted, the man got up from his chair and left. Many others followed suit.

Later, when he was preparing to go home, a member of the audience approached Edward. 'Pritchard, you don't expect us to believe this twaddle, do you. Ha! Utter nonsense that's all I can say. I suspect that you have not been to any of the countries you discuss… let alone engage in the exciting activities you talk so much about!'

Edward could feel the anger rising in him with the speed of a whippet out of a trap. His body tensed. He clenched his fists tightly and stared down at the papers on his desk. Who did this idiot think he was talking to? Red in the face, his eyes cold and hard, he glared at the man. Gaining composure, he picked up his walking stick and pointed it at the startled Gent.

'So, what of it – it goes down!' he replied. He gathered up his papers and stormed from the building.

* * *

CHAPTER FIFTEEN
MOVING IN THE RIGHT CIRCLES

Edward still craved to impress his fellow professionals, and decided it was high time that he bought a property. The most popular place was the up and coming Sauchiehall Street. The westward growth of the city meant that many affluent and influential people wanted to move to the outskirts. Edward wanted to be one of them. He had seen a substantial Villa in Clarence Place not too far from Blythswood Square, where quite recently Madeleine Smith had resided. 'Madeleine Smith?' Mary Jane asked. 'Isn't she that socialite accused of murdering her lover? Such a scandalous affair – the woman caused a sensation and will be the talk of the town for many years to come. Are you sure that we want the family associated with this same area, Edward?' Mary inquired of her husband.

'Mary Jane, the woman was acquitted! She moved out of Scotland ultimately; you cannot hold a grudge against someone who has been found innocent. Justice was done, my dear.'

'Well, I am not too sure about that, she wasn't exactly found innocent was she, the verdict was 'not proven' there wasn't enough evidence they say. But regardless of her, how will we afford such a house; two thousand pounds is an awful lot of money,' Mary Jane questioned, changing the subject.

'I have already agreed mortgage terms with the bank; they are prepared to lend me sixteen hundred pounds, and I am sure your mother and father will give us the rest. I know they want what's best for us, for you and the children.'

Mary Jane sighed, more loans from her family; hopefully, this would be the last time. Edward should then be where he wanted to be, and they could at last progress. With some reluctance, she took out a sheet of writing paper and once again wrote to her mother asking her for more financial assistance.

Jane Taylor was very fond of her son-in-law. Edward was a good husband and an excellent father. The children idolised him. She just wished that he could get on his feet properly! He deserved it. Edward had travelled the world and came from such a distinguished naval family. She and her husband could not have wished for a better match for their daughter; he was like a second son to them. They would do anything to help him on his way. Jane was sure that buying a house in such an affluent area of town was bound to put them in good stead. Mary Jane and the children needed security. Her mind was made up, and she wrote letters to both the land agent to secure the purchase and to Mary Jane who would no doubt be delighted and relieved at her decision.

My Dear Mary Jane

'I have told him (the land agent) to get an order drawn for the money in two sums, one for four hundred pounds, and one for one hundred pounds. This way Edward may hold the one hundred in his hand and pay the four hundred as part of the purchase money. I have done it this way so that the lawyers do not get their hands on it and keep it under some pretence or another. Now, my dear Mary Jane — you must take care that this money is well spent. We have all felt the trouble in getting it. I do not doubt that it would be a source of satisfaction to us all if it is a

means of getting Edward forward in life, and much depends on his going on quietly and preserving. He is now in a better position, and with his industrious and steady attention to his practice, all will be well. Give him my kind love and earnest wishes for success.

Mother

* * *

CHAPTER SIXTEEN
CHANGING CIRCUMSTANCES

Mary Jane lay in her four-poster bed and looked around her bedroom. It was a very modern and comfortable room, decorated to her taste. There was a washstand, a tall mirror, a bookcase and a chiffonier. The furnishings were opulent with crimson damask upholstery which complemented the elegant mahogany furniture. It had not been cheap, but Edward had insisted that they have the best they could afford.

Life hadn't been easy for her and Edward; everything seemed to have happened so fast. What with the fire, and moving to a new house again. The children came in quick succession, and they were all growing up so fast. Her health had not been at its best either, every time she gave birth, she suffered from irritation to her eyes, which was a permanent affliction now. Her eyes were itchy red and sore, so much so that she troubled to see most of the time. At last her family were getting somewhere. Edward's practice was growing, and his patients respected him.

The maid Mary McLeod had been a godsend, and acted as nurse and housemaid and helped with the children whenever she could. Mary Jane did not know what she would do without her. Still, it worked both ways. Mary had a roof over her head and a bit of money in her pocket. Also, Edward from the goodness of his heart was teaching the girl to read. Mrs Lattimer was also an excellent cook, and together with an assistant prepared all the family meals.

* * *

For the past week, Mary McLeod had not felt well. Nausea gripped her first thing in the morning, and she had no energy whatsoever. It was mid-August, and it did not help that the country was experiencing one of the worst heat waves in years. Even at five in the morning heat penetrated through Mary's veins with the speed of an erupting volcano. It was unbearable. Beads of sweat dripped down her forehead, she looked at her face in the small hand-held mirror her mistresses had given her, her face looked pale and gaunt and lacked its natural rosy glow; she would be glad when the rain came. How she hated summer just now, she felt so ill. So, tired.

Mary would like nothing better than to crawl back into bed, and to stay there until the feeling of nausea passed, but she knew that wasn't possible. The willow tree outside her window was unusually silent, mute in the early morning summer air. The dark birds who frequently chirped endlessly to each other as they roosted on the tree's branches were today suspiciously quiet. Perhaps they had moved on to colder climates. Lucky them, she wished she could. Slowly, she got out of bed, picked up her maid's box and begrudgingly made her way down to the breakfast room to start her daily routine.

* * *

Edward sat at his desk in the study. He didn't have the strength to move, and his fingers shook as they relentlessly ran through his beard. He was at his wit's end. He bit down on his lip as he looked down at the letters delivered that morning. Both Clydesdale and City of Glasgow Bank were on his back again, and to add salt to his wounds, his dear mother-in-law had sent him a cheque for ten pounds. Ten pounds – what could he do with that. Nothing! The bank will swallow that up and knock it off his overdraft. He read her letter:

Edward,

Once more let me express the hope that in a very short time you will be relieved from all these troubles. I will do all I can to push the thing on.

Love to Mary Jane and the children.

P.S. Edward, please do not forget the terms on which I advanced you the five-hundred pounds to buy the property, namely that I must have a bond over the property, for the benefit of Mary Jane and the children.

Mother

* * *

His heart was beating fast as he read her words, and the words of the new manager from Clydesdale Bank which were most forceful. The manager stated;

Dear Dr Pritchard,

You have tested the patience of many a bank manager before me, and the bank is no longer prepared to notary any more of your transactions.

He was already behind with the mortgage with The City Bank. He did not know what to do. In a burst of anger, he crumpled the letters up into one tight ball and threw it with all his might across the room.

Edward knew that his options were limited. Even his friend Charles was not willing to 'give' him any more money. In fact, Charles had terminated their friendship. Huh! We will see about that, Edward fumed. Let's see what your new wife and family would say if they knew the truth eh, Charlie boy! No, they won't like that, he seethed.

He looked around the room; he had nothing left to pawn. Well, nothing that would go unnoticed. He looked at the carte-de-visite of him in happier times with his wife and family. He had such high hopes for them all. Where had he gone wrong? He looked out of the window at the street below. It was bustling with people going about their business. What was he to do? Sometimes he didn't see the point in drawing breath and then his thoughts turned to Lavinia Thurgood his favourite boardwalk actress and one-time prostitute to the gentry. Yes, he would visit her.

Seeing Lavinia always cheered Edward up. They had been friends ever since his journey overseas with Charles. Charles depended on Lavinia for many reasons. Lavinia was different to any other woman Edward knew. Outwardly, a confident, independent lady with an air of style and dignity, a striking looking woman with a radiant smile, baby blue eyes, perpetual ruby-red lips, and a clear English peaches and cream complexion, she was the envy of many. Her brown hair gleamed and tied back in a sleek, classic knot. Lavinia was indeed a beautiful woman.

Lavinia, or as she was born, Annie Turner, was thirty-two and lived alone in a grand house on the outskirts of Glasgow. Such a far cry from her squalid roots in the North of England; as soon as she could, she had 'run away with the circus'. Annie loved to sing, and dance and her agility made her an ideal candidate as a trapeze artist. She learned quickly and soon became a familiar figure with the circus as they travelled all over the country. She fell in love with her co-star, who tragically fell to his death one night after a performance in Dumfries. Annie, devastated, decided the time had come to leave the circus and try her chances in the theatre. She moved to Glasgow and changed her name to something more upmarket, and she was on her way. The stage suited her, and quickly she became well known for dressing as a boy in a double act with her co-star Maggie. This is where she had first met Charles. Charles was fascinated by her, and they became inseparable, but not for the reasons you would expect. He came to all her performances, wherever she was, often travelling the width and breadth of the country just to catch a glimpse of her dressed as a boy. Charles became obsessed, and he even paid for Lavinia's apartment and its upkeep, in return she would do him favours. His favourite thing was for her to dress as a schoolmaster and give him the thrashing of his life on his bare backside with a holly branch or a birch whip. Lavinia could not understand it but saw the excitement and joy that Charles derived from these whippings. She had him under her control, Charles liked that.

She persuaded him to set her up in a more prominent apartment, and Lavinia soon realised the power she had over men and how she could dominate them without having sex with them. Soon she had many clients who liked nothing better than to be dominated and spanked by her. One influential man wanted to be strapped tightly to the bed by his ankles and wrists, so he was unable to move, then Lavinia would flog him with a cat o'nine tails. He screamed with pain and pleasure. At first, Lavinia could not understand why a man of such prominent social standing would suffer such pain and be powerless and helpless while he experienced such humiliation. The relationship Lavinia had with her clients always remained confidential. On the outside, and to her neighbours, Lavinia was a healthy, morally upright woman with no sexual thoughts at all. Edward knew different; he was aware that Lavinia was indeed no angel in the house.

Charles had introduced Edward to Lavinia before they travelled overseas. Although Edward found it difficult to resist the temptation, he and Lavinia did not have a sexual relationship. Edward quietly watched on as she gave his friend the beatings he thrived on. It wasn't Edward's thing, but if Charles wanted to pay him to do the same thing to him while they were away, then he must learn. Charles also insisted that Edward peel a piece of ginger root into a small plug and insert it up Charles anus, Charles wriggled and screamed in intense pain as it burned through his body. He would then insist that Lavinia whipped him as hard as she could.

Through the years, Lavinia had become an independently wealthy woman. Money was never a problem to her, and she didn't need a husband to support her. The previous year one of her 'clients' had died and left her the sum of fourteen thousand pounds. With this amount in the bank, she decided that it was time to stop her profession and concentrate on being a Victorian lady. She no longer saw Charles, who had recently married and no doubt didn't want to have to explain to his new wife how he came across the welts and whip marks on his body. Lavinia did see Edward from time to time, especially if she needed a prescription.

She hadn't expected to see him today, still, a pleasant surprise nonetheless. Edward, was a handsome man, and she enjoyed his conversations, he always told her of his adventures and travels abroad, and she found him most entertaining. They had an afternoon tea and played a game of cards, Edward won, although Lavinia did suspect him of cheating. It wasn't until the end of the afternoon when Edward approached her for a loan. Lavinia would not have minded and happily lent him the money immediately, but she didn't like the way Edward asked her; she felt that he was trying to blackmail her. Nobody did that to Lavinia.

'I would hate your little secret lifestyle to become common knowledge,' Edward said.

'Secret lifestyle!' Lavinia fumed, just who did he think he was, she knew judges and solicitors, and then there were some of her more unsavoury friends.

'If you 'lend' me two-thousand pounds, my lips will remain sealed, and I will say no more about it!'

Lavinia couldn't believe the words that came out of her so-called friend's mouth. Did he think she was an imbecile; she hadn't come this far in the world to be threatened by somebody like him. Lavinia had heard enough and in no uncertain terms told Edward to leave her house never to return. As far as she was concerned if he so much as mentioned her name to anyone, then she would make sure that he was dealt with personally from the Chief Police Commissioner, a dear friend of hers.

Edward's plan had failed, he was defeated, not only because of the money but because he had lost a friend, a dear kindred spirit.

* * *

CHAPTER SEVENTEEN
ANOTHER MISTAKE

Mary was dreading telling Edward her news. Pregnant? She had to be; she had not had her show for two months now. Edward would examine her then they'd know for definite; she had to tell him today. He would be kind she was sure. He loved her, he said so often enough. He even told her that one day he would divorce his wife and they could be together properly as husband and wife. Mary so much wanted to be Mrs Pritchard and be with her Edward for life. They were soul-mates. They were destined to be together; she knew how to make him happy.

Edward was far from pleased. His world exploded from the inside; he could not believe the words that came from Mary's mouth. How could he have been so stupid as to let this happen again? He now had to focus on what needed doing. Fortunately for him, his wife and family were away at her parents' – that, at least, was a blessing. Memories of the last look on Lizzie's face came back to him: a look that would haunt him for life. He couldn't go through that again. Nobody would believe that it was an accident, not a second time. He had no choice but to perform an abortion, and to persuade the girl that it was for the best. Edward knew she would believe him. After all, she thought he loved her and that he would marry her. Huh, she certainly had her uses, but as if a servant girl from the Gorbals was any match for him. The girl was delusional. Still, for now, it suited him.

'Mary dear, do not fret! We will sort this out. Together. Dry your eyes.' Edward took his handkerchief from his pocket and tenderly wiped her tears. 'My darling, we cannot have this baby, not yet. There will be plenty of time for us to have more children, but not now, you understand don't you, sweetheart.' He kissed her on the head as he held her close to his chest.

The next day Mary swallowed the female pills Edward gave her. 'What will happen — I mean after I take them?' Mary read the label on the brown bottle. 'Dr Paterson's famous female pills. That doesn't tell me anything,' she said.

'Do not worry, my dear; they are full of herbs!' Edward assured her, looking inquisitively at the label he said, 'See, it says here 'perfectly harmless', nothing to harm you there. It should just feel like your regular monthly time; let's see how you feel in an hour or so!'

An hour passed and Mary felt dreadful, she had been expecting the cramps to come, but nothing happened. Edward insisted that she drink a couple of glasses of Gin. How she hated Gin at the best of times and was wrenching as she swigged it down as fast as she could, but that, together with the smell of the hot mustard poultice he had placed on her stomach, was making her wrench.

'Not long now, my love, just bite down hard on this piece of rubber and then it will all be over,' Edward reassured her as he worked away with the sharp instrument. Sweat poured profusely down Mary's face as her teeth clenched through the rubber bit. 'There – all over.' Mary couldn't hide her pain; she screamed, the agony so intense it felt as if she were a chicken and someone had pulled out her innards.

* * *

October 1864

Jane Taylor decided it was high time that she visited her daughter in Glasgow. Mary Jane seemed to be the one doing most of the visiting, so she was happy to take her turn. Purposely, she didn't announce her visit, let her visit, be a surprise to them. Walking along Sauchiehall Street, Jane reflected on how much the area had changed. Reminiscing, she remembered coming here as a child. It was all moorland then with plenty of willow trees, but not now. Now it was an enterprising high street with shops and coffee houses.

The tobacconist's window looked splendid with all the goods on the show: cigar trimmers, silver toothpicks and a beautiful tortoiseshell comb that Jane could not resist buying for Edward.

At the house, Jane knocked twice on the door admiring the new brass door knocker in the shape of a lion's head, typical of Edward, she thought to herself; she was taken aback when the cook Catherine Lattimer opened the door. 'Oh, I wasn't expecting you! Where is the maid; what's her name, Mary isn't it?' Jane asked.

'I am not sure that I know, madam. I assume she is going about her duties somewhere in the house,' the cook replied.

'And Mrs Pritchard and the children, where are they?'

'They went into town about a half hour ago; they shouldn't be too long I'm sure. Shall I take your coat?'

'That's very kind, Mrs Lattimer.' The cook wiped her floured hands on her apron as best she could, before taking the coat and putting it in the hall closet. This was the second time this week, she had to cover for that girl, taking liberties, she was, and she had a good idea why!

* * *

Edward and Mary had not heard the doorbell, as they frolicked together on the bed. Playfully, Mary reached her arms around Edward and nestled her face into his curly mane; she raised her face to his.

'You do love me don't you, Edward?' she asked.

'You are my heart's desire, the love of my life. I love you more than life itself!' Edward lied. He took a gold locket from his pocket and gave it to her.

'Here, I want you to have this. I love you so much that if something were to happen to my wife, then you would be my wife.'

'What do you mean if something were to happen? Mary said, opening the locket to see a picture of Edward and a strand of his hair?'

'I mean if she were to go away or die!'

Mary put the locket around her neck, she was shocked at his words and did not know what to say, but there was nothing she would like more than to be Edward's wife and the mistress of the house. Using all her female charm, Mary roughly ran her fingers through Edward's hair and gripped it tightly pulling him towards her. Edward liked her being in control; she turned her head and teased her tongue around the soft lobe of his ear. It drove him mad. He grabbed her with both hands and threw her on the bed, kissing her hard on the mouth, he bit her lip, she felt his hardness as he pinned her down with the full weight of his body.

They were so engrossed in the engulfing passion they had for each other, that they did not notice the bedroom door open.

Edward sensed someone in the room; he looked up to see the ashen face of his mother-in-law standing motionless in the doorway.

* * *

CHAPTER EIGHTEEN
DIVIDED AFFECTION

Over the next couple of weeks, a heavy silence settled over Edward and his mother-in-law. Neither mentioned the incident to the other, but the once happy relationship the couple had previously enjoyed was now decidedly strained. Breakfast time was the worst, not wanting to draw attention to the difficulties between them to his wife or children, Edward thought it best to keep up appearances the best he could.

Jane Taylor was not impressed. Her eyes glanced around the breakfast table, watching her treacherous son-in-law surreptitiously as he shifted uncomfortably in his seat, noting his uneasiness as he fidgeted with his food pretending to be unperturbed. His overall demeanour gave him away as he nervously interlaced his sweaty hands and fingers. He must have sensed her eyes on him, as he looked to the floor; she caught him tracing the outline of each floor tile with his eyes. Guilty that's what he was, the filthy heathen Jane concluded.

The children knew something wasn't quite right. They tried to figure out what was wrong between their father and their granny, but they knew it was not their place to enquire any further.

Mary Jane couldn't help being concerned. Her mother was always telling her how proud she was of Edward and how hard he worked. What she could not understand was why her mother's attitude towards her son-in-law had changed so drastically. She decided that it would be best to broach the matter with Edward at bedtime. Sitting at her dressing table, she took the pins from her hair and let it fall around her shoulders. She picked up the tortoise shell hairbrush and began to brush her hair vigorously, waiting for the right time to bring the matter up. Her moment came just as Edward had turned back the sheets on the bed.

'Edward – can I ask you something?'

'Of course, my dear.' Edward hesitated. 'What's the matter?'

'You and Mother; what's wrong?'

'Wrong? What do you mean wrong?'

'You know what I'm saying, Edward, there is an atmosphere between the two of you!'

Edward stayed silent, knowing that he had to cover his tracks the best he could. He had thought this would happen, so he was well prepared.

He took the brush from his wife's hands and brushed her hair, patting her head occasionally as if she were a dog.

'Is it money, Edward? Are we in trouble?'

Edward had cleared his throat before he answered, 'Money… Well, yes in a way it is. I did not want to disturb you with this, Mary Jane. I didn't! It's about the loan for the house. Your mother wants me to sign a deed to make the loan official in case something should happen to you and me. So that the children would be well looked after!'

'Really! I thought she had already spoken to you about it. It's just routine surely, nothing to argue over, is it?'

'Well, no, it's not just that,' he said, putting the brush down on the dressing table. I get the feeling that she doesn't trust me.' Edward chose his words carefully.

'Doesn't trust you, don't be silly Mother idolises you. She always has!'

'I didn't want to upset you with this, my darling, but it's better you hear it from me. I was giving Mary McLeod a reading lesson in the drawing room. To show her gratitude, the girl gave me a peck on the cheek. Nothing improper, you understand. It's just that your mother saw her doing it, and I suspect she assumed something else was going on!'

'A peck on the cheek – you mean she kissed you?' Mary Jane did not expect this revelation.

'No, of course; she didn't kiss me,' Edward insisted. 'It was a polite peck on the cheek… for goodness sake! I hope that you or your mother are not insinuating that I would be interested in a servant girl! Sometimes, Mary Jane, I do not understand you or your family!' Edward shook his head, his temper rising. With a short show of sincerity, he placed his right hand on his heart.

'The girl is grateful for the lessons I give her that is all!'

Mary Jane wasn't stupid; she could almost see the wheels turning in her husband's mind as he conducted his 'defence'. She could just imagine the sort of lessons he would be giving the girl – she knew what type of girls her husband liked, she always had. Mary McLeod fitted the criteria. Still, a blind eye, she would turn, after all, he was her husband. He had married her; he loved her, these servant girls were just that, 'servant girls' and that is all they ever would be. Mary Jane would, as always, keep the status quo of the house. This little 'tiff' between her husband and her mother would blow over. Looking her husband straight in the eye, he met her gaze and didn't flounder for one second. He was so plausible, so believable.

'I see, Edward,' she sighed. 'I will speak to Mother and clear the air.'

'Thank you! As you know, I love her dearly. Tell her that I will sign the blasted piece of paper if she so requires!'

Edward was relieved, glad that the matter was out in the open. He was surprised that his mother-in-law had not confided in her daughter, told her all that she had seen. Well, it was her word against his. He felt sure that his wife believed him! Why should she not?

* * *

The following afternoon, Mary Jane was in the drawing room preparing the monthly household accounts. It wasn't a job she enjoyed. It was always such a chore; there was never enough money it seemed. Edward had insisted that they pay the staff first. Then there were the household goods, food, tradesmen's bills, clothes for the children, dresses for herself; appearances were everything, Edward insisted. Lately, he had spent a considerable amount of money on photographs of himself, handing the carte de visite out to all and sundry. 'Appearance is everything,' he had told her. 'The more people see my face, the better my standing in the community. Recognition will emphasise my public profile,' he proclaimed.

Jane Taylor watched her daughter shuffle invoices backwards and forwards; she saw how she prioritised which needed paying first. Jane took a deep breath; this is not the life she had envisaged for her daughter; she had expected a better life for her.

Mary Jane felt her mother's eyes on her and took the opportunity to address the problem between her and Edward.

'Edward told me that you wish him to sign some papers — for the loan on the house?'

Jane Taylor stared into her daughter's eyes; they were red and puffy, the girl was exhausted; if she were to tell her the truth of what she saw Edward doing with that trollop, that it would destroy her. It would ruin the family. Jane decided there was no point in upsetting her; she was entirely unprepared for what her daughter said next.

'Mother, I do know! I am not stupid. You know how men are; sometimes they cannot help themselves, women throw themselves at him, they always have. He is so handsome, but he is my husband, the father of my children. He loves me. He always has.'

Jane Taylor smiled knowingly. Knowing full well that there was nothing she could say to persuade her daughter otherwise. No point in upsetting the apple cart.

'You must manage your thoughts and your mind.'

'I'm afraid too sometimes. I love Edward so much.' Mary Jane pushed her hair back from her brow, her voice becoming clearer as her confidence returned.

'He doesn't mean it, Mother; he does love me, you know!'

Jane Taylor hesitated, then smiled at her daughter, giving her a reassuring pat on her arm.

'Very well, my dear. I will ask the solicitor to draw up the papers.'

* * *

PART TWO

CHAPTER NINETEEN
AN OCTOBER CHILL 1864

Mary Jane's health was no better. Despite the drapes being closed her eyes hurt, she just could not bear the sunlight through the window. Her head was thumping; she felt as if someone was smashing bricks inside her head. Even the muscles in her face felt numb, and it hurt to smile. Edward examined her and said she had caught a chill. She had not felt like this before; she was perspiring profusely, continually vomiting. Her body smelled putrid. It was midday, and already she had changed her nightdress twice, and she was ready to change it again. Two weeks she had felt this way, and still did not feel well enough to leave her bed. Whenever she tried to get out of bed, she collapsed, her limbs were so weak, and walking was impossible. Her whole body ached – she just wanted to feel better.

Edward was concerned for Mary Jane and remained more attentive to her needs. He insisted on making her meals, just something light as she couldn't handle solid food. The weight had dropped off her, but not in all the wrong places. Everything she ate, she brought straight back up.

The children were upset. They relied on their mother. She tried to keep the family going; they missed the affection she gave them and her morning cuddles and kind words of encouragement. They didn't like their mother being ill; it wasn't like her. Papa had said not to worry, that their mother would soon be back on her feet. They each took it, in turn, to sit with her. Mary Jane adored their visits. Especially the little one, who needed her mummy, she even felt grateful to Mary McLeod who, despite the hostility between them, had been a godsend. Still, Mary Jane was not stupid; she knew the girl was carrying on with her husband. Ideas above her station that one. A servant girl is all she would ever be, Mary Jane reassured herself.

* * *

CHAPTER TWENTY
NOVEMBER 1864-NEW RELATIONSHIPS

Edward was feeling pleased with himself. He had placed an advert in The Lancet for lodgers and was thrilled when two medical students Mr King and Mr Connell wanted to rent the attic rooms. The extra money would come in handy, but more importantly, he looked forward to mentoring them, as first-year students they were impressed with his medical experience. Naturally! He would take them under his wing, show them the ropes. Connell was keen to learn; such a handsome young man, he reminded him of himself in his younger days.

* * *

Mary McLeod was feeling somewhat better, although she still felt a little sad, she couldn't help wondering just who her baby would have taken after? Thank goodness, the pain had gone, if that was what childbirth was like, they could keep it! She didn't fancy going through that again. Still, no doubt it will be different next time. At least there would be a baby to tend after. Someone to cherish and call her own. Her and Edward's child. The thought brought a smile to her face.

Her emotions were all over the place. One minute she was laughing the next bursting into a flood of tears – she couldn't explain why. Edward had been so supportive; he gave her medicine to take the pain away, but it had almost knocked her out, but still, it did the trick.

Mary liked the new students; they brought a freshness to the house. The younger one Mr King had caught her throwing her arms around Edward's neck; she just looked at him with a confident gaze, which no doubt told the young student all he needed to know. Edward had tried to cover the incident up, saying, 'Now, now, my dear, no need to thank me for your medicine, I am a doctor, and as your employer, I must look after you.' Mr King had soon fled off to his room. Mary smiled, she was sure he got the message.

* * *

George King was curious about the relationship between the doctor and the maid. He assumed it was platonic, but, in his mind, he had a nagging doubt, they did seem very close for master and servant. He had seen the way they looked at each other. Still, he knew that Edward liked to look after people and he guessed that this was all that he was doing with the young housemaid. Surely Edward would not jeopardise his family, his reputation, and his career, for any sordid affair – the scandal would ruin him! No, he reassured himself, Edward was too astute for that. The doctor had impressed him and his colleague David Connell. They looked up to him and hoped that one day they too would follow in the eminent physician's footsteps. Edward (as he insisted they called him) had travelled the world; he had given lectures all over the country about his exploits. Edward was such an intelligent and entertaining man. As students, they were so lucky to have found lodgings with such an inspirational mentor, yet that said, the young student doubted that something wasn't all it seemed. He just didn't know what.

* * *

Edward opened his front door as the church clock struck seven. It was a miserable, damp evening, the air thick with fog that had spread across the city like a dark cloak, so dense that he could only just see across the street. He was exhausted. Today, he had seen fifteen patients, most of whom had respiratory problems. There wasn't much he could do for them except tell them to keep as warm as they could and stay indoors. It was the same thing day in day out. Undoubtedly, there was more to life than this? All he seemed to do was work and struggle with money; he was sick of it! His son Horatio interrupted his melancholy mood as he ran down the stairs.

'Papa, Papa, thank goodness you are home. It's mother; she is so ill. Come quick!'

Edward put away his walking stick, took off his coat, and ran up the stairs.

'She's much worse today, Papa, poor mummy she's been sick all day, even Mrs Lattimer couldn't get her to eat any of the broth and mummy loves Cook's soup,' Horatio told his father.

'My poor angel,' Edward said. Taking a cloth from the bed stand, he wiped his wife's brow.

'Edward, I feel so ill; so weak, I cannot even stand. I just go faint and unsafe on my feet. What is wrong with me, what can it be?'

'Now don't fret, it's probably just a chill. You know what a weak stomach you have. My dear, you are soaked let's get this nightdress changed. Horatio, call for the maid we need her to dress your mother.'

'I will make you some tapioca, you must eat something.' Edward left the room, leaving Mary alone to dress his wife and change her bedding.

Alone in the kitchen, Edward took a packet of tapioca from the larder and mixed the contents in an earthenware bowl. He looked around him, checking that nobody could see him through the window. When Edward was sure that the coast was clear he closed the kitchen door, he took the small glass phial from his pocket and hesitated as he read the label 'Tartarised Antimony'. He paused and put the bottle back in his pocket. He couldn't, he shouldn't, but what could he do, his bitch of a mother-in-law was hassling him for money, watching his every move, and the parasite bank manager was on his back.

Convincing himself that all would be fine, he took the phial back out of his pocket and unscrewed the cap tipping the bottle upside down; he watched a drop of the clear liquid as it hit the bowl of tapioca. Just this once he said to himself, as he stirred the mixture. Before opening the kitchen door, he made the sign of the cross, making sure that he did it in the right sequence-forehead, lower chest then both shoulders, reciting 'Forgive me, Father. I have sinned.' He took the bowl of warm tapioca up the stairs to his wife.

* * *

Mary Jane thought she was dying. Never had she felt this ill, she didn't even know what day it was. Her daughter Fanny had told her that morning that it was now mid-November. Where had the time gone? Already she had lost two weeks. Two weeks she had lain in this bed vomiting and sweating profusely. All she wanted was to get well; her children needed her so much. Edward needed her; she struggled to sit herself up, hugging her sore stomach as she moved the bolster pillow under her head. Her hands were weak, but she managed to ring the brass bell at the side of her bed.

Mary answered her call. 'You rang, Madam, is there anything I can get you?'

'Yes, yes. I need to get out of these clothes. I need to be bathed; I can smell the stench of sweat on me. It's disgusting. Help me undress please and change this bedding!'

Mary helped her mistress into clean clothing, and she winced when she saw how thin she had become. For a moment, Mary felt so sorry for her; the woman had been very ill, so bad that Mary didn't think she was going to make it. Although deep down that would please her, she wouldn't want to see her in pain. No, she wouldn't wish that on anyone. Well… almost anyone.

'Why don't you have a couple of weeks away. Perhaps in a few days when you are feeling a bit better?' Mary suggested to her mistress.

'You could see your mother, it's not too far to travel, and the change of air will do you good; I am sure she would be pleased to see you.'

Mary Jane couldn't keep her eyes open, drifting off to sleep, she thought about what Mary said. Yes, change is what she needed, and she decided to tell Edward in the morning and start making the arrangements. For the first time in weeks, she felt calm, content. How she needed her mother, ever since her mother disagreed with Edward, she had not visited as often as she had before. Mary Jane put her head on the clean pillow and fell to sleep.

* * *

CHAPTER TWENTY-ONE
A CHANGE OF AIR NOVEMBER 1864

Mary Jane had been at her parents' house for two weeks. Already she felt better. Her mother had done her hair, just as she had when she was a child, brushing it one hundred times until it shone, her skin was better too. She no longer had the pale grey look to her complexion or the glassy look in her eyes. Today, she had even managed a small walk outside with her mother. How she missed Edinburgh, it was in her soul. The new architecture of the town and the clever way the planners had juxtaposed the new with the old fascinated her. The early history of the old town together with the Georgian style of the new town was incredible. What made Edinburgh so special to her were the green open spaces. It was her home, and she was proud of it. This past week she had almost been back to her old self. Edward wrote to her most days; he was so attentive and so pleased that she was feeling better. Soon she would be ready to go home to be with Edward and the children for Christmas.

* * *

Michael Taylor was worried about his daughter. Something just wasn't quite right. He had a troublesome feeling in the pit of his stomach. He was rarely wrong, and he often put his trust in his gut reaction. He remembered the last time they had visited Glasgow. Edward was much worse for wear, he understood that as a doctor his time was limited, but Michael sensed he was a worried man, a troubled man. He had not seen him for a few weeks, but he'd noticed that his face was pale and narrow and that he smelled of stale cigars and liquor. Something just wasn't quite right. His daughter had been ill far too often for his liking. His wife was also concerned, although Jane was too proud, or should he say too stubborn to admit it. He broached the subject while they were sitting together in the drawing-room.

'Mary Jane, do you think she is any better, my dear?'

'Well, yes, she is much more herself,' Jane replied, putting her needlework down on the stool at her side. 'I do think the poor girl does too much, she tries too hard and is exhausted what with the children, and the house to run. Edward is so busy, and poor Mary Jane, it's all too much for her! Is it any wonder she feels much better away from it all, just a few more weeks to gather her strength. I am sure she will be fine.'

Michael looked at his wife with hooded eyes; unconvinced, he nodded his head and smiled somewhat hesitatingly. 'Yes, I am sure she will. Perhaps it's just the time she needs. Time to take stock.'

Take stock? Jane was not quite sure just what her husband meant by that, but she did detect that her husband suspected that something was amiss. Jane said no more; she was sure it was something and nothing, what she didn't want to do was tell her husband what she had seen between that cheap whore of a maid and Edward. It would cause trouble. She decided there and then that it was time to change her will.

Mary Jane wasn't sure how Edward would react to her mother's will. Admittedly, he would be pleased that her mother had provided for her in the event of her death, but deep down Mary Jane knew he would be fuming. The one thing Edward loved above all else was money. To soften the blow, she thought it best to write to him.

Lauder Road, Edinburgh, November 1864.

Dearest Edward,

I am feeling much better today. I have been for a walk around the park with my mother; the gardens are quite beautiful. I managed to eat a light meal on my return, so my health is improving. I no longer feel quite as sick.

Edward, Mother, has made a new will whereby she has bequeathed two-thirds of her estate to me on the event of her death. If something, were to happen to me then the property would pass to you and the children.

I am hoping to be back at home before Christmas; once my strength has returned.

Your forever loving
Minnie

* * *

CHAPTER TWENTY-TWO
A TIGHT SPOT

Mary McLeod loved having Edward to herself; since his wife had been away, they were closer than ever. While she didn't want to think evil thoughts, she couldn't help thinking how good life would be without her. The children were no bother at all. Still, they had a week yet before the mistress was due back so Mary thought she would make the best of it. Her nerves tingled in anticipation just thinking about him.

That evening, Mary planned a candlelight supper, once the children were in bed, and the cook had gone to see her family. This was the first time she had attempted fancy cooking, but she wanted tonight to be unique, she had even tried on several of her mistress's gowns, but she found all of them hideous. Instead, she decided to settle for a periwinkle satin dress that had been her mother's. She loved it; it was so beautiful and fit her slender body like a glove. Mary couldn't wait to see Edward's face when he saw her in it. For the meal, she planned to cook a meal of chicken with croquettes of rice followed by a sweet jelly. He will like that, she thought; he would be tired when he came home, she knew the perfect way to relax him.

Edward was in a foul mood having received the latest letter from his wife. How dare the evil old witch change her will. He had convinced himself that this was a deliberate act of spite. Well, he would show her. Nobody tried to get the better of him. Edward was far too intelligent for that. He had already borrowed two-hundred and twenty-five pounds against Mary Jane's life insurance policy of one thousand pounds. Money was tighter and tighter.

* * *

CHAPTER TWENTY-THREE
CHRISTMAS DECEMBER 22^{ND,} 1864

Mary Jane was so excited to be home, Edward had collected her from the station and made sure she was comfortable before he went back on his rounds. Poor love, he never stopped; she had brought presents for the children, and couldn't wait to see their faces when they opened them. The boys would love the wooden jack-in-the-box and the girls the tiny china tea set; she had seen the gifts in one of the new artisan shops in Edinburgh, and she just had to buy them. It was the subtle, intricate detail on the tea set that caught her eye. The cups were hand painted with pink and gold flowers, such lovely things.

The servants also had a small box each to open on the day after Christmas. That was to be their day, their downtime. Cook deserved a little something after working so hard in the kitchen making Christmas dinner for the family. It was becoming a tradition now; the newspapers had even begun to give it its name: Boxing Day they were calling it. Mary Jane laughed. Whatever would they think of next?

The bedroom smelled musty. Mary Jane threw the curtains wide and opened a window just enough to let air ventilate. Perhaps a blast of the cold December air would take away the stuffy smell. She rang the bell for the maid. She had let things slip while she had been away. This wasn't good enough, she thought, running her finger along the washstand

and collecting half an inch of dust. Mary came into the room her face flushed from rushing up the stairs.

'You rang, Mam?'

'I did, Mary,' Mary Jane replied, eyeing up the maid with indifference.

'This room is dirty. I cannot be expected to sleep here until the whole room is cleaned to my satisfaction!'

'Dirty, Mam? Where!'

'Please do not question me!' Mary Jane replied, tilting her head upwards to show her authority. 'Look!' she added, showing the girl the dust on the washstand, then thumping the bed with her small fist.

'Look at the dust; this bed is messy and crumpled. I will need clean bedcovers.' She watched Mary's expression as her eyes narrowed. She enjoyed the fact that she had annoyed her, she deserved a reprimand – the girl was becoming far too lazy. She needed to be told, her place and to be reminded just who the lady of the house was, whatever other ideas the deluded girl may have.

Mary was fuming. The woman had been back in the house less than twenty-four hours, and she already had her back up. Jealous old hag, and just because she didn't know how to satisfy her man. Well, Edward was not 'her' man anymore. He belonged to her. If she had her way, she would put pepper in the old hag's bed. Make her itch all over. That would show the nasty withered old sow.

Edward sat opposite his wife in the parlour. He glanced at her as she fiddled with her needlework, her glasses perched at the end of her nose, a needle between her lips as she cut a piece of cotton from a reel ready to be threaded. She was looking a lot better, more her old self, the time away at her parents had apparently agreed with her.

'My dear, can I say how relieved I am to see you looking much brighter, how are you feeling in yourself?'

Mary Jane finished threading her needle and put her sewing down. 'Much better. It is wonderful how a change of air has done me so much good. I am still a little weak, but I think in a few weeks' time I will be more myself.'

'You will still need to take things steady; your body has had a nasty shock, it needs to recover. I will make you a bowl of mutton soup; it will nourish you.' Edward made his way to the kitchen. Making sure he was alone; he took the glass phial from his inside pocket.

Mary smiled, contented. Now back home, things would get back to normal. How she loved her husband and her family, they were all so kind to her.

* * *

CHAPTER TWENTY-FOUR
CHRISTMAS DECEMBER 22^{ND,} 1864

Christmas had been eventful; the children were all growing up so quickly, they were so boisterous and such fun. Mary Jane could not imagine life without them. How she had missed them so when she was recovering in Edinburgh. Six weeks she had been home and had to admit that she felt no better. Her stomach ached so much, and she still could not keep anything down without retching. Edward had decided it was best if he made all the meals from now on and brought them up to the room. Mrs Lattimer had resigned, as the master had caught her giving leftover food to the neighbours and had made such a fuss about it and told her to find another job. The new cook was still finding her way around the kitchen. She had liked Catherine Lattimer; the children adored her, she would make them gingerbread and biscuits and take them to the park with a picnic. Catherine had said not to worry about the children as she would still be popping back occasionally to see how their mum was doing and to take them all to the park. 'Don't worry, hens; I'll not forget you.' This news had cheered the youngest boys up, they loved the park and climbing the Conker trees, and Mary Jane knew she was not well enough to take them.

Mary Jane needed to quench her thirst, she had rung the bell several times for the servant girl, but nobody had come. She cursed under her breath 'stupid, lazy girl, will she ever know her place.' She made a mental note to have a word with Edward, she needed a maid who was more attentive, he could tell her to pull her socks up, or she could start looking for another position.

Mary Jane pulled on her night-cape and drew the drawstring loosely under her chin. Her fingers touched the silky embroidered pattern skilfully sewn in her mother's hand. She loved it. It was her favourite Christmas present. Putting on her knitted slippers, she went downstairs in search of a drink of water. The house was deserted, there was nobody in the kitchen, parlour or the drawing room. The children had all gone out with Mrs Lattimer, but she thought Edward was at home, he didn't have any calls until later that day.

The door to the consulting room was a little ajar; she thought she heard a slight whimper. She peered through the door, standing as still as possible, trying hard not to breathe too loudly. Her fingers were jerking as if in spasm, she daren't move. Through the crack in the door, she saw the unmistakable shape of Edward's head. He knelt on the floor while the maid lay naked on the bed. His head was bobbing up and down while his tongue flicked in and out of Mary's glistening vagina. Mary was squirming with delight as her hands gripped the back of Edward's head, and her eyes were closed in satisfaction. Mary Jane couldn't move. She was shocked and too upset to speak. Edward had never done anything like that to her. Well, she wouldn't let him. Disgusting. That sort of thing was for harlots and prostitutes. She tried to sneak away, but not before she saw Mary's eyes flicker, a smug grin spread across her face.

Mary Jane's legs felt weak as she tiptoed towards the stairs. Her stomach turned over and churned. Oh, God, she prayed. Don't let it happen now; she stood still as she crossed her legs still fighting the terrible loosening of her bowels, and the need to vomit. She had to think fast; she didn't want him to know that she had seen him with that, that whore! She let out a cry as loud as she could muster. 'Edward — help!'

* * *

CHAPTER TWENTY-FIVE
A PRETTY GOOD LIAR

To Edward's astonishment, Mary Jane did not mention the incident with Mary in the consulting room. He had intended to deny it, and blame it on Mary Jane's weak disposition, and suggest that she imagined things. Hallucinating with all the medication she had taken, but this had made it easier. Perhaps she hadn't seen anything after all, although Mary felt sure that she had.

Today, he must visit the pharmacy and purchase some more antinomy. He liked to use a different chemist each time. He did not want to bring attention to himself. The young girl in the chemist already knew him; she had taken quite a shine to him and now prepared his order as soon as he walked through the door. Edward pacified her flirting with her just enough to see her blush; he liked that, so young, and such a sweet looking girl.

* * *

Mary Jane had been bedridden for days. She had spoken to Mary McLeod telling her in no uncertain terms that she knew about the affair with her husband, and that she had seen them together in the consulting room. Mary Jane had further told the young maid that she wasn't the first servant the doctor had slept with, and she wouldn't be the last. 'My husband is nothing but a nasty, dirty man,' she screamed at the maid in anger. Mary McLeod suggested that she go away, leave the household, but Mary Jane disagreed. What would be the point, deep down she knew Edward's fascination with the girl would soon be at an end, and now that the clandestine affair was out in the open, there would be no thrill or excitement left for him anymore. Mary Jane knew her husband too well.

Apart from feeling terrible, Mary Jane was depressed. Her thoughts were running wild, strange notions came vividly to her, outlandish ideas which she couldn't comprehend. She was exhausted in mind and body; she knew she had lived a sheltered life, nothing wrong or unpleasant had ever happened to her. She knew she was lucky, beautiful, healthy children, a lovely home, and a husband. So why was she thinking such terrible thoughts? Her mind was dazed and confused, and her memory is reacting strangely. She thought of Lizzie and the fire in Berkeley Square; she remembered how Lizzie's attitude had changed before she died and how she had become insolent in her manner towards the family, especially Edward. Mary Jane's mind was racing, thoughts entered her head all at once, jumbled, mixed up feelings. Why did Lizzie not wake up? Surely, she smelled the smoke? She couldn't get Lizzie's face out of her head, and then there was Mary McLeod and Edward's affair, and his apparent affection for the girl. The nasty, dirty man! How could he be so cruel? She understood that as a man he had needs, but a young servant girl. A sudden thought entered her mind, remembering the time Mary was ill, Edward attended her every day. She had been pregnant! Yes, it was clear to her now.

Her thoughts turned even darker as she remembered how well she had been in Edinburgh, but ill when she returned home. Something was wrong. It was them! Edward and Mary wanted her out of the way! Why was she sick always after meals or a glass of wine! That's it – they were both trying to poison her – yes, that's what they were doing. It made perfect sense, and the memories were vivid in her mind.

'Drink this, my love,' Edward had insisted, handing her a glass of claret.

'It will put some life into you?'

She remembered the strange bitter aftertaste the wine had left, which at the time she put down to her not drinking any alcohol in a while. She also recalled Edward's reaction when she pulled a face when sipping the wine.

'Don't squirm like that, drink it up! It's your taste buds; they are not used to the wine. You need to be more sophisticated and drink wine more often.'

Doubt set in her head; how could she trust Edward? Edward, the man she adored. Her husband? No, it was her illness, Edward would never do such a thing, not to her, not to his Minnie as he affectionately called her. He loves me, doesn't he? She pushed the niggling thoughts to the back of her mind. Ridiculous, she thought to herself, swearing never to entertain such wicked thoughts again.

Suddenly, Mary Jane began to panic. Why had Edward sacked Catherine Lattimer? Who would cook her meals? The new woman didn't know her; she would not come and sit with her as Mrs Lattimer had. She would be in the house with just the children, Edward and Mary McLeod. Mary Jane shook at the thought, terrified.

In the morning, Mary Jane's problems worsened. Edward had brought her some tapioca for her supper, it was a simple dish and one she could generally digest, but not today, she had wretched it all up as soon as she ate it, she just couldn't keep anything down, not even a small bowl of tapioca. Once again, the sweat poured down her nightdress. She was so weak; she knew that she needed help. Edward tried to comfort her, pacify her. Still, it was not good; the time had come for some intervention. Catherine Lattimer came into the room; it was her last day. Mary Jane gripped her hand tightly, not wanting to let go.

'Please, Catherine, you must help me, ple … ase don't leave me, please not here not on my own!'

Edward watched his wife, and he knew that something needed to be done, and quick. Catherine Lattimer may be getting on in years, and he could not forgive her for giving his food away to strangers, but she was far from stupid. She had a sound sense about her. He wanted the old woman out of the way, but he had to be careful. He led Mrs Lattimer from the room, and had a quiet word with her, not wanting to raise suspicion.

'Mrs Lattimer, I have a problem,' he said humbly, and with sincerity in his voice.

'Would it be possible for you to stay a further couple of weeks? I think you would be such a comfort to Mary Jane?'

Catherine Lattimer agreed, she was delighted, she hadn't secured another position yet, and she needed the money.

Edward was relieved, but in a state of panic, he wasn't sure just what his wife had discussed with the old cook, but never in a month of Sundays would he have thought that his dear wife's drug-infused muddled mind would have suspected him of any wrongdoing. He needed a plan. In his mind, the best course of action was to administer a small amount of antinomy – just enough to keep Mary Jane ill, but not enough to kill her. He couldn't let any doubt or suspicion enter anyone's mind. He also thought that it might be a good idea to ask his wife's second cousin to visit Mary Jane. She would like that, and it would be a pleasant diversion for him. A second opinion is what was needed.

'Edward, please I am not getting any better. There must be something you have missed? Perhaps it is some new type of fever? I cannot eat, I cannot sleep, weight is rolling off me. I have no strength. Something needs to change. I feel like I am going to die!'

Edward took his wife's hand and turned her wedding band around her slim finger. He took a handkerchief and wiped her brow.

'There, there, Minnie my darling. Do not fret so; you are over emotional. You are not going to die. It is nothing serious. It's just a chill that has gotten onto your stomach, these things take time, but if it makes you happy I could ask your second cousin to come check you over and stay a few days?'

Mary Jane felt a little brighter. James was a good doctor, and they were very close, she felt comforted knowing he was coming to see her. James would help her, she was sure of it. 'Oh, Edward, yes, yes, that would be a tremendous relief to me. Would you write to him today?'

Edward wrote to Dr James Cowan, knowing that the letter would take a little while to arrive. In that time, he would administer just enough antinomy to produce symptoms of gastric fever. He was happy. Dr Cowan was old school and much easier to deceive, not like Mary Jane's idiot brother Michael who thought himself knowledgeable in all areas of modern medicine. The imbecile!

* * *

CHAPTER TWENTY-SIX
A SECOND OPINION

Five days later Edward met Dr Cowan in the hallway of their home on Sauchiehall Street; Mary Jane's health had much improved in the days following Edward's letter. She had a few more attacks, but her head felt much clearer, she was beginning to feel far more optimistic about her health. She'd had no more thoughts of madness, how silly of her, as if her Edward would ever consider such an act as to poison her. Just what was she thinking! It would never happen in such a distinguished respectable family as theirs. Never!

* * *

In his letter to Dr Cowan, Edward deliberately stressed his concern about his wife's failing health. He wanted Dr Cowan to believe that Edward was an overly concerned husband who was worrying unduly. He knew he would come as soon as he could.

Dr James Moffatt Cowan had been a doctor for many years, although retired, he had, over the years, treated all types of diseases. Reading Edward's troubled letter, he fully understood Edward's concern; he was bound to treat his wife differently to his other patients. He had said it was urgent that he came and that Mary Jane's declining health was severe. Dr Cowan left for Glasgow the following day.

James had spoken to Edward before he examined Mary Jane, it is evident that Edward was distraught James Cowan tried to pacify him, saying it was understandable for Edward to be oversensitive. However, on examining Mary Jane, he was shocked at her delicate appearance, and the fact that she had aged so; she looked older than her mother! Mary Jane was once a robust girl, but now she was just skin and bones. Her eyes were dark and sunken, her skin pale. She did look dreadful. He felt sorry for her. However, she wasn't as bad as Edward had described in his letter; he didn't think that she was on death's door. He tried his best to keep her spirits up.

'Mary Jane, so lovely to see you. Sorry, I didn't get a chance to see you in Edinburgh, I was indisposed. Please forgive me. Now, what have we here? Let me give you a quick examination.' Putting his cold hands on her wrist, he tested her pulse. How are you feeling in yourself – what are your symptoms?'

'I'm much better than a few weeks ago, yet I cannot seem to keep food down, I'm sick when I eat, and my whole body aches with such terrible stomach cramps. Also, I cannot think straight; my mind is muddled and confused, such wicked thoughts enter my head!'

'Wicked thoughts? We all have those from time to time. Well, all your vital signs seem satisfactory.' He scratched his head; flummoxed. Edward had said it was urgent. He couldn't understand it. In his opinion, her symptoms were not serious or life-threatening. Fever, convulsions and stomach cramps. A chill, perhaps? Edward, as her husband and doctor, knew his wife the best. Still, as soon as he returned to Edinburgh, he would call in and see her parents to express his concerns. Perhaps it would be best if Mary Jane's mother came to stay with her for a few weeks, make sure she took her medicine and was well nourished.

'Edward is right, my dear; you have a gastric irritation, brought on by a chill. You will be back to full health in no time. Until then you must rest, that means stay in bed. I am going to prescribe you a mustard poultice which you must keep firmly on your stomach, and two glasses of champagne and ice each evening to keep those wicked thoughts at bay.'

Deep down Mary Jane knew it wasn't just a chill, why was she losing so much weight, why was she always sick? She had read about cholera, and consumption in the papers and she feared that she might be a victim of one of these terrible epidemics that were raging the country, taking the lives of many in its path. She didn't want to die - what would happen to her children?

* * *

CHAPTER TWENTY-SEVEN
BEST LAID PLANS

Edward was pleased with himself; his plan had worked. He congratulated himself on his strategy 'what a talented man I am.' Nobody suspected his intentions; nobody had his intellect, he made small talk to the ageing doctor as he turned his back on him and without drawing attention he took the bottles of tartarised antinomy and tincture of aconite that he'd bought that afternoon from his medical bag. Time for Mary Jane to have a severe dose of medicine – a violent one to make up for the last week or so.

Edward watched with contempt as the older doctor sat reading a newspaper, contemplating the events of the day. Cowan, thinks himself a good doctor, huh! He's nothing but a quack. Edward chuckled inwardly. Still, it had been worth it to have the pompous oaf in his house for a short while. At least now Mary Jane and that nosy old cook were convinced that Mary Jane was just suffering from a severe gastric fever and that soon she would be back on her feet and back to keeping tabs on him and running the household. No, she wouldn't. He had covered his tracks well. He poured himself a large glass of malt to celebrate his greatness, offering the oaf of a doctor the same.

'I don't mind if I do. I am staying over tonight and not returning to Edinburgh until tomorrow.' However, what James Cowan said next devastated Edward and perplexed him greatly.

'Edward, this is a big house, and four children need plenty of care. There is only one maid and a cook. A new cook, whom, I understand, is not used to this house. It's too much. Mary Jane cannot handle all that as well as being ill!'

What was he implying? Edward had to think fast and try to shrug him off.

'Oh, don't concern yourself with that. The children are no trouble. No need to worry about them!'

Dr Cowan persisted, nothing Edward could say further would change Dr Cowan's mind without raising suspicion.

'I will hear nothing further, stop trying to do it all yourself, Edward. It's too much of a heavy load to bear. I will see Mary Jane's mother when I return. She gave me strict orders before I came that I must report back to her. She will love to come and cluck over her daughter and her grandchildren. You know how she likes to play mother hen! Besides, it will take the burden off you, Mary Jane and the servants. A perfect solution for all concerned.'

Edward was furious, why had he let this man in his house, now all his plans were ruined. The old hag would stick her nose in and complicate matters. She would be wanting to make meals and will be sticking her big nose in the issues that were not her concern. Edward cursed to himself.

He soon regained his composure, realising that it would be more dangerous to refuse that his mother-in-law visit, he didn't want to raise suspicion. Anyway, he was Edward Pritchard. He was invincible. He could manage an old woman, even if it were his wife's mother! He would find great delight in carrying on his deadly plans right under her nose!

* * *

CHAPTER TWENTY-EIGHT
SUSPICIONS

Mary Jane knew she must do something. Her children did not want to come near her. It broke her heart, but she couldn't blame them, she would hate any of them to contract this terrible sickness; she couldn't cope like this much longer. Edward had insisted on giving her champagne and ice as her cousin had prescribed, and then some chloroform, which she hated, and now she felt worse. The night cramps had returned, her limbs were tight and rigid with excruciating pain. The fear had returned to her mind. The time had come to do something, the pain now unbearable, she screamed in agony, and both Catherine Lattimer and Mary McLeod came rushing into the room.

'Mary Jane, my goodness, you put the fear of God in me, whatever's the matter?'

Edward entered the room, hot and flushed from rushing up the stairs. Mary Jane took one look at him besides Mary McLeod, and all her fear and suspicions returned. Suddenly, she was overcome with great distress, terrified of the man she married, terrified of this house of horror. How she longed to go back to the safety of Edinburgh and her parents. Something in her gut stirred and she convinced herself that her husband wanted rid of her! From somewhere deep inside she found a little strength. She remembered her mother telling her about a Dr Gairdner, who lived locally, but who qualified with her brother Michael. *She must see him; he would help her; she must try.*

Mary Jane turned to Catherine and grasped her wrist tightly, not wanting to let go, 'Catherine please, please help me. I need to see Dr Gairdner. I demand that you bring him here!' she screamed, looking her husband straight in the eye with all the contempt she could muster. Edward averted her eyes, feeling alarmed, he looked down at the floor, not knowing quite what to do. The last thing he needed was some know-it-all young doctor poking his nose in, particularly since Mary Jane's body now contained a significant amount of antimony.

Edward had to think fast; it would raise suspicion. He didn't want the cook doubting him yet again.

'Of course, my dear. Mary, fetch Doctor Gairdner, tell him it's urgent. There, there, Minnie there is no need to be alarmed, all this anxiety is making you worse. Calm down.'

A short time later Doctor Gairdner returned with Mary McLeod. Mary Jane reminded him she was Michael's sister. Ah yes, he remembered Michael fondly. Mary Jane apologised for not calling him sooner.

Dr Gairdner took one look at Mary Jane and was alarmed. She was rambling, not making sense at all; her eyes were wild. She was gripped with paranoia, her speech garbled and incoherent. The doctor placed his hands on hers, her hands looked odd, her wrists turned in, and her thumbs inverted towards her wrists. Riddled with cramp, the poor woman must be in agony. She caught Edward's eye, he was looking at her sorrowfully and with pity. Mary Jane snapped.

'If you cry, you are such a hypocrite!'

There was an awkward silence in the room. Edward was alarmed, time for him to gather his thoughts and have all his wits about him, or Gairdner was going to think something very sinister was going on. Edward tried to change the subject petrified of what Mary Jane was going to say next. He remembered that he was Edward Pritchard, and who was this man Doctor Gairdner? A nobody, someone who had qualified with Mary Jane's pathetic imbecilic brother, he had so much disdain for the man attending his wife.

Dr Gairdner was puzzled by Mary Jane's behaviour. Feeling cold, he turned to the fire to warm his hands; Mary Jane cried out.

'Oh, you cruel, cruel, unfeeling man – you cannot leave me like this, what sort of a doctor are you!'

The doctor tried to soothe Mary Jane and in a reassuring voice assured her that he wasn't leaving her, he was merely warming his cold hands on the fire.

For the first time, Edward realised that his wife knew his intentions. She knew he was trying to destroy her. She knew he wanted to be rid of her. No longer could he dominate her. Knowing that he had to act fast, he grabbed Dr Gairdner by the elbow and ushered him from the room. Mary Jane tried her best to protest, but nobody was listening.

'As you can see, doctor, my poor wife is under the influence of alcohol. I didn't think it proper to prescribe her champagne, not in her delirious state, but Doctor Cowan insisted. Mary Jane is not herself; please excuse her ramblings, she doesn't know what she is saying. It's not her; it's the drink!' Edward said with a sneering voice of satisfaction.

Dr Gairdner shook his head in agreement. 'Yes, I can see that my good man,' Gairdner reassured him, patting Edward on the arm. They returned to Mary Jane in the sickroom.

Mary Jane felt irate and excitable, she tried to take advantage of Dr Gairdner to try to make him see what was happening to her, but her words came out slurred. She couldn't think straight. Her chance had passed, the two people who could help her were Catherine Lattimer and Doctor Gairdner, but she couldn't convey her message to them. She was doomed.

'Hypocrites, you are all hypocrites together!' she moaned.

'Good gracious, the young doctor exclaimed.' He was puzzled by his patient's anger and her outburst. Well, it cannot be every day that a young doctor was called upon to diagnose the symptoms of someone suffering from the results of poisoning by tartar emetic.

Edward smiled. 'It has been so hard, to see my Minnie, my lovely wife change in this way not easy at all! Do you think that she could be suffering from catalepsy?' Edward slyly guided the young doctor towards this incorrect diagnosis.

'Catalepsy?' the doctor was puzzled. Little was known about this disease, especially for a newly qualified doctor such as Gairdner was. He scratched his head not wanting to admit that he felt a little in awe of the older doctor's knowledge and professionalism and didn't want to appear incompetent to him.

'Yes, you could be, right… it could indeed be catalepsy. I will prescribe a simple, light diet, no medicines and no stimulants. I will call and see her again in the morning.'

Edward was pleased with himself; he couldn't help sniggering; once again, he did not need to worry about another doctor in the house, catalepsy indeed – what an idiot. The blithering fool had no idea what he was talking about. Stupid man. Ignorant soul. A doctor indeed.

In the morning, Dr Gairdner was relieved that Mary Jane was feeling a little better. She had at last slept, which was a start, and had even managed to eat a boiled egg. However, Doctor Pritchard told him that morning that he was taking over his wife's care from now on. The young doctor was somewhat taken aback.

Dr Gairdner was also baffled by Mrs Pritchard's illness. It was all bizarre, and something troubled him for some reason. Mary Jane's face haunted him; she looked so desperate and afraid. So much so that he thought it best to write to her father.

Dear Michael,

I have over the last few days attended to your daughter's health. In my opinion, her health is waning. It is my professional opinion that she would benefit from a change of scenery, a plain diet and rest. I do not believe that she is getting the attention she requires in her present environment. It may be a good idea for her to stay with family, perhaps with her brother Michael for a short while, where she can be monitored and nourished without distraction.

Regards
Dr Gairdner

* * *

Old Michael Taylor was once again concerned. Earlier that day he had written to Edward suggesting that his daughter should come and stay at her brother's house in Edinburgh. Edward had replied that while he agreed that it would indeed be a good idea, his wife was not fit enough to travel, although in the last few days she was feeling a little better.

Michael showed the letter to his wife who was not happy with her son-in-law's response and went upstairs to pack a bag. No need for their daughter to come away from her home and children. Jane would go to her; she would look after her just as she had when she was a child. And as her mother, she would nurse her back to health. Jane would show Edward and that floozy of a maid, but she did not intend letting them know of her planned visit, she preferred to surprise them all.

* * *

CHAPTER TWENTY-NINE
MOTHER COMES- FEBRUARY 10TH 1865

Mary McLeod heard someone open the front door, to her knowledge the family were not expecting anybody, and who would walk straight in unannounced? Concerned, she made her way to the hallway, where, to her surprise, Mrs Taylor stood taking off her top-coat.

'Why, Mrs Taylor, you startled me, we were not expecting you; is there something wrong?'

Jane looked the girl up and down, and for a moment stood irresolutely still, her stronger will conquered and stopped her speaking her mind to this young harlot. Still, there were things she would like to say to this girl, but she was far too much of a lady for that, and besides, now was not the right time. Jane would say her piece to her one day, without a doubt. Very slowly her eyes disengaged with those of the young girl, and with a bowed head she passed her and walked up the flight of steps.

'I will be with my daughter, should anyone need me!'

Mary raised her eyebrows behind the woman's back and proceeded to follow the woman up the stairs.

Jane Taylor was upset to see her daughter in such a poor state of health; she looked so thin and weak, if only she had come sooner.

'Mary Jane, you poor dear. I have come to nourish you back to health; I will stay with you until you are back on your feet.'

Mary Jane mustered a weak smile and heaved a sigh of relief, even laughing hurt all the muscles in her face – everything was such a great effort. She was delighted to have her mother here; she felt a surge of relief come over her. At last her prayers had been answered. She felt like a child again, with her mother there to protect her, then no evil would bestow her. She watched her mother as she struggled to open the bedroom window.

'Good gracious, when was the last time this was open, it's so stuffy in here; fresh air is what you need, it will do you a world of good.'

Mary Jane could not answer her; she put her hand over her mouth as her mother reached for the bowl on the bedside cabinet, she had picked it up just in time before Mary Jane vomited for the fifth time that morning.

Edward was not at all pleased that his mother-in-law had decided to nurse his wife, she was such a formidable woman; there she was fussing over her child like a lion with its cub. The interfering old hag had even decided that it was best to sleep in the same room as her, the sheer impertinence of the woman. What was he to do? Over the last few weeks, there had been a couple of bouts of sickness in the house, one of his children and the lodger Connell had also suffered. He assumed they had tasted some of the food intended for Mary Jane. Edward decided that to combat any further doubt; he must carry on pretending to be a loving husband and devoted son-in-law. The last thing he needed was to create suspicion, or plant a seed of doubt in Jane Taylor's mind; she was as sharp as a knife that one. No, he had to be careful.

* * *

Mary Jane craved for tapioca; it was the first time in months that her taste buds had desired anything. Her mother had a word with the cook, but there was no more tapioca left in the kitchen. Mary Jane's son, Kenneth was more than willing to go to the local shop for a packet; he liked to go to the store on his own as the shopkeeper was a friendly man who always gave him a biscuit.

Mrs Lattimer prepared half of the packet of the tapioca and left it on the hall table. Twenty minutes later, Mary took it to her mistress. Mary Jane couldn't eat it; her appetite failed her. Jane Taylor, never one to waste good food, took the bowl from her and ate a large spoonful herself. Instantly Jane felt ill; she held her stomach as it rumbled, was violently sick almost straight away and had to lie down. She couldn't be sick, who would look after her daughter. The last thing she needed right now was the same disease as her daughter; two ill women in one house were no good to anyone.

Jane Taylor was far from stupid; she was unable to sleep. She couldn't help thinking *what was in the tapioca.* There must have been something added to it. Her suspicion deepened. Could it be the cook, was it sour grapes for losing her job? No, she wouldn't be so stupid? But what was the reason for her daughter's illness? Her anxiety deepened, her head ached, the pain had become unbearable, she took the brown bottle from her pocket and took a couple more drops of Battley's Sedative Solution. She had taken it for years and couldn't imagine life without it. So much so that she had sent that girl Mary to the chemist a couple of days ago, to refill her prescription, well at least the girl was good for something.

* * *

CHAPTER THIRTY
MRS LATTIMER'S PREDICAMENT

Catherine Lattimer wanted to keep her job; she enjoyed cooking for the Pritchard's. The trouble was, the doctor had caught her giving leftover food to the unfortunate beggars in the street. The doctor wasn't happy, and wanted her to leave sooner, but had softened with the mistress being ill, and asked if she could work a little longer. That poor woman looked dreadful; she had no strength at all and was pining away. Catherine had said so to the doctor. But the doctor had merely told her not to have such dreadful thoughts.

Those bairns needed their mother; she had promised them that she would still be popping in and that she would always take them to the park. Little Kenneth cried, he didn't want Mrs Lattimer to leave. The cook had explained to the children that she was older and needed to rest. Besides, Mrs Taylor was there to look after them and their mother now, and the new cook seemed kind, she had sampled her apple turnovers, and although she didn't like to admit it, they were as good as hers, if not better. Mrs Mary Patterson was her name. Gracious me, another Mary in the household. God forbid she would turn out to be the same as the other Mary. No, nobody could be like her, a vixen that one!

* * *

CHAPTER THIRTY-ONE
INTERFERENCE

Jane Taylor remained respectful to Edward. The poor man must be so worried what with the children and the house to look after and a sick wife to attend to as well as his other patients.

Mary Jane did not say a word to her mother about her wicked thoughts and doubts. She had accepted that her outbursts must have been down to the alcohol Dr Cowan prescribed. Anyway, she didn't want to trouble her mother any longer than she had already. Her mother was not getting any younger.

Jane Taylor was not happy and confided in Edward that she thought that for some reason someone was tampering with Mary Jane's food and that this was the source of her illness. In no uncertain terms, she told him that she suspected Catherine Lattimer as possible revenge for the family asking her to leave their employment.

'Women can be vindictive if scorned,' the old lady had told him confidently.

Edward once again pacified his mother-in-law. Mollifying her anxious thoughts with his tender, over-the-top concern, he reassured her that she was mistaken and that no such thing would happen in this respectable household.

'Well, to settle my mind I will be cooking all Mary Jane's meals from now on!

Edward decided there and then that he could not tolerate any further interference. The foolish old woman had just signed her death warrant. She must die, and she must die soon.

* * *

CHAPTER THIRTY-TWO
CAUGHT IN THE ACT

Edward and Mary's lovemaking had become more frequent and more intense since Mrs Taylor arrived at the house. One afternoon they were having a fumble in the consulting room when they heard steps at the door. Mrs Taylor's voice was shouting Edward. Once more she saw Mary in a state of undress and her son-in-law with a guilty look on his face. In that instance, she realised that Edward was not the man she believed him to be. Strange things were happening in this house, and perhaps these two were the cause of it.

What she needed to do was to keep a closer eye on matters. Turning to Edward she declared. 'I am shocked at your behaviour, shocked beyond measure!'

Her anger turned to Mary as she prodded her firmly on the shoulder, and you are nothing but a whore! Pack your bags; I will not have you in this house!'

Edward didn't let Mary know he was worried. He assured her that she was not going anywhere.

'This is my house. I am the master of it. I decided who comes and goes!'

Hoping that his mother-in-law would not confide in his wife, she was too ill to be upset any further. Perturbed, he worried that she would insist on taking her daughter back to Edinburgh. That would ruin his plans. As luck would have it, he saw her coat hanging in the lobby. Looking through her pockets, he found a bottle of Battley's. Edward knew what to do; he slipped the bottle into his pocket.

* * *

CHAPTER THIRTY-THREE
'NEVER, IN THIS WORLD!'– 24ᵀᴴ FEBRUARY 1865

The following day Jane Taylor couldn't get up, she had eventually fallen asleep on her daughter's bed after hours of pain and vomiting. She knew just how her daughter felt. She managed to ring the bell loudly – not easy with her delicate fingers. Jane needed something to stop her sickness; her head was thumping, she took another couple of drops of her solution that was on the bedside table, and waited for the pain to subside. It didn't.

Mary didn't know what to do for the old woman, so she called for Edward. Edward knew her time had come.

'Fetch a cup of hot water, Mary, as fast as you can.'

Jane took a sip of the water and felt much worse; her head hung loosely on her breast. She didn't have the strength or inclination even to hold her head up.

Edward knew there was nothing else he could do. Suddenly, an idea came to him; he called the medical students to fetch help.

'Quickly, Connell, bring Doctor Paterson — go on boy as quickly as you can.' Edward continued to hold Jane's hand which was as cold as a dead fish.

'Just after ten o'clock, Dr Paterson arrived. Greeted in the hall by an anxious Edward.

'She was all right one minute,' Edward lied. 'She was sitting in the parlour writing letters when without warning she fell from her chair, myself and Connell carried her upstairs to her chamber. Mind you; she does take a drop if you get my meaning, doctor!'

Dr Paterson met with an extraordinary sight in the sick room. Mrs Taylor was lying on the bed fully clothed beside her daughter who was shaking frantically with anxiety, her hair wild and her eyes bulged with fear.

Paterson took one look at Jane Taylor and knew that she was a lost cause. She was exhausted and paralysed on her left side. Her pulse was indiscernible, her skin clammy and her breathing laboured and heavy. The old woman's pupils were dilated. The doctor knew what the problem was. In his mind, the old lady could not be helped, and he became more concerned with Mrs Pritchard who seemed on the verge of collapse. Dr Paterson noticed that this woman had peculiar rosy cheeks and a high-pitched voice and was visibly disturbed to see her mother so close to death. Pritchard had told him that his wife and mother-in-law were recovering from a severe bout of gastric fever. Paterson was not convinced. In his opinion, he could almost believe that Mrs Pritchard was suffering from the symptoms of poisoning. However, Dr Paterson would never consider breaking the etiquette of the medical profession. Besides, he had not been asked to give his opinion on Mrs Pritchard, but if he had then poison would be his diagnosis. What a sinister house; if he were right who would be administering poison? Who would know the dose to give her? And who would be able to procure such poison? His thoughts returned to the patient.

'This woman is under the influence of some powerful narcotic – some opiate I would say!' The doctor attempted to rouse her, but Jane did not have the strength to respond.

'Opiate? Well, that will be the Battley's, she uses it for her terrible headaches, she has suffered from them for many years and swears by Battley's she does!' Edward gave the doctor a knowing look.

Edward looked at the sorry state of his mother-in-law as she lay on the bed next to his sick wife. Impulsively, he tapped his mother-in-law woman on the shoulder and proclaimed.

'You are getting better, darling!' on which Dr Paterson stood and shook his head, as he remarked.

'Never, in this world, Pritchard! The woman is dying!'

'I think this time she has taken too healthy a swig of Battley's, she would not listen.'

Dr Paterson had heard enough, and without saying another word, he left the room, walked down the stairs, picked up his hat and coat and left the house.

The next day Connell was once again sent to Dr Paterson's house to ask him to attend Mrs Taylor. Dr Paterson refused. In his opinion, Mrs Taylor was beyond his help.

* * *

CHAPTER THIRTY-FOUR
THE DEATH OF MRS TAYLOR –
25ᵀᴴ FEBRUARY 1865

Jane Taylor had an attack of vertigo and rigours and soon became comatose with paralysis of her left side. Her breathing was slow and laboured, and she was involuntary passing faeces. She died at one o'clock on 25th February two weeks after her arrival at her daughter's home. The cook, Mary Patterson, along with the help of a neighbour, Mrs Nabb, proceeded to wash and dress the body. As they laid her dress on the floor, they came across a brown glass bottle in the pocket of her nightdress. Mrs Nabb couldn't resist taking the top off and smelling it, 'Phew, that's strong, smells like laudanum.' She read the dosage on the bottle of the Battley's Solution and handed it to Mrs Patterson who placed it on the bedside table.

On hearing of this Edward asked to see the bottle, and in a loud voice exclaimed.

'Good heavens, has she taken all this since Tuesday!' He cautioned the women not to mention it to anyone as it may lead to trouble, knowing full well that the gossiping neighbours and the cook would be falling over themselves to be the first to divulge this new information.

* * *

The following day Edward was on his way to the chemist to buy some more antimony when he came across Dr Paterson quite by chance.

'Good day, sir.' Edward took off his hat to greet the doctor.

'Good day,' the doctor grunted, the last person Dr Paterson wanted to see today was this wretched man.

'Would you be good enough to call on my wife, sometime tomorrow, she is no better, and in need of a second opinion, unfortunately, I cannot be there myself as I have to go to Edinburgh for the funeral of my dear mother-in-law – God rest her soul.'

Dr Paterson agreed, knowing that he would not have to see this man.

On examination, the following day the doctor took a closer look at Mrs Pritchard. Her appearance had changed dramatically since he last saw her, and not for the better! She appeared lethargic and depressed, although he did not communicate this to the patient; his observations convinced him that his diagnosis was poison. Asking her what her symptoms were, she responded 'sickness and a constant thirst'. Paterson grew more and more uneasy. What was he to do, he couldn't very well turn around to her and say, 'I believe you are a victim of poison', nor could he accuse her husband of trying to murder his wife. Instead, the doctor told her to take small pieces of ice to relieve her thirst, a small glass of champagne and brandy to strengthen her, and foods such as beef tea, and chicken soup. In his opinion, the damage had already been done, all the medicine he could administer could not change that. As he packed away his equipment, Mary Jane suddenly grabbed Dr Paterson by the arm and in an anxious voice said, 'doctor, when you last called to see my mother did you believe that she was dying?' Mary Jane looked anxiously at the doctor waiting for his response still clinging tightly to the concerned doctor's arm.

'I was sure of it!' the doctor said without hesitation, 'I knew she was dying and I told your husband so!'

The doctor's words had an extraordinary effect on Mary Jane as if something inside her had clicked and all her thoughts and fears now made sense; she clasped her hands together as if in prayer, looked up to the ceiling and burst into tears.

'Good heavens, is it possible?' she garbled incoherently.

Doctor Paterson didn't know what to say; it wasn't his place to offer his opinion. Affectionately he patted the grieving lady on the arm and bade farewell, he swiftly left the house, hoping that he would never set eyes on any of the Pritchards again. He had decided that under no circumstances would he sign the death certificate for Mrs Taylor — and that he would tell the registrar that the death was unexpected and mysterious.

* * *

CHAPTER THIRTY-FIVE
NO DEATH CERTIFICATE

Michael Taylor was distraught; it had all happened so fast. His wife had been in good health two weeks ago; he was heartbroken when he received the wire. Edward had explained that it had been paralysis following epilepsy and there was nothing anybody could have done. Michael went to Glasgow as soon as he could.

Edward asked him to call on Dr Paterson for the death certificate, explaining that it would be better if he asked being her husband. Michael found Dr Paterson very brusque and uncooperative, and to Michael's astonishment, the doctor refused without explanation, to provide a death certificate, he said;

'This I cannot do, as to do so would be contrary to professional etiquette.'

As soon as Michael left the doctor's house, the doctor took pen to paper to Mr Struthers, registrar, who had sent him a schedule to fill in.

6, Windsor Place, Glasgow, 4th March 1865.

To Mr James Struthers, the registrar.

Dear Sir. I am surprised that I am called on to certify the cause of death in this case. I only saw the person for a few minutes a short period before her death. She seemed to be under some narcotic, but Dr Pritchard, who was present from the first moment of the illness until death occurred, and which happened in his house, may certify the cause. The death was sudden, unexpected, and mysterious.

Yours faithfully
James Paterson, M.D.

Edward was not unduly alarmed, and luck was on his side once more. The registrar's office misplaced the letter sent by Dr Paterson, but the records did state that both Dr Paterson and Dr Pritchard had attended the sick old lady, the registrar assumed that he'd sent the request to the wrong doctor, and sent another to Dr Pritchard. Edward completed the form stating that Mrs Taylor had died of paralysis and apoplexy. That should have been the end of the matter, and only Dr Paterson would ever doubt that the old woman's death had been due to natural causes.

* * *

CHAPTER THIRTY-SIX
CHEESE

A black mist had settled over Mary Jane; she missed her mother so much. She had no energy and was inconsolable. Why hadn't her mother stayed in Edinburgh, perhaps if she had, she would still be alive, maybe if she'd remained there with her, then she wouldn't feel like this! The sadness flowed through her veins and deadened her mind. Her heart ached, not even the voices of her children, or her husband could abate her depressed mood.

Her dressmaker had called on her yesterday and was shocked at the mistress's appearance. Now Mary Jane was a shadow of her former self. She remembered the times when Mary Jane would need her clothes, taking out as she had put on weight. Not now. Now she could make two dresses out of just one of her dresses. She didn't like to see her like this.

'Why don't you go to Edinburgh for a while, the air suits you better there?' the worried dressmaker suggested.

She asked Edward if he thought it would be a good idea, but Edward would not hear of it, 'You cannot stand, let alone travel!'

She knew he was right; she so missed her mother, she felt so lost without her. Mother had even slept in her room and made her meals, now Edward must look after her himself. Her head ached so much, and her heart raced so fast, she couldn't stop the tears from rolling down her face.

Edward felt confident now that his mother-in-law and that busy-body cook were out of the way. His thoughts turned to Mary and how much she meant to him. For his love of the girl, he had to proceed with his plans. Putting the next part of his plan in place, he decided to placate Dr Paterson; he needed the doctor on his side. Edward called on him and thanked him for his wife's care and how her health had significantly improved following his suggestions on a diet. Still, he needed to cover his tracks; Mary Jane's idiot brother was always writing to him asking how his sister was. Under no circumstances did he want him coming to see her and sticking his nose in!

In the meantime, he continued to buy tartarised antimony and tincture of aconite, a little at a time. One day at the dinner table with the family he had cut a piece of cheese which he sent up to Mary Jane. Unbeknown to others this piece of cheese had been dipped in a solution of tartar emetic. Mary McLeod took the cheese for Mary Jane. Mary Jane asked Mary to taste it for her. Mary did and felt a burning sensation in her mouth, the cheese tasted strange. The cheese was taken back to the kitchen where Mrs Patterson ate it and was violently ill, and had to stay in bed for a few days.

Shortly after this incident, Edward asked the cook to make his wife an egg-flip, he said he would fetch the sugar for it. He returned with two sugar-lumps which he added to the mixture. Mrs Patterson again sampled the dish and spat it straight out, declaring that it had an extraordinary taste. Mary Jane ate the egg-flip and soon after became very ill. Following the incident with the cheese and now the egg-flip Edward knew what was happening; the cook was tasting the food intended for his wife. Why would she do that; was she just greedy, or did she suspect something more sinister? Edward was growing more and more uneasy by the day.

* * *

Mary Jane rang the bell in her room continually, but no one answered. Mrs Patterson eventually heard it. She had also learned that no one except the doctor and Mary McLeod could attend the mistress, she heard them both in the consulting room, but for some reason, she couldn't open the door, something heavy was blocking it from the inside. She then started to go upstairs to attend to Mrs Pritchard, whose bell ringing was more frantic, when she saw the doctor come out of the consulting room with Mary McLeod close behind him.

Edward saw the look on Mary Patterson's face, once again he was worried it was just a matter of time until the cook put two and two together, she had tasted the food, she had herself become ill, now she had seen him and Mary together. If she had not done already?

That evening Mary Jane's condition worsened. She became delirious; it was clear that her health had taken a turn for the worse. Edward sent for Dr Paterson; he felt confident to have a second opinion, after all, he had no notion of the doctor's suspicions.

Dr Paterson was horrified at the drastic change in Mary Jane; her eyes were sunken, she had a nervous expression in her eyes, her pulse was weak and rapid. Despite being delirious, she recognised the doctor and held on tightly to his hand. Dr Pritchard had explained that his wife had not slept in five days, so perhaps her appearance was to be expected. Paterson prescribed a mixture consisting of thirty drops of a solution of morphia, thirty drops of ipecacuanha wine, five drops of chlorodyne and an ounce of cinnamon water, suggesting that this prescription should be repeated if there was no relief.

Mary Jane Pritchard couldn't take this level of pain much longer, she tossed and turned her head on the pillow, her body rigid, she rolled her eyeballs upwards and showed the whites of her eyes as if asking for divine intervention, her prayers were soon answered. She died at one o'clock the following morning.

* * *

CHAPTER THIRTY-SEVEN
DEAD — SHE'S NOT DEAD

Edward knew his wife was dead, but for now, he didn't want to believe it. Five minutes earlier he had asked Mrs Patterson to prepare a mustard poultice for his wife. Upon her return, he had lifted his wife's nightdress from her stiff, cold body and asked the cook to place it on her stomach. She refused. 'No point in putting mustard on a dead body!' Edward knew he had to be careful with this woman.

'Dead, she's not dead, she's just fainted.'

'She's dead, as a doctor you should know that better than me!'

Without warning, Edward gave out a cry of grief.

'Come back, come back, my dear Mary Jane. Don't leave your dear Edward!' He turned to the servants, demanding that they bring him hot water.

'No amount of hot water will bring her back, she's gone,' Mrs Patterson asserted.

'She's not dead, no she's not. She can't be — not my Minnie; she's just drunk too much wine; Patterson prescribed it.' Distraught, he made an astonishing remark.

'What a brute, what a heathen. Quick, King has a rifle in his room, fetch it and shoot me!'

For a few seconds, Edward felt remorse. His equanimity soon returned knowing that he had to put on a show for Mary Patterson. It could be that she remembered the incident with the cheese and the egg-flip. Edward was quite aware that if the authorities carried out an autopsy on Mary Jane, then that would be it, his time would be up. Edward was mindful of the fact that in the 1860s murder was looked upon as a terrible crime, and hanging was the punishment. Edward felt no remorse over Betty Chandler, Lizzie or his mother-in-law, but Mary Jane had been the mother of his children and his wife.

Too late for regrets now the deed had been done, he recovered from his slight twinge of guilt and began to replay the role of grieving husband. Leaving Mrs Patterson to wash the body, he sent Mary McLeod to inform Dr Paterson that Mrs Pritchard was dead, and there was now no need for him to call any further.

Edward went to his office and wrote letters to the family, and a letter to Clydesdale Bank with regards to his account being overdrawn by £131 12s 4d.

131 Sauchiehall Street
Glasgow

Sir,

I am acutely aware of the overdraft, and nothing short of the substantial affliction I have been visited with since the year commenced in the loss of my mother-in-law and this sad day my wife, after long and severe illness would have made me break my promise. If you kindly tell Mr Readman, to whom I am well known, that immediately I can attend to business, I will see him on the matter; please ask him if he can wait till after my dear wife's funeral on Thursday.

I am sir, yours faithfully.
Edward W Pritchard. 18th March 1865

On returning from the post box, he was still concerned about Mary Patterson; he couldn't get her face out of his mind. Now home, he sought her out to have a quiet word with her and to show his feelings as the grieving husband.

'Mrs Patterson, my wife walked up the street with me. She asked me to take care of our children, especially the little girls; she didn't mention the boys, and then she left me!' He broke down and wept openly. Crocodile tears.

The following Monday, Edward certified his own wife's death, entering the cause of death as gastric fever, stating that the duration of her illness was two months.

* * *

CHAPTER THIRTY-EIGHT
ANONYMOUS MAIL & ARREST

The Procurator-Fiscal received an anonymous facsimile. The contents of which read;

March 18th 1865, Glasgow.

Sir,

Dr Pritchard's mother-in-law, died suddenly and unexpectedly about three weeks ago, in his house at 131 Sauchiehall Street, under strange circumstances, and at least very suspicious. His wife died today, also sudden and unexpected and equally suspicious. We think it right to direct your attention to the above as the proper person to act on this matter and see justice done.

Amor Justitiae.

* * *

On 20th March 1865, Edward was at his father-in-law's house in Edinburgh, where his wife's casket lay before she was taken to Grange Cemetery the following Thursday, for interment beside her mother. Edward did a bizarre thing and demanded that he be allowed to open the casket and in full view of the priest, his children and all the family, and with 'lots of feeling' he bent down and kissed his wife fully on the lips. Edward then wept like a baby. Nobody knew what to say; they were dumbfounded, the priest had seen nothing like this before and hoped he would never see it again, to him it was the most incredible sight he had ever witnessed.

Edward was ecstatic as he sat on the train back to Glasgow. At last, he was free. Free from not only the burden of marriage but also from his wife's interfering family. He had conquered everything he set out to do. On reflection, he did feel a slight twinge of remorse for Mary Jane after all she was his wife and the mother of his children. He had no sympathy for his mother-in-law, the nosy old bat, in his opinion, it served her right, how dare she try to interfere in his life, criticise him and upset his plans. Lizzie and the others meant nothing to him and were all insignificant. As for those incompetent doctor's, well, Edward smiled once again; he had outsmarted them all, Cowan, Gardiner and Paterson – fools the lot of them.

Yes, he was content with the details of his atrocious plot, just a few more days and the casket and his crime would be concealed forever, he could then move on with his life. However, his elation didn't last long as he stepped off the train at Victoria Street station, he turned to see a man standing behind him. The colour drained from Edward's face as he realised that the man was Superintendent McCall, one of Glasgow's finest police officers. Edward's heart could almost be heard above the station clock it was beating so hard. Surely, the Superintendent wasn't there for him? But his fears were soon realised as the officer promptly grabbed him by the elbow and ushered him to a quiet corner of the platform where he immediately arrested him on suspicion of the murder of his wife.

Did they not know who he was! What evidence did they have? Edward convinced himself it was all a misunderstanding, and that it would all be sorted out swiftly. Still, he remained stunned at the charge brought against him. Although inside he was livid; he tried to keep as calm as possible; not wanting to give the police any reason to doubt him.

* * *

CHAPTER THIRTY-NINE
SUPERINTENDENT MCCALL

Dr Paterson allegedly penned the anonymous letter, but who, when questioned strenuously denied he was the perpetrator. While Edward was away in Edinburgh, the police had made themselves busy in the house of horror on Sauchiehall Street. They had instigated a rigorous search of the home. They had removed various bottles from the doctor's consulting room and elsewhere. They had taken clothes and bed linen worn by Mrs Pritchard before her death. A post-mortem examination had been carried out by Doctor's Maclagan and Littlejohn on the body of Mrs Pritchard; they could find nothing to indicate that her death was due to natural causes.

The following day Edward William Pritchard appeared before Sir Archibald Alison of Lanarkshire and emitted a declaration upon the charges made against him. Meanwhile, Mrs Nabb had provided the police with information about an illicit affair between the doctor and his maid Mary McLeod. Mrs Nabb left nothing out as she revelled in every minute detail of the sordid affair that she could recall.

Superintendent McCall was a dedicated police officer and had served on the force for many years, and in all his numerous investigations he left no stone unturned. An imposing man by Victorian standards, tall, balding with a thick set of fashionable whiskers to compensate, he was well known in the community and feared by thieves and vagabonds. McCall's investigations had revealed that

Pritchard's finances were in disarray, and there was an insurance policy on Mrs Pritchard, but not significant enough to warrant such drastic action such as murder? The superintendent was baffled. If the doctor did kill his wife, then why? What was his motive? Not for the love of a servant girl. Surely not? Was the wee girl the instigator? The superintendent concluded it was time to bring the young lassie in for questioning.

* * *

Mary McLeod appeared at the police station on the charge of murdering her mistress. She was horrified. And she had no idea what to say. Mary was so nervous, petrified, what if they didn't believe her. Her nails were already bitten down to the quick as she nibbled at their frayed edges like a famished mouse.

McCall was shocked at Mary's youth and her innocence. What was the doctor thinking of, seducing such a simple, naive young girl? When he began his questioning her face crumpled, she collapsed into a flood of tears. 'Murder the mistress… me… No, I never!' The Superintendent's questioning was relentless, and Mary became exhausted, hoping upon hope that they believed her and would let her go. She even wouldn't mind returning to the Gorbals, and her pig of a father, she just wanted them to release her. The Superintendent wouldn't give in.

'You were in on it, weren't you, Mary?'

'N… no, I knew nothing!'

'Come on, Mary; you wanted the doctor to yourself, didn't you! You planned it together so you could be the mistress of the house, that's the truth isn't it, Mary?'

Cold sweat glistened on Mary's crumpled brow. With hands clasped tightly on her stomach, she constantly fiddled with her knuckles, weaving her fingers in and out of each other. She just wanted to curl up into a ball and be invisible.

'No! it's not the truth. I knew nothing about Mrs Pritchard's death. She was sick, that's all I know!'

'Me and Edward — well, yes — we were intimate, but murder! I know nothing about his wife's death!'

'He took your virginity, didn't he?'

'Yes, but it wasn't like that – he loves me!'

The Superintendent looked Mary straight in the eye and smiled a knowing smile. He'd heard it all before. A young girl, the older man, always grounds for trouble.

'Were you going to have his baby? Is that the story, Mary? You wanted his wife dead. You wanted him all to yourself, didn't you? You can tell me, Mary. Confess, you'll feel better for it!'

'I was pregnant, yes, but Edward got rid of it for me. It wasn't the right time you see!'

'He got rid of it? What do you mean?'

'Abortion, he performed an abortion on me. The mistress knew all about it!'

The Superintendent was shocked at Mary's revelation, not wanting to believe what she had just said.

'The mistress knew that you were carrying on a sexual affair with her husband?'

'Yes, yes, she found out. Her mother knew too; she caught us together in the consulting room!'

'And what did they say to that?' The Superintendent was intrigued.

'Err, I don't know, they weren't happy. Edward dealt with it. You had better ask him.'

'Oh, I will, Mary. I will.'

Superintendent McCall kept up his vigorous interrogation, but after a few hard hours was satisfied with Mary's story and release her without charge. Mary was not off the hook just yet, as she was to be a prime witness for the prosecution. Edward wouldn't like that.

Meanwhile, an examination of the books of the chemist Messrs Murdoch Brothers and the Glasgow Apothecaries Company, Sauchiehall Street, where Edward kept accounts further satisfied the authorities of Edward's guilt. The reports showed recent purchases of tartarised antimony, aconite and other poisons and in quantities unexplained with regards to that of an ordinary General Practitioner.

* * *

CHAPTER FORTY
A CHARMING MAN

Edward was charming them all, right from the outset he had decided that if he were to get them all on his side, then his chances of an acquittal would be improved. His attitude was so calm and peaceful that he could not be considered remotely capable of murdering his wife. Not his Minnie, he loved her and told everyone how much he loved his wife and family. He even carried around a picture of the whole family, which he kept close by him, showing it to anyone that crossed his path. This show of affection ensured that everyone knew that he genuinely cared for his deceased wife and mother-in-law.

His peaceful attitude convinced Even the prison guards that met Edward Pritchard that he must be innocent. There must be an entirely plausible explanation for Mrs Pritchard's death. While he was in North Prison he turned to prayer; he remained quiet and courteous, determined to impress those around him with his impeccable manners and his intellect and to show them how foolish they were to bring such a diabolical charge against a man such as he. Edward even tried to keep his anger at bay when the prison denied a little pomatum for his hair and beard. It was vital that he kept up appearances. Now he would be on the stand with streaks of grey in his hair and beard. What difference does it make to them denying me such an essential part of my makeup? The fools.

The police had taken Edward's diaries, and read segments from them, yet again the authorities found it virtually impossible to believe that this smooth-tongued gentle-mannered man could be responsible for the murder of his wife. When the police read his diary for the date Mary Jane died, the charges against him seemed unfathomable.

18th March 1865

Died here at 1 a.m. Mary Jane, my beloved wife, aged 38 years – no torments surrounded her bedside, but, like a calm, peaceful lamb of God passed Minnie away. May God and Jesus, Holy Ghost; one in three – welcome Minnie. Prayer on prayer till mine be o'er; ever-lasting love. Save us, Lord, for thy dear son.

* * *

CHAPTER FORTY-ONE
CHANGING OPINIONS

On 22nd March 1865, Mary Jane's body was interred in the Grange Cemetery. Edward was apparently both shocked and inwardly relieved to hear this news.

'She is at peace at last and is now with Mummy. Please, God, look after them both; they are gentle souls!' His inner peace didn't last long when the authorities informed him that portions of his wife's body had been reserved for chemical analysis. Modern ideas and modern medicine, Edward being a more traditional physician hadn't bargained on that one.

* * *

Public interest in the case was intense, and every step of the inquiry pursued in the press. In the public's eyes, it was all nonsense! Edward had declared his innocence. There was no motive, why would a middle-class man of Edward's standing want to kill his wife? He had nothing to gain. Surely, he must be innocent. Edward retained the services of Messrs Galbraith & Maclay as his agents, who restricted the news reports to the press. Before their engagement, daily reports on the case and subsequent propagating sensational theories were common fodder for the broadsheets. Every note that he'd written and every diary entry had been scrutinised and analysed. They must think he was stupid, Edward knew that if there were to be any suspicion that he had covered his tracks, the only thing they would find would be complimentary. Superintendent McCall had shown him a few of the letters he had written to his father-in-law and other family members, which, in Edward's opinion supported his case.

8th March 1865

Dear Michael,

Mary Jane progresses slowly towards convalescence – still very fickle in her appetite, requesting something and when it is brought unable to take it.

15th March 1865

Dear Michael

We are all in grief at Minnie's wretched nights – no sleep and the sickness has been worse yesterday and today.

If you have any Champagne or Port Wine, bring over a little. She fancies it; it is the only thing that supports her.

Your affectionate son-in-law
Edward

* * *

Much was Edward's dissimulation with the case that neither the Taylor family or any member of the Pritchard family thought that he was guilty. Even his sister, who he hadn't seen for years, supported him. They all expressed their confidence in his innocence. Edward had charmed them all.

To his absolute delight, the press was also on his side; the prison warders had shown him the cutting from the local paper. Edward began to relax; it was all going to be well.

Glasgow Daily Mail
17th March 1865

The circumstances of the unfortunate double bereavement which has fallen upon Doctor Pritchard's family, although peculiar, have nothing in them so far as is yet known which would implicate Doctor Pritchard and his unblemished public character. He is considered free from the least taint of guilt till conclusive evidence be brought against him.

Since Doctor Pritchard settled in Glasgow some six years ago, he has shown an abundance of talent amongst a wide circle of patients; he engaged with the public institutions – such as the Glasgow Atheneum of which he was a Director. Many of his vast and exciting talks have become widely known.

An author of numerous medical papers and amongst others entertaining guides about Yorkshire and the watering place of Filey, where he lived before moving to Glasgow, where he gained an additional reputation. Thus, the prominence he has attained adds heightened misfortune to his present situation.

* * *

However, general feelings were about to change as the result of chemical analysis taken from tissue samples on Mary Jane's body. Edward had always been against modern medicine, and he believed that science did not play a part in it. How wrong he was.

The Reinsch process was applied whereby tissue samples were immersed in hydrofluoric acid along with copper foil, which facilitated the slow extraction of antimony. Mary Jane's body contained an unmistakable presence of antimony. The news reached Glasgow on 28th March and because of these findings, Edward was fully committed for trial, and a warrant issued for the exhumation of Mrs Taylor's body. The public was in a frenzy. Up until now, there had not been any suspicion surrounding the death of the doctor's mother-in-law. The same test was applied to Mrs Taylor's remains with the same results. Two murders. The public was excited and braced themselves for a sensational trial.

* * *

CHAPTER FORTY-TWO
BLAME THE SERVANT GIRL

Edward sensed the change of loyalty and began to panic; he needed a plan. Thinking fast, he decided that his best course of action was to blame Mary McLeod. Well, it was all her fault. If she had not come into his home, then none of this would have happened. Mary Jane would still be alive! Yes, Mary McLeod was the actual killer. Poor little Mary from an abusive, humble, home, she had tempted him into sin with her come-to-bed eyes, wicked ways and slender body. Not surprising he had been tempted, the girl had put a spell on him. All he had done to the brazen hussy was offer her kindness, and she had abused his kind-heartedness. The girl had needed him, and all he had done was to try to better her and now look where he was.

Edward needed to convince the police and the public of the truth and assure them that he wasn't the one to blame here. People knew that he was an affectionate husband, a loving father, a good doctor and an admirable man. Mary McLeod was just a housemaid who was obsessed with her master and murderously jealous of his wife. Yes, that is what he would do. Nobody would miss a young servant girl like her, and she would not be bright enough to defend herself against him. A stupid young girl infatuated in believing that once she had disposed of her mistress, then she could have the handsome doctor all to herself. Edward persuaded himself that his plan would work and that the public would believe him. It all sounded like a plot from an Edgar Allan Poe novel. After all, he was a doctor with friends in high places, a perfect gentleman and a model of married decorum, his mother-in-law, was an old lady who had died a natural death, and Mary McLeod, well she just told dreadful lies. Convinced, he immediately requested to speak to his defence team. They needed a strategy. He would soon be free.

***

PART THREE
THE TRIAL

The trial opened after a delay. Under the Habeas Corpus Act (Scotland) 1701 a trial must be fixed within sixty days and completed within one hundred days of the 'date of intimation'. If this is not possible, then the prisoner must be released. Dr Pritchard's indictment was served on 31st March 1865, and the trial began on 3rd July the same year and expected to last five days. This meant that the one-hundred-day rule would expire during the trial. After consultation it was agreed that adjournments of the trial would not count, thus allowing the trial to go ahead just within the limit.

* * *

Day 1 Monday 3rd July 1865 -10 am.

The High Court of Justiciary, Criminal Court of Edinburgh.
Judges Present
The Lord Justice Clerk (Lord Glencorse - John Inglis)
Lord Ardmillan - (James Crauford)
Lord Jerviswoode - (James Baillie)

Counsel for the Crown
The Solicitor General. (Lord George Young)
Adam Gifford and James Arthur Crichton, Esqs;

Advocates-Depute.
Agent -
Mr Andrew Murray, Jun. W.S.

Counsel for the Panel. (Defence)
Andrew Rutherfurd Clark, William Watson, and David Brand
Esqs; *Advocates.*
Agents-
Mr Henry Buchan, S.S.C., Edinburgh; Mr James Galbraith, of
Messrs. Galbraith & Maclay, Writers, Glasgow.

* * *

Before the commencement of proceedings, the learned judges
took their seats on the bench. The prisoner was then placed
at the bar and formally charged with the crime of murder, and
the indictment read out to him. This claimed that he had
unlawfully administered tartarised antimony, aconite, and
opium to his mother-in-law Mrs Jane Taylor in tapioca, porter
and beer and that he added it to a medicine named Battley's
Sedative Solution. Furthermore, that between 10th and 25th
February 1865 he was also charged with administering on
repeated occasions in February and March 1865 tartarised
antimony and aconite to his wife Mary Jane Pritchard in
articles of food and medicine.

Edward listened intently as the charges against him were
read out, his expression subdued, but he managed to maintain
a sense of tranquillity in his demeanour, seldom changing
position, and gazing steadfastly at the witnesses; he nodded
nonchalantly once the speaker had finished reading the
indictment.

The trial heard before Lord Justice Clerk; Lord Glencorse
(The Right Honourable, John Inglis), who eight years earlier
had served as counsel for Madeleine Smith; a sensational trial,

which, with Inglis's brilliant defence, ended with the accused being acquitted as the jury deemed the case 'Not Proven'. The case caused an uproar throughout the country with people still debating the socialite's innocence. Some thought that she had got away with murder. This case was considered Inglis's most famous achievement, and his address to the jury considered a masterpiece of forensic eloquence.

As a lawyer, Inglis stood alone among the men of his generation; he had a higher judicial reputation than many other judges did. As a magistrate, Lord Glencorse was courteous, dignified, and patient in his manner and the discharge of his high office. Well respected by his peers, and renowned for his soundness of judgement, he was also responsible for much public work, particularly in higher education. He was a tall man with wiry bushy sideburns, a prominent nose, and a formidable stare.

The Solicitor General of Scotland prosecuted the case, assisted by Mr Gifford and Mr Crichton, while Mr Clark, Mr Watson and Mr Brand defended Pritchard.

Public interest in the case was immense and replicated the same level of excitement as that of the Smith trial. Special regulations were in place with strictly controlled admission to the courthouse during proceedings. This grim fascination with the case brought crowds from all over the country, hoping to catch a glimpse of the handsome, calm, collected doctor accused of poisoning his wife and mother-in-law.

On the day of the trial, at an early hour, people queued outside hoping to get a place in the courtroom, and members of the public besieged every entrance to the court. When the doors opened, the crowds flocked in, and the courtroom became jammed to capacity, while others were left disappointed to be refused admission.

* * *

CHAPTER FORTY-THREE
THE JURY

The all-male jury, *(It was considered unsuitable for women to be appointed to a jury. The opinion was that women lacked either the Constitution or the intellect required to serve as jurors, frequently succumbing to their emotions either by fainting or by voting for an improper verdict)* having been empanelled. Headed by Mr George Sim, a writer from Glasgow, and occupations held among the jurors consisted of farmers, ironmongers, grocers, plumbers and gas-fitters.

Lord Justice Clerk addressed the jury of their regular duties.

'Gentleman of the jury, the task you are called upon to discharge, the most solemn which a man can perform, is to sit in judgement and to decide on an issue which depends upon the life of a fellow human being who stands charged with the highest crime for which a man can be arraigned. Your responsibility is to try this case, according to the evidence before you, which shall be brought, and according to that alone. You must discard from your mind anything that you have ever read or heard or any opinion that you may have formed. If the evidence before you should satisfy the prisoner's guilt. Then, you will have discharged your duty to society; to your consciences, and to the oaths you will have taken, by fearlessly pronouncing your verdict accordingly. However, if the evidence fails to produce a reasonable conviction of guilt in your minds, God forbid that the scale of justice should be inclined against the prisoner by anything of prejudice or pre-conceived opinion.'

The chairman of the jury agreed with the statement made, and the long-awaited trial began. The judge and the other magistrates, followed by the jury, took their seats, and when they were all seated Edward William Pritchard was then escorted into the dock.

Silence fell over the court, and all eyes watched the accused as he entered the room. Edward had taken special care of his appearance, believing that once the people and more importantly, the judge and jury saw how dignified he was, then they would soon acquit him. Edward had chosen his attire carefully and decided to wear his black mourning suit as a mark of respect to his much-missed dear departed family. With a little effort on his part, the public would realise that he was grieving. After taking his seat, he took a long look around the courtroom, consciously trying to get an inkling for the type of people he had to endure. Edward's brother, Charles Augustus Pritchard, secretary of the navy in chief at Plymouth, wholeheartedly believed in his brother's innocence and with permission from the court sat at his brother's side throughout the trial.

Edward was thankful that his parents were not alive to see this, and not at all surprised that his elder brother Francis Bowen was unavailable for most of the trial. Typical of him – so much for family loyalty and solidarity. His sister Emma-Louisa and her husband Raymond had made the journey from Dublin; he was surprised at that, as they had never been particularly close. The Taylor family also refused to believe Edward's guilt and decided amongst them that there must have been a terrible misunderstanding.

* * *

Mr Watson for the defence moved for a separation of the trial of the two charges together on the grounds of 'incompetence of the proceedings to try both deaths together.'

The solicitor general responded: 'The two murder charges are inseparable parts of the same story, and as such should be tried jointly.'

Mr Clark for the defence argued that: 'The danger to the prisoner is, that though there may be independent evidence sufficient to prove either of the charges, yet taking the two together the jury may hold that there is enough to prove both.'

The motion was refused.

Edward was then called to the bar, and the clerk of the court read out the charges against him and asked,

'How say you?'

Edward, pulled himself up to full height pushed his shoulders back, lifted his bearded chin and looked directly at the judge, and in a clear, distinct voice, said.

'Not Guilty.'

Raised whispers spread all around the courthouse. The drama appealed to Edward, at last, he had his stage, and he intended to play his role the best he could under the circumstances. Although the whole scene had made him tired and weary, he tried his best not to show it. Worried, he hadn't slept for a few nights waiting for this day to arrive. However, he knew he looked pale but handsome, and he could sense the ladies admiring his good looks. Edward made sure he had a crisp white handkerchief in his pocket, and that he wept at all the appropriate moments, remaining sad, thoughtful, and reflective throughout the proceedings.

The judge banged his gavel.

'Silence in court, the defendant's statement is important.'
The room fell quiet as the clerk recorded Edward's plea.

* * *

CHAPTER FORTY-FOUR
EVIDENCE FOR THE PROSECUTION

The first witness to be called was Catherine Lattimer, the family's former cook. This day couldn't come soon enough for her. She was haunted by the look of agony on her mistress's face the last time she saw her. She was cross with herself for not speaking up sooner and alerting the authorities. Questions kept going through her mind. 'Why didn't she realise that Mrs Pritchard and her mother's food was tampered with, and why didn't she do something to stop it!' Perhaps if she had both women would be alive today. Today was her chance to get it off her chest, time to do her duty and put the record straight.

She had dressed smartly and had borrowed her sister's best hat. She didn't want anybody looking down their noses at her. Catherine took the oath and glared straight at the doctor as he sat smugly in his seat. Just look at him dressed all in black, he was a hypocrite in her eyes. How she hated him and that whore Mary McLeod. The weeks leading up to the trial, Catherine had time to reflect on the suffering those two vulnerable women went through and she thought of all the times she had held her mistress's hands trying to warm them and relieve them from the twisted pain of cramp.

The times Mary Jane rolled on the bed in pain, clutching her stomach and writhing in despair. No, a more terrible and painful death, Catherine could not imagine, why had she not done more and alerted the authorities? Still, she was pleased that she had done the right thing in the end, and by telling the truth today, it would hopefully go some way in ensuring that the doctor got what he deserved. She had prepared for this day for months, now she felt ready and took a deep breath, and waited for her name to be called.

The solicitor general rose from his seat and stood up straight, in an authoritative voice he said, 'I call Catherine Lattimer to the stand.'

Catherine ambled towards the dock, nerves had set in, and her legs felt heavy. An officer of the court had to help her up the step to the bar.

'Your name is Catherine Lattimer, and you are a widow, is that correct?'

Before answering Catherine put her hand in her pocket, and clasped the cross of her rosary beads. Her faith would guide her through this. Of that she was sure.

'Yes,' she replied in a quiet voice barely anyone could hear. 'That's right.'

'Mrs Lattimer, can you speak up please so that the jury can hear you.'

Catherine took a handkerchief from up her sleeve blew her nose, and cleared her throat.

'Sorry, Your Honour,' she said in a much louder tone.

The solicitor general nodded his approval.

'How long did you work for the prisoner, Doctor Pritchard?'

'Five years. I started just after my husband passed away. I left his service on 16th February last. I was a cook. I was supposed to leave on 2nd February, Candlemas Day, but the doctor asked me to stay longer due to Mrs Pritchard being so sick.'

'Could you describe the house on Sauchiehall Street?' Catherine scratched her head. What a strange question, still, she tried her best to answer it.

'The house, well… it's large. Four floors, one of them a sunk level. On that floor, there are two bedrooms, kitchen, larder and cellar. I had to sleep with her, the maid. That I don't miss!'

'With her? For the benefit of the jury could you please clarify as to whom you refer?'

Catherine cleared her throat before answering; she had spotted Mary McLeod in the crowd as soon as she came in, and was waiting for an opportunity to tear into her. Catherine pointed her finger straight at her.

'Mary McLeod, the floozy!' Catherine rolled her eyes and tilted her chin upwards as she answered. The courtroom was abuzz with whispers as people strained their necks to look at the red-faced young servant girl seated near the front of the court.

'Order, order! This court is in session. The judge banged his gavel.

'Mrs Lattimer, please keep your opinions to yourself they are not relevant in this courtroom. Could you please stick to the questions, without surreptitiously casting aspirations?'

Catherine nodded her head, glad that she had caused the commotion she wanted. Anything to embarrass that whore made her happy.

'Yes, sorry, Your Honour.'

The solicitor general looked down at his brief and continued with his line of questioning.

'When did Mrs Pritchard's illness first come to your attention?'

'Well, that would be when I came back from visiting my brother in Carlisle. Unfortunately, he was dead when I got there, so I wasn't away long. When I returned, Mrs Pritchard was ailing and said she had caught a cold. She looked terrible. Although, not confined to bed then, but was laid up two days after. The poor woman had attacks of vomiting, and the weight rolled off her, she didn't look herself. She was a little better when she came back from time away at her parents' house, just before Christmas, but the sickness started again about a week later and seemed to get worse after she'd had anything to eat.'

Catherine could feel herself getting upset, she tried to control her emotions, but her throat felt tight. Taking a deep breath, she said, 'It's just so dreadful. Why did I not do something! I should have known!' The tears fell freely, Catherine reached for her handkerchief, as she did, she caught the doctor's eye, he gave her a cold purposeful stare which seemed to bore straight through her.

Outwardly, Edward's face was expressionless, but inside he was foaming, he had employed this woman, kept a roof over her head, provided her with food and this is how she repaid him. God knows he would never understand the mind of the working class. No loyalty. Such stupid, short-sighted people.

Catherine regained her composure; she had decided right from the day of the doctor's arrest, that no longer would the doctor intimidate her. She could see straight through his lies and his fancy language and cleverly orchestrated manners. There he was pretending to be the big man, then there he was carrying on behind his wife's back with a servant girl. A liar that's all he was, and not a very pretty one in her opinion. Catherine cleared her throat, took a deep breath, and continued answering the questions.

The Solicitor General

'Did you observe the state of Mrs Pritchard's hands?'

'Yes, I did, they were horrible; her fingers were straight out and the thumb twisted underneath them. She seemed to have no power to put them straight. I remember telling the doctor that it was bizarre, for the mistress's fingers to be bent and twisted like that. The cramp so severely afflicted Mrs Pritchard, and she was so distressed and tearful at the seriousness of her condition. It just wasn't normal! She didn't just have a cramp in her hands; she had it in her stomach as well, she must have been in agony. The pain seemed to affect her speech as well; it was higher than normal more like a squeak sometimes.'

'Did Mary McLeod wait on Mrs Pritchard?'

Once again Catherine couldn't help turning her nose up at the mention of 'her' name. Catherine took a deep breath and in her best sarcastic tone replied.

'Huh, yes, she did. Well, that was one of her duties, amongst other things!' She shook her head.

'Mrs Lattimer, was Mary McLeod responsible for serving Mrs Pritchard her meals – please just answer the question?'

'Yes, she was, until Mrs Pritchard's mother came to stay, then I cooked the meals, and she (Mary McLeod) served them.'

'Thank you, Mrs Lattimer, can I ask, did you speak to Mrs Pritchard about her sickness?'

'I said it was strange that nothing would do her good!'

'Did you see her that night again?'

'Later the same evening. It was about eleven o'clock when I saw Mrs Pritchard last. She was better, but not well.'

'When did you see her next after that?'

'I saw her the next day, about eleven o'clock in the forenoon. She was in bed, but a good deal better. She did not complain about anything, neither of weakness nor sickness, she stayed in bed until her mother came to visit. I would see her most days make sure she was as comfortable as could be expected.'

* * *

The Solicitor General, Mr Gifford, stepped briskly round from the dock and faced the full court with perfect composure.

'During the years you were in the Pritchard's' service, before the time you have mentioned – after your return from Carlisle – was Mrs Pritchard ever sick?'

Catherine studied the question for a few minutes.

'Oh well let me see, no I do not think so. I do believe that Mrs Pritchard's sickness began after I went back in October, after that she confined herself to bed, but, she went into the drawing-room sometimes; she did not lie in bed all day.'

'Do you remember when Doctor Cowan came to see her?'

'Yes, it was about two or three days before her mother, Mrs Taylor, came. He came one day and went away the next. He remained all night and left sometime the following evening.'

'Was the prisoner at home?'

'Yes, so far as I know, he was never from home during the time I have been referring to.'

'Did anything remarkable occur on the night of the day that Doctor Cowan left?'

'Yes, it was either that night or the next that Mrs Pritchard had the first cramp. She was in agony and screamed out in pain.'

'From which room did you hear the screams?'

'From the top bedroom, she had gone back there round about the 1st February; she said she felt more comfortable there than in her room. She had a nasty attack though not long after. Screamed out in terrible pain she did, it would be round about the eleventh when she went back to her room. The second attack would be the day before I left –around six in the evening.'

The Solicitor General (Mr Gifford)

'When you heard her cry out about midnight, was that not the night Doctor Cowan left?'

'Yes; I think that would be the night that Doctor Cowan left.

'Mrs Lattimer, you say that Mrs Pritchard was taken ill at around six in the afternoon, the day before you were due to leave your employment with the family. You also think on the night Dr Cowan left, Mrs Pritchard cried out with pain about midnight is this correct?'

'Yes, that's right, sir.'

The solicitor general looked towards the judge who adjusted his reading glasses to the end of his nose and checked his pocket watch, he – and no doubt the jury – had heard enough for one morning. He banged his gavel and in a slow, clear voice said;

'Thank you, Mrs Lattimer. This court is adjourned until 2.15 this afternoon.'

* * *

CHAPTER FORTY-FIVE
THE PRESS

The Broadside publishers scrambled to be the first to compose a ballad and report on the first day of the trial. One reporting of the doctor's first appearance in court read;

He is as popular as rumour has made him out. The Prisoner is a tall, stout well-built man, rather prepossessing, and with sharply defined features. A good-looking fellow, with a beard, much admired by the other sex, and envied by many people.

He came to the dock, frankly pale, and worn from his months in prison, yet cheerful overall. Pritchard composed himself well for the day and looked the most relaxed and unconcerned person in court.

I observed that he almost wept when as a loving husband, it was proper that he should be moved — wept or did something dexterous with his pocket handkerchief, which could pass for weeping. He is to all extents and purposes a human crocodile.'

* * *

CHAPTER FORTY-SIX
MRS LATTIMER - CONTINUED

With the recess over, the court was back in session, and the solicitor general continued his line of questioning with Mrs Lattimer.

'Mrs Lattimer when you heard the calls of pain from your mistress what did you do?'

'I went upstairs to see whatever was the matter. Mrs Pritchard was in agony. The doctor was with her. Sorry, I mean the prisoner.' Purposely, she looked directly at Edward as she corrected herself. 'The mistress was in such pain, and in deep grief about her mother. She looked emancipated, thin and weak. She also seemed to be under the influence of chloroform – she wasn't quite insensible, but not right.'

'Was she very excited?'

'Very much, the doctor was with her, but he didn't say anything, as far as I can remember. He remained calm, and held the mistress's hand and tried to soothe her.'

'Did Mrs Pritchard say she wanted to see another doctor?'

'Yes, that she wanted to see Dr Gairdner, she told the prisoner too.'

'What did she say to her husband when Dr Gairdner came?'

'Said she didn't blame him. The prisoner I mean.'

'Mrs Lattimer I want you to recollect the occurrences of that night. When you went up to the bedroom and heard Mrs

Pritchard cry out with pain about midnight, did you hear her say anything to her husband?'

'Yes, she said they are all hypocrites together!'

'Was the doctor weeping?'

'Pretending to cry if you ask me! Mrs Pritchard said to him if you cry again, you are a hypocrite.'

'Mrs Lattimer! Please just answer the question. Moving on, do you remember did Mrs Pritchard have a severe attack after her mother came to stay?'

'Yes, she had cramp two or three days after.'

'Was the prisoner there when the attacks happened?'

'I don't remember if I'm honest. I left shortly after, but I still went back to see Mrs Pritchard and the children.'

'Do you remember what Mrs Taylor said to you before she died?'

'Yes, she said: "Well, Catherine, I don't understand my daughter's illness; she is one day better and two days worse." That was the last words she ever told me; she was dead soon after.'

'Mrs Lattimer, there has been much talk about the preparation of tapioca, can I ask who it was that told you to make this for Mrs Pritchard?'

'It was Mary McLeod; she said that Mrs Pritchard would like a little tapioca.'

'Where did you get the tapioca?'

From the local shop Burton & Henderson the grocers, young Kenneth went to fetch it. It came in a paper bag, as always.'

'Had the bag been opened when brought to you?'

'No, I did not notice whether it had or not.'

'Did you take it to the ladies, or send it up?'

'There was about half a breakfast-cupful made, and Mary

McLeod took it up to the dining-room to Mrs Taylor. She said she was not to take it to Mrs Pritchard herself, but that Mrs Taylor would take it to her.' 'Do you know how long it stood after preparation before it was taken up?'

'Yes, about half an hour or twenty minutes in the dining-room.'

Mr Clark – 'How do you know?'

'Mary McLeod told me that it was there.'

The Solicitor General

'Did you see it there yourself?'

'No, I cannot say I did. I said it was rather thin. If I had known it would stand so long, I would have done some fresh. I thought the standing had made it worse!'

'Did you put anything into the tapioca?'

'No, nothing except tapioca and the water.'

'Any salt?'

'I don't think there was salt or sugar in it. Mrs Pritchard liked to put sugar in anything she got herself.'

'So, you did not put any substance into the food that could hurt anybody?'

'No, I did not!' Catherine replied in a raised voice, somewhat perturbed by the question.

'Did you ask Mrs Pritchard what she thought of the tapioca?'

'I did, she said, "Catherine it wasn't very good, it was rather tasteless." Mrs Taylor said the same, which is not surprising as it had stood so long!'

'Thank you, Mrs Lattimer. No further questions, Your Honour.'

* * *

Mr Clark for the defence began his line of questioning.

'Mrs Lattimer, did the doctor keep any medicines in the house?'

'Yes, he held chloroform, I don't know what else, I think he gave prescriptions for medicine, there were a good many bottles in there, but I couldn't tell you what they contained.'

'Was the consulting room, which included these bottles, locked?'

'No, it was not always locked.'

'Was Doctor Pritchard in the house at the time Mrs Pritchard ate the tapioca?'

'No, sir, he wasn't.'

'Thank you, Mrs Lattimer, no further questions.'

Catherine was so glad that was all over, she felt proud of herself, and had done what she had set out to do. Tell the truth, and hope that the jury believed her enough to send the murdering scum of a doctor to the gallows. As she left the bar, her eyes met with his cold, cruel eyes. Horrid. It was the whore's turn for the witness box yet, that should be interesting. Let's see if the young slut can tell the truth. Just how does that girl live with herself, was the question Mrs Lattimer asked herself.

* * *

CHAPTER FORTY-SEVEN
MARY MCLEOD

Mary McLeod hadn't slept for days. She looked and felt terrible, her face pale, and her hair lank and untidy. All Mary could think about was this trial, and what she needed to say. She knew she would be the talk of the town. 'That's her, the servant girl who fell for her master.' Why did she take this job in the first place, and why did she fall head over heels with the doctor? What had she been thinking? She thought about it now, and all she saw was a dirty old man leering after a young girl. She just wished she'd dared to walk away and find someone her age and live a normal life; now she felt responsible for the death of two women. Why did she not realise? Why did she not see through Edward's silver tongue and philandering ways? The trouble was, despite it all deep down she still loved him.

So, the day had arrived, Mary needed to be careful what she wore, not wanting to feel like she was the one on trial here. Not that she had much choice, her wardrobe was hardly debonair. Eventually, she decided on a simple pale blue dress and chose a bonnet that would blend nicely with it. She covered her arms with a knitted shawl which had been her mother's, hoping that it would bring her some luck, not that it had done much for her mother. God rest her soul.

Mary walked up to the courtroom virtually unnoticed, the usual spectators and press vultures were already gathered outside hoping to catch a glimpse of the key players. Soon they were bombarding her with questions.

'Mary, tell us about the doctor, do you think he is guilty? Did he, do it?'

'Mary, did you know what was going on, come on Mary you must have known!'

Women waited around in groups whispering; it didn't take them long to recognise her, and they began looking her up and down like she was a mannequin in a shop window. Mary sighed, she would be so glad when all this was over, she couldn't stand it, and the trial had just begun. Once finished, she would feel better, she wanted to move away, and go somewhere where nobody knew who she was. Get a new job and start again. All being well Edward would come with her, and they could get married and start a new life. Mary pushed passed the crowds, gave her name to the official in charge and made her way into court. The solicitor for the defence was waiting for her.

'Mary, you need to answer the questions put to you firmly and as truthfully as you can. Don't elaborate on detail, just stick to the point,' the solicitor reminded her. 'I would lose the bonnet if I were you, don't want people thinking you have ideas above your station, do we?'

Reluctantly, Mary removed her bonnet and tied her hair back the best she could. She so wanted to look smart, and now she felt inadequate. She was no different to anyone else, why did the people around her try making her feel inferior. Her downfall had been in her bad judgement of character and for trusting and loving the doctor, but she was no murderer. People need to understand that. Her nerves were in tatters as she took her place in the court waiting for her name to be called. She didn't have to wait long, a few minutes later they called her.

The courtroom fell silent as Mary made her way to the stand all eyes on her observing her as she took the oath. She glanced at Edward; she hadn't seen him since the day of his arrest. He looked so pale and tired. The butterflies were still dancing in her stomach when she looked at him. She must be stupid, but she didn't suppose that you could help your feelings, or who you fall in love with.

The judge asked for silence in court, and the solicitor general began his questioning.

'For the benefit of the court, please state your full name, your age and your occupation.'

'Mary McLeod and I will be seventeen next October. I entered the service of Doctor Pritchard at Whitsunday, 1863. I was a housemaid and nurse. I was only fifteen when I went.'

'Thank you; do you remember when the mistress of the house, Mrs Pritchard, first became ill?'

'The mistress seemed to be sick quite often, but to my thinking, she became much worse since February this year.'

'Do you remember when Mrs Pritchard went to Edinburgh to visit her mother?'

'Yes, it was in November last year. She'd perked up when she came back, although I did see her retching in the pantry once, and I fetched her some hot water to settle her stomach.'

'Where was the prisoner at that point?'

'Upstairs, in his bedroom.'

'At what time of day did Mrs Pritchard become ill?'

'Usually, around forenoon and on a night-time after she had eaten.'

'How do you know that she was sick at night-time?'

'Sometimes, she would tell me herself, and I had to move the slops from her bedroom, and sometimes the doctor, I mean the prisoner, would remove them.'

'How do you know that?'

'Well, there was no one else in the room to do that.'

'Then it is your own opinion that he did so, and Mrs Pritchard never told you that the doctor had taken away what she had vomited?'

'No.'

The Lord Justice Clerk picked up pieces of paper from the desk in front of him and rifled through them with his fingers. He was angry with Mary; the girl was assuming answers to the questions and not telling what happened; thus, she was purposely misleading the jury.

Gathering his composure and in a firm, harsh tone asserted his authority, 'Miss McLeod, you must try and speak out; it was from you not speaking out that the mistake was very nearly arising, and it might have been a severe one!'

Mary hung her head, and looked down at her hands, and fidgeted; she hated all these questions, she just wanted today to be over. Much to her dismay, the questioning began again.

'Before Mrs Pritchard went to Edinburgh in November 1864 was there any doctor attending her besides her husband?'

'No.'

'Did she get any medicine as far as you know?'

'Yes, but I could not say what.'

'Did you procure it for her?'

'Yes, it was some white liquid in a doctor's bottle.'

'Was the liquid clear like water, or white like milk?'

'It was white as milk, but what it was I don't know.'

'Did she get anything else?'

'Yes; red powders.'

'Where did these powders come from?'

'I ordered them.'

The solicitor general raised his eyebrows at Mary's answer; he hadn't expected that.

'You ordered them. How?'

'The doctor gave me a prescription to get them.'

'Oh, I see. And some of these powders were in the consulting room when the prisoner was apprehended?'

'Yes, it was me who told the Inspector where to find them.' At this Mary felt the doctor's eyes staring at her, a cold, hostile stare. Mary ignored him and glanced away.

'Now, did Mrs Pritchard take to her bed permanently after returning from Edinburgh? Was this before Dr Gairdner came?'

'Yes, the mistress had been confined to bed sometime before Dr Gairdner came.'

'What seemed to be the matter with her when she got into bed?'

'Mrs Pritchard didn't complain much, except about her hands and feet being cold.'

'Was anything else the matter with her hands and feet, except cold?'

'Not that I remember.'

'Did she have a severe attack of vomiting at any time?'

'Yes, sometimes worse than others.'

'Sometimes worse than others.' The solicitor general repeated Mary's words verbatim. 'From what you saw of her, can you tell me was Mrs Pritchard sick before or after she'd eaten?'

'Usually, after she had eaten something.'

'Who took the food to her when she was in the bedroom?'

'Sometimes I was me and sometimes Catherine Lattimer.'

'Was it ever taken up by anyone else?'

'Occasionally the doctor took her breakfast up.'

'Did you ever hear the victim cry out in pain?'

'Yes, I had seen her scream out when she had an attack of the cramp.'

'Was her husband there at that time?'

'Yes, he was rubbing her hands and feet, and putting hot and cold water on them.'

'Was he excited, or quite restrained and calm?'

'He was excited, crying and upset because his wife was ill.'

'Before you went away to fetch Doctor Paterson, did you hear her say anything to her husband when he was upset and crying?'

'Yes, I heard her say something to him after I returned.'

'Do you recall what it was?'

'She said, "don't cry you, hypocrite, if you cry, it was you that did it," as far as I can remember.'

The packed courtroom fell silent at Mary's latest revelation, up to now sympathy had been with the doctor, but feelings were now beginning to change.

'Now, I do not want to press you about anything, but I wish you to remember as accurately as you can. Was what you had just told us now not said before Mrs Pritchard stated that she wanted to see another doctor?'

'I think it was after.'

'Now, after this did Mrs Pritchard become very unwell till her mother came?'

'Yes, she did. Her mother came a few days later, but I continued as her housemaid.'

'Did she ever complain of a great thirst?'

'Yes, she did and of a great heat in her head, and pain in her stomach.'

'After Mrs Pritchard's mother came to stay, was Mrs Pritchard confined to bed?'

'On the whole yes, she would get up for short periods, but not for very long, Mrs Taylor, her mother, slept in the same room and attended upon her.'

'Really! But you continued to be housemaid to wait in the chamber. Is that correct, Mary?'

'Yes, that's right, sir, I still saw both ladies several times a day.'

'Did Mrs Pritchard continue to be sick each day?'

'She was much the same.'

'Miss McLeod, was Doctor Pritchard in the house all the while that Mrs Taylor was with her?'

'Sometimes, if he was not working.'

'Was he commonly there when she and her mother had dinner?'

'Often, but not every day.'

Once again, the solicitor general could feel himself losing patience with this witness if only the girl would concentrate on answering his questions precisely.

'That is not an answer to the question. Was the prisoner commonly there when his wife had dinner?'

'Not so often as not.'

'When Mrs Pritchard had a cup of tea who poured it for her, did the doctor pour it?'

'Yes, sometimes he would, but if not, then it would be the cook or me.'

'After Mrs Taylor's death on 25th February who was in the habit of taking Mrs Pritchard's meals up to her?'

Mary found the questions tiresome and didn't understand why they wanted to know such detail. She just wanted to sit down, rest her feet and have a cup of tea.

Mary hesitated, then she shrugged her shoulders and screwed her face up before answering,

'Her breakfast and lunch were taken up to her by the doctor or one of the children. That is, the doctor took them up himself from the dining room or sent one of the children up with them, or he would send me.'

'If it was you, did you take it to her direct from the kitchen?'

'Yes.'

'Before Mrs Taylor's death, did she send you to the druggists to buy a bottle of Battley's Solution?'

'Yes, Mrs Taylor sent me.'

'How long was this before her death?'

'It was the Monday before.'

'Where did you buy it?'

Mary was indeed getting agitated at the line of questioning, why he asked such questions was beyond her.

'Murdoch Brothers, Mrs Taylor gave me a brown bottle to be filled.'

'How much did you pay for it?'

'Mary tutted, 'Eight shillings and fourpence.'

'So, on your return did you give the bottle straight to Mrs Taylor?'

'Yes.'

'Did you see the bottle again after Mrs Taylor's death?'

'Yes, in the bedroom.'

'Did you find it in her pocket?'

'No, it was at the side of her bed.'

'Before you went away to fetch Dr Gairdner, what did Mrs Pritchard say about a doctor?'

'She said, "Mary be sure to go; I want another doctor" Please.'

'Was Doctor Pritchard crying?'

'No, I think it was after that he was crying.'

The Lord Justice Clerk intervened.

'You are not sure whether it was before or after?'

'I am not certain. I saw the prisoner crying after I returned, but I am not sure if he did so before.'

The solicitor general resumed his questioning.

'Are you really satisfied that he was not crying before you went away to the doctor?'

Mary scratched her head. 'I do not know whether he was crying before or not, but I am certain that he was crying after I returned.'

'Now, what was it, she said to him after you returned?'

Mary just shook her head and looked up to the ceiling. How many times did she have to answer the same questions, all they were doing is wording them differently, trying to catch her out, well they could wait.

'Now, I do not want to press you about anything, but I wish you to remember as exactly as you can. Was what you had told us now not said before you went to the doctor when Mrs Pritchard was crying out that she wanted another doctor, and telling you to go?'

'I think it was after.'

'Now, after this did Mrs Pritchard become very unwell till her mother came?'

'Her mother came a day or two afterwards.'

'Did her sickness continue until that time?'

'Yes.'

'And anything else excepting sickness – cramp?'

Mary rolled her eyes in annoyance. 'I do not think the mistress had cramp between that night and the time that Mrs Taylor came.'

'After Mrs Taylor came, how was Mrs Pritchard – was she confined to bed chiefly?'

'As I said before. Mrs Taylor slept with her and attended upon her, sometimes she was much the same, at times she was a little better, and on other occasions, she was worse.'

'Did she complain of great thirst?'

'Yes, as I said before! A great heat in her head and pain in her stomach.'

'Was Doctor Pritchard in the house all the while that Mrs Taylor was there.'

'He was not in the house all day, but was living at home.'

'Miss McLeod, do you remember Mrs Pritchard asking you to taste a piece of cheese.'

'Yes.'

'Did it make you very thirsty?'

'No, I do not recall.'

'Did you never say that you were sick after eating a small piece of cheese?'

Mr Clark, for the defence, objected to the question – the question was put again, but re-worded.

The Solicitor General

'After eating a small piece of cheese, did you feel any peculiar sensation in your throat?'

'Yes; I only tasted a minuscule bit, it had a burning sensation, but not a thirst as such.'

'Did Mrs Pritchard take the rest of the cheese?'

'No; it was left uneaten.'

The solicitor general was tired of this witness; he found her difficult, and uncooperative. Well, she would sit up and listen to his next stratagem. Questions, which should change people's allegiance of the whole case.

'Had Mrs Pritchard, in her lifetime, ever seen the prisoner using any familiarities with you?'

Mary gasped with embarrassment; she couldn't believe what he just asked her, she wished she was a snail who could disappear and crawl into a protective shell. She couldn't speak; everyone was staring at her like a pride of lions stalking their prey. Shocked looks of surprise and disapproval spread around the crowded courthouse. Mary almost fainted and asked for a glass of water. Mr Gifford for the defence jumped to his feet and objected to the solicitor general's line of questioning and thankfully for Mary she was removed from the courtroom while the parties deliberated.

* * *

Edward watched Mary as the guard ushered her away. Just the sight of her slender body excited every part of him. In his life, he had made love to many women, but none of them captivated him as Mary did, but today he saw her in a different light, no longer was she the smouldering siren he thought she was. No, she was nothing but a young, insignificant servant girl who thought she could get the better of him. For the first time since this charade began, he felt guilty. Oh, what had he done, and more to the point, why had he done it? That was a question even he could not answer.

* * *

Mr Gifford and Mr Watson, for the panel, both objected to this question. Their reasons being that in the first place the question asked was not sufficiently precise and, in the second, as disclosing the intention of the prosecutor to follow up a line of examination for which he thought laid no foundation in the libel, the question now put was not limited in point of time. He believed that this had no connection whatsoever with anything contained in the libel. Furthermore, they had received no notice for this line of questioning, and the defence did not know the ground on which the Crown put their claim to go into this line of examination unless they were suggestive of motive.

The Solicitor General

'My friend must have been aware, from the investigation, that this line of examination is necessary. Bearing in mind the way the prisoner and this girl lived before the time referred to in this libel, and down to the very period of his wife's death. I must, therefore, proceed with this line of enquiry.'

The Lord Justice Clerk

'Yes, I agree, please continue.'

Mary once again took her place at the bar, and the examination resumed by the solicitor general.

'Did Mrs Pritchard ever see her husband use any familiarities towards you?'

Mary, although uncomfortable, answered as confidently as she could.

'Yes; she did.'

'What were they?'

(No answer.)

The Lord Justice Clerk

'Miss McLeod this is very unpleasant, but there is no avoiding it, and you must tell us the whole story. What was it?'

Mary knew that the mistress had probably seen them doing much more, but she didn't care if she had sworn on oath, to tell the truth, she was not admitting to it, she couldn't live with being branded a harlot. Once again, she crossed her fingers, then replied. 'She saw him kissing me!'

The Solicitor General

'Whereabouts in the house?'

'It was in the consulting room.'

'And Mrs Pritchard came in just at the time?'

'No, I think she saw us through the door, it was slightly open.'

'Did she speak to you about it afterwards?'

'Yes, I told her that I wanted to leave and go away, but the mistress, she would not let me.'

The Lord Justice Clerk

'What did she give as her reason for not letting you go away?'

'She said she would speak to the doctor.'

'Did she tell you anything else about him?'

'Yes, she said he was a nasty, dirty man.' Mary sniggered, remembering her mistress's face as she'd spat the words out.

The Solicitor General

'When did the doctor first use any familiarities with you? Was it shortly before this?'

'It was not long after I started working there.'

'Did he get the better of you?'

(No answer.)

'He had a connection with you, had he not?'

Embarrassed, Mary looked down at the floor trying to hide her blushing face. 'Yes,' she answered quietly.

'Did you become pregnant with him?'

'Yes.'

'When did this happen?'

'Last year, after Mrs Pritchard had seen him kissing me. The prisoner said, he would see to it and put it all right.'

'Did he give you any medicine?'

'Objection!' The defence bellowed.

'Mr Clark, are we going into questions leading to this, that he gave her medicine for procuring an abortion?'

The Lord Justice Clerk

'I would first like to know if a child was born. Were you delivered of a child?'

Mary was horrified, she had been dreading them asking this question. She didn't know what to say; the courtroom was so quiet you could almost hear her breathing. Ashamed, she dropped her head and once again looked at the floor, she didn't have the strength to lift it up and answer the question. Instead, she said nothing. Mary could sense the Lord Justice Clerk's annoyance and frustration. Mary bit down hard on her lip, desperately seeking the confidence to answer and get it over with, but still, the words would not come out of her mouth. She hunched her shoulders to make herself look smaller, holding her hands at her side, she did the sign of the cross on her side.

The question was repeated, in a firmer authoritative tone.

'Was there a child born?'

(No answer)

Still, Mary could not bring herself to respond; she was traumatised, she couldn't formulate any words, it was as if she had suddenly gone mute.

'Miss McLeod, you need to answer the question – I shall put it another way! Did you have a miscarriage?'

Swallowing before she spoke, she answered,

'Yes.'

For a second the courtroom went quiet. People stood with their mouths wide open, not quite believing what they had just heard. Mary caught sight of Catherine Lattimer's face, which had a smug grin of satisfaction all over it. Mary had never been so embarrassed; she just wanted the Lord to strike her down dead, there and then.

* * *

Since this revelation, the atmosphere in the courtroom changed. Was it an abortion or did the girl only miscarry her unborn child? If it were aborted, then this would alter the course of the trial altogether. An illegal abortion performed by Doctor Pritchard himself would not bode well with the judge or jury. Since 1861 the laws on such horrendous acts had been brought in to kerb this malpractice, and anyone found performing such could expect several years in prison. No, the doctor was not looking so innocent now, and his usual persona as a calm, confident physician who couldn't possibly murder his wife and mother-in-law was now beginning to be questioned.

Edward, shuffled uneasily in his seat, not looking at anybody or anything. He just stared straight in front of him. He knew the question would come up, but in all honesty, he'd expected Mary to lie. What on earth was she thinking of admitting to an abortion, they had agreed it would be their secret, so why did the stupid girl open her mouth now. Edward was disappointed, he believed they were kindred spirits, that above everyone he could trust Mary, but not now at the first chance she could she had dropped him right in it. Why could she not be strong and keep her silly, immature mouth shut? This revelation would take some explaining. He watched on with contempt as the degrading testimony continued.

'When did that take place? Was it in the winter?'

'No.'

'Was it in the late summer/autumn?'

'Yes.'

The solicitor general intimated that the next question he meant to put was whether the prisoner gave her anything to produce the miscarriage.

Edward turned a whiter shade of pale, knowing full well that the implications of this question would have upon the case, which, if the judge were to allow this into the trial, then it would incur more charges for him. Illegal abortion was a serious crime. He prayed that his defence team was on the ball. Fortunately for him, they were, and they objected immediately.

Mr Clark (Defence)

'If this matter is to be investigated, then we should have had notice. It is an issue that the prosecutor could have raised on a separate indictment, or under this indictment on a separate charge, and is entirely different from the two murder charges!'

The Solicitor General

'It is material to the ends of justice that we should show not only the footing on which the prisoner was living with this girl at the time but also, being a medical man; he in the course of that illicit intercourse. He used his professional skill and knowledge of his art for such a purpose. It is material concerning the charge made against him in this indictment that he used his professional expertise for another purpose upon his wife and her mother.

'The bearing of that on the other evidence, not only for the prosecution but the defence, it would be improper and might be prejudicial to the ends of justice, to dwell on. However, it is impossible not to feel that it is of importance, for the consideration of the jury concerning the whole circumstances that may be brought out in evidence on the prisoner's side. It may be signs of good character, evidence of his living together with his wife on such terms as to exclude all notions of such a crime as is imputed to him. That the jury should know how he was living in his own house, and to what uses at the time in question, he was applying the skill and practice of his art.'

Mr Clark (Defence)

'The prosecutor argues that he is entitled to use the alleged commission of another crime as proof of this crime. Nevertheless, he does not suggest that as a motive he wants to use this evidence for showing that, because the prisoner used his skill in this inappropriate manner, it is probable he may have used it in the more atrocious behaviour charged against him in the present indicant. That is simply, that I suggest, putting the prisoner on trial for a crime not charged against him in this libel. Therefore, it would be an entirely competent charge if the public prosecutor thought it his duty to make the charge and to put it in the indictment. He has not done so, presumably because he knew he could not prove it. Therefore, he brings this girl as a witness to put the prisoner on his trial for an offence, which suggests that as a doctor the prisoner misused his knowledge, and as a result, he could be defamed. If the prosecutor wanted to charge the prisoner with this additional crime, the proper course was to have charged it specifically in the indictment!'

The Lord Justice Clerk, after consultation with the other judges, held that the proposed question was not competent and the trial continued.

'Did this improper connection continue long after you had the miscarriage?'

'Yes.'

'Was the connection continued when Mrs Pritchard was in Edinburgh visiting her family?'

Mary had reflected on this question before she answered, her time with Edward was probably the only time in her life that she had been truly happy. If only she had known then what was to happen, she'd have run as far away from that house and the bloody doctor as fast as she could. Mary ignored the question. Instead, she hung her head, hoping that they would all leave her be. Unfortunately for her, the questioning started to become even more personal and intrusive.

'Had the prisoner any connection with you whatsoever while Mrs Pritchard was in Edinburgh visiting her family?'

Still, Mary could not bring herself to answer, thinking that if she said nothing, then no one would believe wrong of her.

The solicitor general was finally losing patience with this girl, did she think he was just going to stand here and let her ignore his questions? Well, if she did, she was in for a shock.

'Miss McLeod, it is necessary that you should answer the question. I sympathise with your excruciating position, but it is necessary that you should do so! Now did the doctor have any connection with you at that time?'

Reluctantly, Mary lifted her head, and without looking at anybody quietly answered, 'Yes.'

'Thank you, and before the prisoner's wife turned ill, did he ever speak of marrying you?'

'Yes.'

'Did he speak of marrying you after his wife became ill?'

'No.'

'When he said he would marry you, did he speak of his wife?'

Once again Mary didn't answer. Instead, she looked above the solicitor general's wig and took a furtive look at Edward, he even twitched his eyebrows at her, what a bastard she thought to herself, what a complete idiot she had been, why had she been so stupid?

'Did he tell you that he would marry you if his wife died?'

This time Mary found the strength from somewhere to look the doctor in the eye when she replied, she was now beyond caring. He didn't care what happened to her, so why should she care about him.

'Yes, he did.'

Gasps of unbelief rippled throughout the court; people were mesmerised by the stupidity of this young girl.

'Now, Miss McLeod, after I have suggested the matter to you, you will be kind enough to repeat what he did say to you.'

Mary didn't answer, once again, she was rigid with fear.

The Lord Justice Clerk, banged his gavel, not at all happy with this reluctant witness.

'Can I remind you that you are under oath? Now, can you please give us the exact words.'

Still, Mary hesitated, not wanting to get Edward into more trouble, perhaps he was just playing the game and once he was free then like he always told her they would be together.

The solicitor general lost it and tore into Mary in a loud and domineering tone. 'You cannot possibly like standing there, but you must if you do not answer the question. What were the words the prisoner said to you?'

Unperturbed, Mary still hesitated, and stood there quietly for a further few minutes, doing herself no favours at all.

'Did the prisoner ever give you any presents?'

'Yes, after his wife died, he gave me a ring, and a locket with a photograph of him inside and a lock of his hair. I tore the picture up though once he was arrested. I didn't want to see his face anymore.'

'When the prisoner talked of marrying you, do you think that he said it in jest?'

'Yes, I do,' Mary lied, remembering the compromising sexual position he was in when he asked her to marry him.

'You say that the prisoner appeared to be speaking in jest to you when he proposed, now you must tell us his exact words – there can be no more delay about it, the thing must be done!'

Still, Mary refused to answer.

The Lord Justice Clerk finally lost his temper.

'This is the last question you have got to answer, but if you do not answer it, I shall be obliged to send you to prison. Now, you may choose between these two things. The question you have got to answer is, what exactly did the prisoner say to you about marriage? Do you understand?'

At the mention of the word prison, Mary changed her attitude, that would be typical of Edward she would be the one in jail and no doubt he would end up free. He had the look of the devil, he did. She decided she needed to conform and get this over with as quickly as possible.

'He said that when Mrs Pritchard was to die, and if she died before him, and I was alive, he would marry me.'

The solicitor general was at last satisfied, he did understand that the questions he asked the girl were difficult and that she was only young, but if she was old enough to involve herself with a married man, then she should also be prepared to accept the circumstances.

'You may go now. This court is adjourned until ten o'clock tomorrow morning.'

Thank goodness it was all over, Mary had never felt so scared in her life. Hopefully when the trial was all over her and Edward could finally be together, somewhere where nobody knew them. With that thought in her head, Mary held her head high and left the courthouse.

* * *

CHAPTER FORTY-EIGHT
FORMING OPINIONS

By profession, George Sim considered himself an accomplished writer, although to be honest, he had only had a couple of articles printed in Charles Dickens' periodical *Household Words*, and not much since. George wanted to break into novel writing and complete his half-finished manuscript, but with an endless amount of rejection letters, he felt disillusioned with the whole industry. Nevertheless, he kept on writing determined that one day he would get the break he desired. After all, women were writing novels now and achieving some success, so there was hope for him yet. George was in the fortunate position of not having to work. His late father had left him a considerable sum which would help him see his days out.

As a person, George was a likeable chap, an old-school Gentleman who prided himself on his ability to converse with anyone whatever their status in life. George, when talking to others, remained cool and collected while keeping a respectful chaste. He rarely spoke about his work, nor did he divulge too much of his personal life, believing that his merits would shine through in due course without the need to sing his praises. His strategy was to be courteous and harmonious, always, putting people at ease was George's forte. It allowed others to express themselves, and reveal valuable information, while he retained his courteous and well-bred manner.

George lived his life around this, and it had always served him well among his peers, who considered him to be a reliable and popular man and an excellent judge of character.

George had been delighted to be asked to be a juror in such a notable and high-profile case. He didn't live too far from the Pritchard house on Sauchiehall Street, and quite close to where Madeleine Smith had once lived. He would have enjoyed being on the jury of the Smith trial. Since the 'non-proven' verdict George had become quite obsessed with the lady and the circumstances of her trial, so much so, that he had loosely based his novel on her.

After hearing the two women's evidence, he had a good idea where the Pritchard case was heading, he particularly liked the cook, Mrs Lattimer, and in his opinion, she was an honest, God-fearing woman, who wanted to tell the truth and let justice do its job. Now when it came to the young maid, Mary McLeod, his opinion was divided. George could not decide if she did, in fact, have any involvement in the case, and that if Doctor Pritchard did in fact murder his wife and mother-in-law, then could it be that this young slip of a girl had anything to do with it. After all, she did have a lot to gain. The evidence stated that the doctor had promised to marry her, could it be that Mary was not the innocent little thing she portrayed and that underneath the façade was a sharp, talented, manipulation poisoner. George could not make up his mind. He needed to confer with the rest of the gentlemen of the jury.

The coaching inn where the jury was sequestered was comfortable enough, the food pretty good and plentiful. Thomas Stark loved his food, and liked nothing better than to wash it down with a couple of large brandies in the lounge and talk about events of the day, this was the first time he had been called to a jury, and he found the whole process fascinating.

George Sim was good company, an intelligent and articulate man whom he had seen in Edinburgh, and once or twice in his tobacconist shop, although until this trial commenced, they had not spoken to each other. As this was the first day of the trial, there was plenty to discuss. They were both in agreement about Catherine Lattimer, she had no reason to speak anything but the truth, and to just report her recollections as accurately as she could, but the young lassie, Mary McLeod, was a different matter altogether; if she was involved, what were her motives? Did she intend to marry the doctor and be mistress of the house? Well, yes, they both agreed it was a plausible theory, but could a girl of just seventeen orchestrate the murder of two women, at this stage both men were unsure.

'Quite a revelation today, George, what are your thoughts on the abortion business? Throws an entirely different light on the doctor, don't you think?' Thomas asked George as he lit his cigar and swirled the amber coloured brandy around his glass.

'It does, but let us not yet jump to conclusions. It could well be that there was a legitimate reason for this?'

'A legitimate reason, such as?' Thomas replied, not too convinced by his friend's train of thought.

'Well, it could be that the doctor sympathised with the girl's plight and performed the abortion himself as he didn't want the girl going to some unscrupulous back street abortionist?'

Thomas studied this for a moment, he did see the logic in his colleague's thinking, but still, he remained unconvinced.

'Yes, but an abortion! Why would a doctor of Pritchard's standing perform such a thing on a servant girl, knowing the strict laws on such a horrific and diabolic act? Unless, of course, it was his child. After all, he wanted to get rid of it quick without anyone knowing or raising unwanted suspicion?'

'Yes, exactly we have much to deliberate over.' George had heard enough for one day, he was tired and wanted to retire to bed early, so that he could be fresh for the second day of the trial. He didn't want to miss anything through lack of sleep or overindulgence.

* * *

CHAPTER FORTY-NINE
SECOND DAY-TUESDAY,
4ᵀᴴ JULY 1865.TEN O'CLOCK

Next to take the stand was Mary Patterson; she had looked forward to it. She hadn't worked for the Pritchard's long, but she knew something wasn't quite right there. The first time that she entered the house, she sensed something amiss. Like Mrs Lattimer before her, she intended to tell the truth as she saw it, no more, no less. She was called to the stand and immediately examined by Mr Gifford.

'Mrs Patterson, please tell us when you started working for the Pritchard's and anything else you remember from that time.'

'I began working for the Pritchard's on 16ᵗʰ February last. Before then I had never met any member of the family. At that time, the household consisted of Doctor Pritchard and his wife, their four children, Mrs Taylor, Mr King, Mr Connell, Mary McLeod, Mrs Lattimer oh and the washerwoman Mrs Nabb called in occasionally. Mrs Pritchard was not well and confined to her room, so it was left to Mrs Taylor to give me my orders.'

'Did Mrs Pritchard say anything to you, the first time you met?'

'Yes, I first met her the evening before her mother's death. Mrs Taylor had been ill around nine in the evening, Dr Paterson had been called in. Mary McLeod went to fetch him, so I went upstairs to see if there was anything I could do to help.'

'Did you hear anything going on in Mrs Pritchard's room?'

'Yes, when I entered the room I heard Mrs Pritchard saying to her mother, "Mother can you not speak to me?" The following morning Dr Pritchard told me that Mrs Taylor had gone.'

'What did you do then?'

'I went into the room and saw Mrs Taylor dead. I was sure of this as I put my hand on her forehead and she was cold. I shut her eyes as they were just staring as cold as a kipper. Came on quick though, her death, I mean, as I talked to her around seven the night before and she seemed tired, but she seemed fine to me.'

'What was Mrs Pritchard doing at that time?'

'The mistress was beside herself, uncontrollably upset, she knelt beside her mother rubbing her hands with hers, trying to bring her back to life. The doctor sought to get her to go into another room, but Mrs Pritchard didn't want to leave her mother. She just could not believe that her mother was dead. Doctor Pritchard even said that he would carry her downstairs if she wished.'

'What did Mrs Pritchard say to that.'

'She glared at him at first, then said "I would rather walk".'

'What happened then?'

'Then Mrs Nabb the washerwoman came, and together we dressed the body.'

'Were her clothes on when she died?'

'Yes, they were, I took her dress off and laid it on the floor.'

'Did you feel or hear anything in Mrs Taylor's pocket?'

'Yes, on taking her dress off I found a brown glass bottle, a key and a letter.'

'Was there anything in the bottle?'

'Yes, it was half-full of brown liquid, something like laudanum.'

'Did you uncork the bottle.'

'I didn't, but Mrs Nabb did, she read the label which said two drops equal to three of laudanum. Mrs Nabb said it smelt like laudanum!'

'What did you do with the bottle?'

'I put it on the dressing table next to the bed.'

'Was Doctor Paterson in the room at the time?'

'No, but Doctor Pritchard was.'

'Did he make any remark to his wife?'

'Well, when Doctor Paterson did not come, Mrs Pritchard said to him, "Edward can you do nothing yourself". The doctor didn't like that and replied, "What can I do for a dead woman, recall her life". He then took the brown bottle that we found in Mrs Taylor's pocket.'

'What did he say when he took the bottle?'

'Well, he raised his eyes and hands in amazement and said, "Good heavens, has she taken this much since Tuesday". He then took the bottle away saying he wanted to show it to Mrs Pritchard.'

'What happened after, did you wait on Mrs Pritchard or was it Mary Mcleod?'

'Usually, it would be Mary McLeod. I do remember the day before Mrs Pritchard died, she rang the bell in her room, but nobody answered it so I went to the consulting room to see if I could find the doctor or Mary McLeod. The door was ajar, but nobody answered, but I know the doctor was in there with Mary McLeod as I saw them both come out as I reached the top of the stairs.'

'There were two occasions where you tasted food given to Mrs Pritchard, is this correct?'

'Yes, Mary McLeod asked me to eat a small piece of cheese and some egg flip, which tasted bitter. I had a burning in the back of my throat and grew sick immediately after eating them, and I had to go to bed, I was sick all through the night.'

'When did you next see Mrs Pritchard?'

'I saw her the night before her death; I went to her room as the bell was ringing again. She was in a state of excitement, her hands rigid with cramp. I tried rubbing them to improve circulation, but it didn't seem to help. Then Mary McLeod asked me to make a mustard poultice for Mrs Pritchard, so I went down to the kitchen to prepare it. When I returned, the doctor was lying on the bed next to his wife, and Mary McLeod stood at the foot of the bed. The doctor pulled up the mistress's nightdress and asked me to apply the poultice, but I refused. I said there was no use putting mustard on a dead body!'

'When you said that, what did the prisoner say?'

'He said, "Is she dead, Patterson?" I replied, "doctor you should know better than I!" He insisted that she wasn't dead and that she had only fainted, he then went on to ask for hot water to revive her, and he wailed "do not to leave your dear Edward" and requested that I bring Mr King's rifle and shoot him. I got angry with him then and asked him not to provoke the Almighty with such expressions; it just wasn't right. I said, if God were to shut your mouth and mine, I don't know how we would be prepared to stand before a righteous God.'

'What did the prisoner say to that?'

'He said, he admired my wisdom, and then went on to say that Doctor Paterson had been tending to his wife and that she must have drunk too much wine. I heard nothing further until Superintendent McCall came to the house and asked for Mrs Pritchard's clothes and bed linen, which she had before her death. Catherine Lattimer was there at the time, and we gave the police the half-opened packet of tapioca, which was untouched since the mistress's death.'

Cross-examined by Mr Clark

'You said you did not know that Mrs Taylor was in the habit of taking Battley's Sedative Solution?'

'No, I wasn't.'

'And the prisoner told you to say nothing about it?'

'That's correct; I don't think he wanted to tarnish her memory.'

'Did you understand him at the time to mean that you were not to say that Mrs Taylor was taking that solution?'

'I understood him to mean that we were to say nothing about finding it in Mrs Taylor's pocket.'

'He said not to say that Mrs Taylor had been taking it? That was all you understood?'

'Yes, that was all.'

'When you tasted the cheese in the morning, did you tell the prisoner that you had been ill.'

'No, I did not.'

'You never did at any time?'

'Well, yes I did; the morning after I tasted the egg flip. I asked how Mrs Pritchard was, and he said she had had a terrible night. I said me too, and that I had been sick and vomiting during the evening. The doctor was in the pantry at the time and, as far as I remember, he was gargling his throat after coming down from the bedroom.'

'All you said was that you had been vomiting?'

'Yes.'

'Who was in the house the night you made the egg-flip?'

'Mr King and Mr Connell, and Mary McLeod. All the people that usually slept there.'

'After you left the mixture in the pantry, you did not see it again until Mary McLeod brought it down to the kitchen?'

'No.'

'Thank you; you are free to go.'

Edward had observed Mrs Patterson throughout her testimony, and he had to admit he had been impressed. Who would have thought that someone as ordinary as this cook could recall the events of the household with such detail? At least his Mary had the decency to only answer questions when forced into it. As the cook spoke, he watched the expression on the juror's faces. The trouble was, he didn't know how her testimony had gone. He couldn't decide if she had given anything away, he hesitated for a moment, trying to recall, no he didn't think she had, only the obvious and how distraught he had been after the death of his wife. Well, that was only to be expected, the jury would understand that. He regained his composure and gave a half smile to the jury, hoping that they would see that he was a compassionate, industrious and loving father, who could not possibly be guilty of such a heinous crime.

* * *

CHAPTER FIFTY
THE BOTTLE

Mary McLeod was recalled, and examined by the solicitor general.

'Miss McLeod, you were in Doctor Pritchard's house after his wife's body was taken to Edinburgh – is this correct?'

'Yes, I was.'

'On Tuesday, the police were in the house, and you saw Superintendent McCall there?'

'Yes.'

'Did you give him a bottle?'

'Yes.'

The solicitor general then produced the bottle marked as evidence 85.

'Is this the bottle you gave him?'

'It is very like it. It is the same looking bottle and the same looking label.'

'Did the bottle you saw after dressing Mrs Taylor contain a dark-coloured liquid?'

'Yes.'

'Where did you find it?'

'It was in the chest of drawers when Mrs Taylor and Mrs Pritchard died, but they had moved it to the lobby by the time Superintendent McCall came to the house to search, and in one of the drawers of that chest of drawers I found the bottle and I gave it to him.'

'Was there any other bottle like it in the house that you knew of?'

'No.'

Evidence for Prosecution

The Lord Justice Clerk

'How did you come to look for the bottle in the drawers?'

'Superintendent McCall asked me to look for the bottle found in Mrs Taylor's pocket after her death.'

* * *

Jessie Nabb was then called and examined by Mr Crichton.

'My name is Jessie Nabb, and I am a washerwoman, and have sometimes been employed by Doctor Pritchard's family. I remember being sent for the night that Mrs Taylor died, between twelve and one in the morning, to assist in dressing the body. Mrs Patterson and I prepared the body. I saw a bottle found in Mrs Taylor's pocket. (Shown evidence no. 85.) Yes, that is the bottle, and the label is the same. The bottle was about three-parts full of a brownish liquid, which did not come under the name.'

The Lord Justice Clerk

'You say that it stood at the lower edge of the label?'

'Yes, that's right.'

'Did you see what he did with it?'

'Yes, Mrs Patterson put it in the drawers.'

'In the drawers or under the drawers?'

'I think it was under the drawers because we were both on the floor at the time gathering up the clothes.'

'Did you see the prisoner after that?'

'Yes, he came into the room and said that Mary McLeod had told him that we had found a bottle in Mrs Taylor's pocket. He asked Mrs Patterson to give it to him, and she knelt and gave it to him. He looked at it, and said, "Good heavens, has she taken all that since Monday?" He told me she ought not to have got a girl like that to buy it for her, but she ought to have asked him to buy it for her, and he would have got it. Then he said she had been in the habit of taking it for years.'

'Did he say anything about Mrs Taylor's illness?'

'Yes, he told me she had been indulging in liquor for a few days and had taken an overdose of the opium.'

The Lord Justice Clerk

'By which you understood him to mean Battley's mixture?'

'Yes, sir.'

'Did he say anything more about it?'

Jesse hesitated for a second and looked the doctor straight in the eyes.

'He told us to say nothing about it because it might lead to trouble.'

'When did he say that?'

'At night in the bedroom.'

'Did he speak to you again about this bottle?'

'Yes, the next morning in the consulting room, between eight and nine o'clock. I had gone in to make up the fire. The doctor told me to say nothing to anyone about the bottle. I asked if it was dangerous, and he said yes, it was poisonous when one took too much of it.'

'Do you remember seeing Mrs Pritchard one day in January when you were there?'

'Yes, I cannot remember the date, but I know it was in January.'

'Did you hear anything before you went into the room?'

'Yes, I heard Mrs Pritchard retching very much indeed. I wasn't sure if I should intrude. I waited for a little. But then the mistress rang the bell very violently, and so I went in and there she was in agony leaning over the basin stand, she asked me to fetch her a drink of cold water.'

'Did she ask for anything else?'

'No, she told me to put her to bed, and get her a bottle of hot water for her feet, as she was freezing.'

'Did you see Mrs Taylor just before she died?'

'Yes, on a Wednesday night, during the week in which she died.'

'Did she say anything to you about Mrs Pritchard's illness then?'

'Yes, she said she could not understand Mrs Pritchard's illness, for she was one day well and another day very ill, and that she had been very ill the night before.'

'Did she say how ill she had been?'

'Yes, she stated that she had been very ill—sick and vomiting all through the night.'

'Were you washing in Doctor Pritchard's house after Mrs Taylor's death, upon the ninth of March?'

'Yes.'

'Were you in Mrs Pritchard's bedroom that night and were some soiled bedclothes taken off the bed by you?'

'Yes. I took them off the bed, as they were disgusting.'

'When you say disgusting did they appear soiled with vomit?'

'Yes, very much so, she told me she had been sick, but that she was not aware of it till she awoke in the morning.'

The Lord Justice Clerk

'Had Mrs Pritchard spoken to you frequently about her sickness?'

'Very seldom. I saw very little of Mrs Pritchard. If I'm honest.'

'Did she ever tell you how she was when she was in Edinburgh?'

'Yes, she said she felt much better when she was in Edinburgh.'

Cross-examined by Mr Clark

'Mrs Nabb you told us the conversation that passed between you and Doctor Pritchard when he came in at the time you and Mrs Patterson were dressing Mrs Taylor's body. Have you told us all that was said?'

'Yes.'

'Was Mrs Patterson present during the whole of the conversation?'

'Yes, she was.'

'Was anybody else present besides Mrs Patterson and you?'

'If you mean Mary McLeod no, she wasn't there.'

The Lord Justice Clerk

'When you showed Doctor Penny the quantity of liquid that had been in the bottle, was there anything in it?'

'No, it was empty.'

'Did you see the bottle more than once?'

'I only saw it the night I was in Mrs Taylor's room, and when I saw it again, it was empty.'

'Thank you. No further questions, Mrs Nabb.'

* * *

CHAPTER FIFTY-ONE
A GOOD MENTOR

The next person to take the stand was Thomas Alexander Connell, examined by the solicitor general.

Thomas had been shocked by the charges brought against the doctor. Dr Pritchard was his mentor, and as a student, Thomas looked up to him. The doctor was a knowledgeable, kind man; nothing was too much trouble to him. Undoubtedly, this was all just a mistake that would soon be sorted out. Thomas's father disagreed, as a doctor himself, he had heard many tales of Dr Pritchard and his underhanded ethics and philandering ways. He was glad that his son was no longer under the doctor's influence. He only wished it were under different circumstances.

Thomas had spent weeks writing down all he remembered, he had stated to the police of course, but he so wanted to give a good account of his time with the Pritchards.

Gingerly, he took the stand and began his deposition.

'I am a student of medicine. I boarded with Doctor Pritchard as a medical student. I went to him in November 1863; I remained till after his wife's death. I was in his house when his wife went to Edinburgh in November last. I spent the Christmas and New Year holidays with my father at Helensburgh, and I was away when Mrs Pritchard returned. I found her at home when I came back. I returned shortly after the New Year. She appeared to be in pretty good health at that time. I knew she had been ailing before she went to Edinburgh. After my return in January, I observed that she became unwell again. She told me she had a cold. She did not complain about anything else. I remember her complaining in the prisoner's presence of being unwell one night in the third week of January. It was in the dining-room when the prisoner and I were there. She said she felt sick and would go to bed. It appeared to come to her suddenly, and she left the room. I don't remember her ever coming down to her meals after that. I did not see her again till after her mother's death. She never said much to me about how she felt. That was the only occasion that I remember when she complained of illness in my presence. I next saw her the week after her mother's death. During that time, I asked the doctor every morning at breakfast time how she was. Sometimes, he said she was much better, and sometimes he told me she was no better. He did not mention what the matter was with her.

'Shortly before her death, and after Mrs Taylor's death, he told me that he thought it was gastric typhoid that ailed Mrs Pritchard. He had not before that given any name to her illness. He mentioned sickness as one of the symptoms of her disease. He said the sickness came on whenever she had anything to eat. He referred to this several times. He never mentioned cramp as a symptom of her disease. I heard that from Mrs Taylor. The only sign of an illness which the prisoner told me of was the sickness. Mrs Taylor said Mrs Pritchard was sick every time she tasted the food, followed by attacks of cramp in her arms and hands. She said the pain came on after tea and at night.

Mrs Taylor once spoke to me about being sick herself. She told me she was sick after taking some tapioca prepared for Mrs Pritchard. Mrs Pritchard had refused to take it, and she, Mrs Taylor, had taken it, and about an hour and a half after she started with sickness and vomiting, which continued about an hour. I understood her to say it was severe. She also said she was pleased that Mrs Pritchard had not taken it, as it might have proved fatal to her in her delicate state. She said she would send the tapioca back to the shop, for it was terrible.'

The Solicitor General

'Did she say that her sickness and vomiting were like those with which Mrs Pritchard was afflicted?'

'She said something of the kind, but I cannot remember the exact words.'

'But although you don't remember the phrase, the idea she conveyed to you was that her attack was like Mrs Pritchard's own?'

'Yes.'

'When you last saw Mrs, Taylor did she appear ill to you?'

'I had seen her on Friday. It did not seem to me that there was anything the matter with her. I always thought her a strong, healthy old lady. She took tea that night with the prisoner and myself and the rest of the family in the dining-room just as usual about seven o'clock. She left the dining-room shortly after, as she was in the habit of doing. She went to Mrs Pritchard's room after tea. I next heard her about half-past nine o'clock.

'The prisoner came into the room and said Mrs Taylor was taken suddenly ill and asked me to go for Doctor Paterson. I wondered what was the matter with her, and he said he thought it was apoplexy. I went to fetch Doctor Paterson, and he came about ten minutes after. I was not present when Doctor Paterson was in the room. I saw

Doctor Pritchard for a few moments shortly after Doctor Paterson left. I asked him whether Mrs Taylor was any better. He replied that she was not. I asked if it was apoplexy, and he said it was. The next I heard of Mrs Taylor was the following morning. The prisoner came to my room early and said something which at first, I could not catch, but when I awoke and understood him, it was that Mrs Taylor had died about half-past twelve o'clock, very calmly and peacefully.

He told me afterwards she was unconscious for some time before she died, but that she had recovered consciousness for a few minutes immediately before her death. I left the house the next day and returned on Monday the sixth of March. I saw Mrs Pritchard that day in the drawing-room. I asked her how she felt, and she said she was well. The prisoner was in the room at the time. I thought, from her appearance, that she was getting better. She seemed a little better, but her face looked somewhat haggard. I saw her again about a week before her death, in the drawing-room. She appeared much the same in health as when I had seen her before. She did not tell me anything about herself. The prisoner was not present, and she asked me to go for him, which I did. She did not say why she wanted him. I never saw Mrs Pritchard alive again. I asked the prisoner about her every morning. He told me she was getting better, and that he thought she was improving.'

The Lord Justice Clerk

'How long did he continue to say that?'

'Until the day she died. He complained of being worn out by sitting up so often at night watching her, but that she had often done the same thing for him when he was ill. I understood him to mean that he did not grudge sitting up, for she had done as much for him. On the night before Mrs

Pritchard's death, about nine o'clock the prisoner gave me a doctor's prescription to get for him and told me to go to the Glasgow Medical Hall, Elmbank Street. I went and got two phials containing a liquid preparation, which I gave to the prisoner. I brought the prescription back from the chemists, and gave it to Doctor Pritchard, along with the phials. The prisoner, when he gave me the prescription, said it was for his wife. Mary McLeod told me of Mrs Pritchard's death on the following morning.

I used to be frequently in the prisoner's consulting-room, but not for six months before Mrs Pritchard's death. I went in when I wanted to get a book from the library. There were a few tinctures kept in a cupboard in the consulting-room. There were no tinctures or any other medicines held elsewhere that I am aware of. The prisoner was not in the habit of making up drugs for his patients, to my knowledge. It was not his practice to send prescriptions to his patients since he came to Glasgow. I never saw him doing experiments with chemicals or compounding drugs in the consulting-room or elsewhere.'

* * *

The next person called was Richard John Christian King, examined by Mr Gifford. Unlike his friend and fellow student Mr Connell, Richard thought there was something very wrong in the Pritchard household, and he had for some time. However, at no point had he suspected that the doctor and head of the household was slowly poisoning his wife and mother-in-law. He did think that the doctor was carrying on with the young maid Mary behind his wife's back, but he hadn't interfered, it wasn't his business, besides he valued his lodgings, they were hard to find in Glasgow.

'My name is Richard John Christian King. I am a medical student. I went to board with Doctor Pritchard at the end of October last. Mrs Pritchard seemed to be in good health then. I remember her going to Edinburgh. She was a little delicate before she left. I remember her coming back. She was kind of well when she returned, but got worse soon after. I am not sure that the prisoner ever spoke to me about her. He described her complaint as gastric fever. After her return from Edinburgh, she occasionally confined herself to bed. I remember Mrs Taylor coming. Mrs Pritchard was confined to bed then. I saw Mrs Pritchard only once while her mother was there: that was in the drawing-room. I remember the morning after Mrs Taylor died. I saw her that night between seven and eight. She was in the consulting-room writing letters. She appeared to be quite well. I next heard of her at ten o'clock. The prisoner told me that she was dangerously ill. I asked what the matter was, and he said it was apoplexy.

I went to bed between eleven and twelve and was woken after twelve by one of the servants, who told me the prisoner wanted me. I got up and saw him; he asked me to go to the telegraph office and telegraph to Mr Michael Taylor, Edinburgh, that Mrs Taylor, his wife, was dangerously ill. The prisoner told me at that time that she was severely ill; he did not say that she was dead. I went and telegraphed accordingly.

When I returned, the prisoner asked me to go back to the office and telegraph that she was dead. He then told me that she was dead before, but that he did not want to alarm the old gentleman. After Mrs Taylor's death, I never saw Mrs Pritchard as she was always upstairs. I remember the night before her death. I came in about eleven and went to bed. I awoke between a quarter and half-past twelve by Mary

Patterson. I rose and went into the prisoner's bedroom. He was in bed beside Mrs Pritchard. Mrs Pritchard was dead. The prisoner said she was not dead, and asked me to go for Doctor Paterson. I went and saw Doctor Paterson, and told him to come, and he said he would. When I returned to the house one of the servants met me and said that the doctor was not to come. There was no reason given to me for his not coming. I then went down to the Victoria Hotel for Mr Michael Taylor, of Edinburgh, Mrs Pritchard's father, who was living there. I can't remember which of the servants it was who told me to go to the Victoria Hotel, but it was one of them. I brought Mr Taylor up to the house. I slept in the room next to Mrs Pritchard's. I have heard her vomiting during the night not frequently, but more than once – five or six times. I did not hear her vomiting in the mornings. There is nothing more I can add to my testimony, which I haven't already said. I can only tell my account as I remember it.'

* * *

CHAPTER FIFTY-TWO
DR WILLIAM TENNANT GAIRDNER

Examined by Mr Gifford

'I am a Professor of Medicine at the University of Glasgow. I know the prisoner. I remember receiving a message requesting me to call at his house on the night between the eighth and ninth of February; I think between twelve and a half past one. I cannot come nearer the time. I had not retired for the night, as I was preparing for a lecture next morning. The message was to come and see Mrs Pritchard. I went immediately. I had never seen her before, so far as I know.'

The Lord Justice Clerk

'Never as a patient?'

'No.'

Mr Gifford

'You met Dr Pritchard at the house?'

'Yes.'

'Did the prisoner take you to his wife's bedroom?'

'Yes.'

'Did the prisoner tell you before he introduced you what was the matter with her?'

'In general terms. The prisoner said his wife had been very sick, and that her stomach was not able to bear food. I think he told me she had been some weeks so.'

'Did he say anything more?'

'Not just at that time.'

'When he had introduced you, did he continue to speak to you about her symptoms?'

'At intervals; but I cannot remember exactly.'

'How did you find Mrs Pritchard – was she in bed?'

'I found her in bed, lying on her back, with a considerably flushed face, and in a state of pretty considerable excitement. She, then, I think, told me herself, that she had been sick.'

'You said that the prisoner went on to speak of her symptoms? Did he say anything about spasms?'

'He did, but I cannot remember whether I got the first information of the spasms from him or her. The only thing I recollect was after the seizures became known to me, and he then said that it was catalepsy.'

'Did he mention that any other medical man had seen her?'

'Yes, he mentioned that Doctor Cowan, of Edinburgh, had seen her and that he had ordered stimulants, and he said that his wife had had chloroform, but whether by Doctor Cowan's orders or not I do not know.'

'Did he say his wife had had the stimulants?'

'I think so. The prisoner told me his wife had some champagne.'

'You spoke to Mrs Pritchard, I suppose?'

'Oh, yes.'

'Did she say anything about having sent for you?'

'Yes, she began by apologising for not having sent for me sooner. She stated that Doctor Cowan was an old friend of the family, that though she had wished to send for me, she had sent for him on that account, and made a kind of apology to me for not sending for me before. I told her there was no necessity for an apology because all that she had done was perfectly natural and right.'

'Did she say anything about her brother?'

'Yes, she said she was aware that I was a class-fellow of her brother, Doctor Michael Taylor, of Penrith. We had a good deal of general conversation about her symptoms.'

'What state did you find her in?'

'She had been sick. I found her to some degree exhausted, but not by any means extremely so. She had a pretty good pulse. There was nothing in her symptoms indicating immediate danger, and the most remarkable thing about her was the violent state of mental excitement she was in, and the spasms of the hands.'

The Lord Justice Clerk

'There was no immediate danger from exhaustion?'

'I thought not, from the state of the pulse and the general aspect of the patient, but the most striking symptom was the excitement and the spasms in her hands.'

Mr Gifford

'Did you observe the spasms in the hands?'

'Yes, I did. The patient held her hands outside the bed-clothes above her head, and I saw that the wrists were turned in, and the thumbs somewhat inverted towards the wrists – a very peculiar state of the hand. I think it was owing to her mentioning this that Doctor Pritchard used the word catalepsy.'

'Did you form any opinion as to the cause of her excitement?'

'In all honesty, I thought that she was intoxicated. I attributed it to the combination of champagne and chloroform.'

'Did you make any further examination?'

'Yes, I then withdrew to the fire to warm my hands, as I wanted to warm them before I examined her person. I had no sooner moved towards the fire than she began to scream out at the top of her voice, "Oh, you cruel, cruel man," or something like, "you unfeeling man, please don't leave me." I was startled by her outburst, so I returned to the bed, and said I was not going to leave her. I then returned to the fire and was warming my hands. While I was doing so, she got into a state of most violent, hysterical excitement, screaming out various exclamations, which, after a little while, I ceased to take any notice of, because I thought she was not responsible for them, being, as I considered, temporarily intoxicated.

The general purport of them was to the effect that I was incredibly unfeeling in leaving her alone and going to the fireside. I returned to her and examined her person. I took up the bedclothes and examined the belly, and I asked both her and Doctor Pritchard if there was any chance of her being pregnant – pregnancy being a frequent cause of vomiting. There wasn't, and then, after various other inquiries, and feeling her pulse, looking at the state of her skin, and her general health. I concluded that she was not in a state to give any evidence at all about her previous history that night, and I gave the orders I thought necessary, and left her.'

'Did you order the discontinuance of the stimulants?'

'Yes. Definitely.'

The Lord Justice Clerk

'To whom did you state that?'

'To Doctor Pritchard and Mrs Pritchard, but I repeated it more emphatically to Doctor Pritchard than to her, because I told him very decidedly that I thought this was very improper treatment, and that she was to get no stimulants whatsoever until I saw her again.'

Mr Gifford

'From what you observed, did you see any symptoms of catalepsy in her?'

'No.'

'You formed a definite opinion that there was no catalepsy?'

'I may explain that I hardly know what catalepsy is. It is not a disease within typical medical experience at all. Most of what we know about it is from books, and most of it is fictional. I, therefore, don't presume to be an authority upon catalepsy.'

'Do you remember her using any expression while you were there, to you or anyone, about hypocrites?'

'I cannot say. The patient used lots of language in her agitated state, of which I took no notice, and, in fact, deliberately and intentionally ignored.'

The Lord Justice Clerk

'You intentionally paid no attention to it?'

'Yes, I thought it was as well to show her that I did not wish to give attention to such expressions.'

'Were any of the servant's present?'

'I have great difficulty in remembering that. My concentration was on Mrs Pritchard. I have some recollection of Catherine Lattimer, though none of the other servants.'

'You left that night?'

'Yes.'

'Did you say anything to Doctor Pritchard before you left?'

'I spoke to him in strong terms about the impropriety of this practice of giving stimulants and said it was appalling treatment. He said Doctor Cowan had ordered it. He rather seemed to indicate that he concurred with me in disapproving of the champagne, but asked me if she was to get no more chloroform. I said, no, no stimulants and no medicine till I see her again.'

'Did you arrange when you were to see her again?'

'Yes; I was to see her the same day of which this was the morning. I called between twelve and one o'clock on the ninth of February.'

'Did you see Doctor Pritchard?'

'Yes, I did. He said Mrs Pritchard was better and quite quiet.'

'Did you go to Mrs Pritchard's bedroom?'

'We went to her room, and I found her quiet, and free from fever. I had a general conversation with her, and I assured myself that Mrs Pritchard was feeling better and that she had not vomited since I last saw her, but she still had the remains of the spasms in her hands.'

The Lord Justice Clerk

'That was about twelve hours after your former visit?'

'Yes.'

Mr Gifford

'Was Doctor Pritchard there the whole time?'

'Yes, he was. I was only there about ten minutes. I stated that the patient was still to get no stimulants and no medicine. If her appetite returned then to get her a plain boiled egg, and milk and bread, but nothing else, and that she needed a diet as simple as possible. That is, nothing that would produce sickness or sit heavy on her stomach.'

'Did you say anything more to Doctor Pritchard?'

'I just repeated in general terms what I had said to her.'

'Did you form any opinion as to what was the matter with her?'

'I was very much puzzled. I thought the patient was intoxicated the evening before drunk, in fact, but beyond that, I formed no opinion.'

'Did you think her case required severe and constant attention?'

'Yes, my impression was that if I had been a general practitioner, in attendance upon her, I should probably have seen her every day or twice a day, but there was a doctor in the house, and my habit is to act as a consulting physician.'

The Lord Justice Clerk

'You considered that you had been called in by the prisoner as a consulting physician?'

'Yes.'

'Were you ever sent for again?'

'No, I had to leave town for a distant engagement on Friday, and before leaving town, I wrote a note to ask how Mrs Pritchard was, and I received an answer back to say that she was better. I then left for my engagement and returned on a Saturday afternoon. On my return, I had another patient waiting for me, and while engaged with this patient, Doctor Pritchard called and left word that his wife was better and that I need not call.'

Mr Gifford

'Did you write to your friend Doctor Taylor, in Penrith, about the case?'

'Yes, I think it was on the ninth of February, after my second visit. My reason for doing so was that I was puzzled and that I thought the practice dangerous insofar as stimulants were concerned at least, and that I wished to be backed up and aided by his assistance.'

'Were there any symptoms of gastric fever upon Mrs Pritchard so far as you observed?'

'I did not think there was any fever at all.'

Cross-examined by Mr Clark

'You said you did not understand the meaning of the word catalepsy, which the prisoner used?'

'It was not I who applied the word to the case!'

'I thought you said you did not understand the meaning of the word as used?'

'No; it seemed to me to have no application to the case.'

'Had you known the prisoner before?'

'Yes; I think for one or two years. My connection with Doctor Pritchard has been chiefly seeing a few cases with him in consultation.'

The Lord Justice Clerk

'You knew him as a medical man for a year or two previous?'

'Yes.'

'What was it you observed in him?'

'I have no distinct impression, except I think he was rather a careless man in his ideas.'

'Was that through ignorance, do you suppose?'

'I cannot tell.'

'Was he a skilful man in his profession?'

'I had not enough to do with him to form an opinion.'

'You said you wrote to her brother after you saw her the first night?'

'Yes.'

'Did you indicate to him that there had been anything more than improper treatment, or that there had been any foul play?'

'No, but I did suggest to him that it would be in Mrs Pritchard's best interest if she were to stay with him for a while, unfortunately for her, Doctor Pritchard rejected this suggestion giving the reason that his wife was not fit enough to travel.'

* * *

CHAPTER FIFTY-THREE
DR JAMES PATERSON

The Lord Justice Clerk, Lord Inglis observed the next witness as he took his place at the bar. Patterson looked like a typical middle-class doctor, overweight, ruddy complexion and with a constant layer of sweat on his forehead. His eyes were dark, bead-like, and were too close together. Lord Inglis considered himself impartial and did not often form an opinion of someone or their actions before he had heard all the facts and each side of the story, but on this occasion, there was something about Dr James Paterson that troubled him deeply. He had read his notes thoroughly and found it difficult to believe that this man, a doctor for over thirty years and who suspected the poisoning of two women, did nothing to alert the authorities. Why did he not go to the police? Why did he not speak up at the time? Perhaps if he had spoken up Mrs Pritchard would be alive today, and maybe it may not have been too late for Mrs Taylor. Lord Inglis listened to this testimony carefully.

* * *

Doctor Paterson, was ready to give his evidence; he just hoped that it wouldn't take too long. He had planned to dine at his gentleman's club this evening and wanted to be on top form to enjoy it. He most certainly didn't want any unpleasantness with his friends because of the wretched Pritchard fellow. He took his place at the bar, wiped his forehead with the back of his hand and nodded at the judge, who did not acknowledge him and quickly turned away.

'I am Doctor James Paterson, and I am a doctor of medicine in Glasgow. I have been in practice there upwards of thirty years. I was formerly Professor of Midwifery at the Andersonian University. I resigned about two years ago.'

The Lord Justice Clerk couldn't help himself and in an unmistakably unpleasant tone interrupted the witness.

'Eh! What is that – I never heard of such a place.'

Dr Paterson could not quite believe his ears, was the eminent lord deliberately trying to ridicule him, was this a blatant attempt to undermine his status and professional authority? The doctor was furious, but remembering that he was on oath replied with decorum.

'My Lord, it is not properly speaking a University, but an Andersonian Medical School!'

The Lord Justice Clerk sat back in his chair and looked directly at the red-faced doctor.

'Ah, I can understand that.'

Still fuming, but with a degree of composure, Dr Paterson continued.

'I reside at No. 6 Windsor Place, Sauchiehall Street, a division of the street in which Doctor Pritchard and his family lived. I remember Doctor Pritchard called me to his house on Friday evening, the twenty-fourth of February.'

'Was this your first visit?'

'Yes, it was the first time that I ever crossed his threshold. It was late evening between half-past ten and a quarter to eleven.'

'Did you see Doctor Pritchard?'

'I met him in the lobby or hall of his own house.'

'Tell us, if you please, what he said to you.'

'He conducted me into his consulting-room on the first floor, and then he stated that his mother-in-law, while in the act of writing a letter, had suddenly been taken ill and had fallen off her chair to the floor. She had been conveyed upstairs to the bedroom about half an hour or an hour before I came. I asked if he could assign any reason for the suddenness of the attack. He said his mother-in-law and Mrs Pritchard had been partaking of some bitter beer, as I understood, for supper, soon after which they both became sick and vomited, and both complained that the beer was much more bitter to the taste than usual.'

'Doctor Paterson, please tell us what Doctor Pritchard said to you on your first arrival in the consulting-room, when he and you were alone together?'

'The doctor stated that the women could not have taken more than one-third part of a pint each because there was still some remaining in the bottle. I said I did not think it possible that strong beer could produce such an effect, and that the attack must depend upon some other cause. I then asked him about the previous state of his mother-in-law's health, and especially about her social habits, when, by a particular insinuation, he led me distinctly to understand that she was in the habit of taking a drop occasionally.'

The Lord Justice Clerk

'Drinking spirits, you mean?'

'Yes, he also stated that Mrs Pritchard had been very poorly for a long time with gastric fever; and that some days previously he had telegraphed for his mother-in-law to come through to attend to her in her illness. We then went upstairs to the bedroom. On entering, I observed Mrs Taylor on the outside of the bed. She was lying on her right side with all her clothes on, and on her head a cap with a small artificial flower. She had all the appearance of having had a sudden seizure. Mrs Pritchard, in her nightdress, with her hair very much dishevelled, was in the same bed, but underneath the bedclothes, and sitting up immediately beyond her mother. On examining Mrs Taylor, my impression was that she had previously been in good health.'

The Lord Justice Clerk

'Was she dead or living?'

'She was still living.'

The Solicitor General

'Did she appear to be a healthy-looking old lady?'

'Yes, I should say so. Mrs Taylor seemed rather above the ordinary size, good-looking, well-formed, altogether a very superior-looking person for her station of life, and certainly not having the slightest appearance of being addicted to the use of spirituous or intoxicating liquors. On examination, her face was rather pale, but the expression was calm and placid. Her eyelids partially closed, the lips were rather livid, the breathing slow and laborious. The skin was cold and covered with a clammy perspiration. The pulse was almost imperceptible, and she seemed to me to be unconscious. On opening the eyelids, I found both pupils very much contracted. From those symptoms, and judging from her general appearance, my conviction was that she was under the influence of opium or some other powerful narcotic, and I at once pronounced my opinion that she was dying and there was nothing further that I could do for her.'

'You stated that to Doctor Pritchard, who was beside you all the time?'

'Yes, I did, but on my doing so Pritchard said something in an undertone of voice, being apparently unwilling that my opinion should be heard by the ladies, which was quite natural. We retired a little from the bedside, near to the fireplace, and I then stated that she was dying. Pritchard said she had frequently had attacks of a similar kind before, but never one so severe. I said that nothing we could do would have the slightest effect, but that, as a last resource, we might try mustard poultices to the soles of the feet, the calves of the legs, and the inside of the thighs, and as quickly as possible administer a strong turpentine enema. Pritchard at once proceeded to prepare the medicine and said he had shortly before administered a glass of brandy. The old lady lay apparently comatose; but on being roused a little, and the head and shoulders slightly elevated, a degree of consciousness ensued, and the pulse became perceptible at the wrist.'

'Was that rousing the first thing you had done to test whether she was conscious or not?'

'It was.'

'And what you meant by saying that she was seemingly unconscious is that the symptoms indicated unconsciousness.'

'Yes; I directed Pritchard's attention to the pulse, and he then tapped the old lady on the shoulder and said, you are getting better, darling. I couldn't believe my ears, and I looked at him, shook my head ominously, and said, "Never in this world." I was shocked.'

The Solicitor General

'She gave no promise to you of recovering?'

'None. A slight fit of retching came on, and the lady vomited a small quantity of frothy mucus, immediately after the coma returned, and her breathing became more oppressed and laboured. I then concluded that the case was utterly hopeless, but Pritchard administered the enema. I afterwards left the room and went downstairs, accompanied by Pritchard, to the consulting-room. I repeated my opinion that she was under the influence of narcotics.'

The Lord Justice Clerk

'Meaning under the influence of opium or some narcotic?'

'Yes, Pritchard then said the old lady was in the habit of taking Battley's Sedative Solution, and that she had recently purchased not less than a half-pound bottle of the medicine, and that he had no doubt, that she might have taken a good swig of it.'

'You know Battley's Solution?'

'I know it, but I seldom use it.'

'Had Mrs Taylor the appearance of a lady who had been in the practice of using such a medicine?'

'My impression was that she was not what is called an 'opium eater' or one who used opium to any great extent. She presented no appearance of that.'

'Thank you, Doctor Paterson. Would you now tell us what you observed of Mrs Pritchard?'

'While attending to Mrs Taylor, I was very much struck at the same time with the appearance of Mrs Pritchard. She seemed exceedingly weak and exhausted. Her features were sharp and thin, with a high, hectic flush on her cheeks, and her voice was feeble and peculiar – in fact, very much resembling the voice of a person verging into the collapsed stage of cholera. The expression of her countenance conveyed to me the idea of a semi-imbecile person. At first, I was inclined to attribute her appearance to the recent severe attack of gastric fever, of which the prisoner told me, her symptoms, which were aggravated, of course, by the consternation and grief naturally caused by the dangerous condition of her mother. At the same time, I could not banish from my mind the idea, or rather the conviction, that her symptoms betokened that she was under the depressing influence of antimony.'

On hearing this, the solicitor general shook his head and raised his eyebrows.

'You mean that that impression or conviction you created entirely by her appearance?'

'Yes, and the general symptoms of the case. I then left, and went home about half-past eleven.'

The Solicitor General

'Were you sent for again during that morning about one o'clock and did you afterwards get another message not to come because Mrs Taylor was dead?'

'Yes, a little before one o'clock someone rang my doorbell. I was in bed, but Mrs Patterson happened to be sitting up. She opened the door, and a girl asked me to come directly and see Mrs Taylor. I refused to go because I was confident that I could be of no help to the old lady. Furthermore, the previous day's work had tired me out, and I was very unwilling to rise, but I sent my compliments to Pritchard, saying that if he thought I could be of use, he was to send back word, and I would then rise and visit her.'

* * *

The solicitor general could not believe the sheer arrogance of this man. 'He would not rise!' Knowing that the poor old lady was dying. Some doctor!

'Your house was only a short distance from his in the same street? Two-hundred yards at the most. Did any message come back?'

'No message came back, and I did not go, but about ten o'clock on Saturday morning, of the twenty-fifth, an elderly gentleman called upon me, a Mr Taylor, who was the husband of the old lady.'

'Did he inform you that she was dead?'

'Yes, he came for the death certificate, which I refused to give.'

'You refused to give the death certificate?'

'Yes, I said I was surprised that Pritchard had sent for a certificate, and that, as a medical practitioner, he should have known that it was not given to the friends, but to the district registrar.'

'Did the registrar request full details of the death?'

'Yes, on Friday the third of March, I received through the post-office a schedule from the registrar, in which I was requested to fill in the cause of Mrs Taylor's death, and the duration of her disease, which again I refused to do.'

'You refused to do that?'

'Yes, I did; and sent it back with a note accompanying it, directing his attention to the circumstance.'

'When did you see the prisoner after that?'

'On Wednesday the first of March. I met him accidentally in Sauchiehall Street, near my own house. On coming up to me, he said I had been correct in my opinion about his poor mother-in-law, and he added that he would feel obliged if I would visit Mrs Pritchard next day at eleven o'clock, as he was going to Edinburgh to attend Mrs Taylor's funeral. I at once agreed to his request and went to see her on Thursday the second of March, about eleven in the morning. Mrs Pritchard was in bed. She was still very weak and prostrated, and in a soft voice, she expressed her satisfaction and her gratitude at my visit. Then she asked me if I thought that her mother was dying when I first saw her. I said, most definitely, and that I had told her husband so. She then clasped her hands, looked up to the ceiling, and feebly exclaimed, "Good God, is it possible." Then she burst into a flood of tears. I put some questions as to the previous state of her mother's health, and especially if she was habitually addicted to the use of Battley's Sedative Solution.

Mrs Pritchard told me that her mother's health had generally been good, but that she occasionally suffered from what she called 'neuralgic headaches' and for the relief from these attacks, she did take a little of Battley's Sedative Solution, but not that she was in the habitual use of that medicine. I then questioned her about herself. She told me that for a considerable time she had suffered from sickness, retching, and vomiting, with severe pains in the stomach and throughout the bowels, accompanied by attacks of high heat and uneasiness about the mouth and throat, and a constant, urgent thirst.

I examined her tongue. It was very foul and of a lightish brown colour. Her features were still very sharp and deeply flushed. Her pulse was weak, contracted, and very rapid. Her skin was moist, and altogether she presented an appearance of a large general prostration. Her eyes were watery but bright and intelligent. I prescribed for her small quantities, at short intervals, of champagne and brandy to recruit her strength; small pieces of ice occasionally to relieve the thirst and irritability of the stomach. If she tired of these, I said, she should have recourse to granulated citrate of magnesia as a cooling, effervescing drink. I also recommended small quantities, at frequent intervals, of easily digested, nutritious food, such as beef-tea, calf-foot jelly, chicken soup, arrowroot, and so on. I then prescribed twelve grains of calomel, twenty-four of blue or grey powder, twelve of powdered ipecacuanha, and six grains of aromatic powder, the whole to be carefully mixed, and divided into six equal parts – one powder to be taken every day.'

'Did you give the prescription to Mrs Pritchard herself?'

'Yes, I did, and told her to show it to Pritchard when he came home in the evening, I never saw Mrs Pritchard again until within four or five hours of her death.'

'Between the visit of which you have given us an account and the last time you saw her before her death, did you see her husband?'

'Yes, I did. On Sunday evening, the fifth of March, about nine o'clock, he called at my house and told me his wife had been much relieved by the medicines and treatment I had prescribed, and that she greatly relished the small quantities of champagne and brandy, and felt refreshed by the cooling, effervescing draught. He said that she was still very weak and the stomach still irritable. I recommended the continuance of stimulants and nourishment and more particular attention to the state of the stomach and bowels. Nothing more passed at that meeting.'

'Then the next occasion you must speak of is that visit a few hours before her death.'

'On the seventeenth of March – the Friday – Pritchard called upon me. Personally, I think about a quarter to eight o'clock in the evening, and requested me to go with him to see Mrs Pritchard.'

'Did you go?'

'I did. I went up to the bedroom. Mrs Pritchard was in bed in a sitting position, supported with pillows. Her altered appearance shocked me. She seemed quite conscious. I went up to her bedside, and she caught my hand, and I could see a half-smile of recognition upon her countenance. She soon began to mutter about having been vomiting. Pritchard was standing beside me, and he volunteered the observation that she had not been vomiting – that she was only ranting. She complained of great thirst, and Pritchard poured some water out of a carafe into a tumbler, and gave it to her to drink, saying, "Here, some nice, cold water, darling." She swallowed it. As I previously remarked, I observed that her appearance had changed dramatically from what it had been when I last saw her. She had a peculiarly wild expression; her eyes were fiery red and sunken. Her cheeks were hollow, sharp, pinched-looking, and flushed. Her pulse was feeble and exceedingly rapid. Her tongue was a darkish brown colour, and she immediately began to grasp with her hand, as if to catch at some imaginary object on the bedclothes. She muttered something about the clock, and Pritchard said he thought she referred to the clock on the drawing-room mantelpiece. There was no clock in the bedroom.

I asked Pritchard how long had his wife been entirely confined to bed. He said only since morning, and that yesterday she was in the drawing-room amusing herself with the children. I again expressed surprise at her alarming condition. He told me she had not slept for four or five days or nights. I was shocked and said to Pritchard that we must endeavour to do something to relieve her, and, if possible, procure sleep. We left the bedroom and went downstairs, and I then prescribed thirty drops of a solution of morphia, thirty drops of ipecacuanha wine, five or ten drops of chlorodyne, and an ounce of cinnamon water. The preparation was to be repeated in four hours if the first draught did not give relief. That is, did not procure sleep.'

'Did you write the prescription?'

'No, I did not. Pritchard prescribed at my dictation.'

'Did you ask him to write it?'

'No, I said it was unnecessary to write it, it was a simple draft that he might make it up himself. I was anxious to save time and give relief as soon as possible.'

'What did he say to that?'

'He said he kept no medicines in the house except chloroform and Battley's Sedative Solution. I asked if he did not keep a small stock to meet any emergency, and particularly for night work, and he said he did not!'

'Did that strike you as strange?'

'Yes, it certainly did.'

The Lord Justice Clerk

'You mean that it is not a usual thing for a medical practitioner?'

'Yes, it is normal for medical men in extensive practice to keep medicines in stock, especially if they have much night work to go through.'

The Solicitor General

'And he wrote it to your dictation?'

'Yes, so far as I know.'

'What happened next?'

'I then left the house, and I heard no more until about one o'clock on the following morning when my doorbell rang loudly. A young man requested me to see Mrs Pritchard immediately, as she had become much worse, and was thought to be dying. I proceeded to dress at once. In less than three minutes after that my doorbell rang again, this time by a servant girl, and when I opened the door said, "You need not come Mrs Pritchard is dead!" So, I did not.'

'You did not go to the house again?'

'No, I never crossed the threshold of the house except on these occasions.'

'Did you ever say to the prisoner that you thought his wife, Mrs Pritchard, had taken too much wine?'

'I never did.'

'Doctor Paterson, please confirm that you have mentioned to us accurately everything you ever prescribed for her?'

'Yes.'

Cross-examined by Mr Clark

'You mentioned that Mrs Taylor had not the appearance of having been in the habit of using opium?'

'Yes, that is my candid opinion.'

'Have you had experience in cases of that kind?'

'I have.'

'What led you to believe that she was not addicted to the use of opium?'

'If a person is in the habit of taking opium to any great extent, you find that, as a rule, they are not of good colour. They are thin in features and hollow about the eyes; in fact, not of a healthy appearance generally.'

'And Mrs Taylor, being stout and healthy looking, so far as you could judge, you concluded that she was not addicted to the use of opium?'

'Well, I do not say that she never took opium at all, but merely that she was not a habitual consumer of opium.'

'Do you mean that she did not take it continuously, though she might take it by way of medicine?'

'Yes, that is what I meant.'

'After you saw the patient, you thought the statement was not consistent with facts?'

'I didn't think so.'

'Now, when you were with Mrs Taylor that evening, did you examine the condition of Mrs Pritchard attentively?'

'No, I only glanced at her. I did not talk to her. I formed a diagnosis from the symptoms that were present.'

'What, by merely looking at her?' Mr Clark was astounded at this witness's lack of compassion for his patient.

'Yes, just as I am in the habit of forming an opinion of any patient I see for the first time.'

'You did not examine her at that point as a patient, did you?'

'No, certainly not.'

'But, you formed the conviction that she was under the influence of antimony?'

'Yes.'

'Had you ever seen a case of poisoning by antimony?'

'Yes, two or three.'

'What were they?'

'Young children.'

'Did you ever see a case of poisoning by antimony in the case of an adult?'

'No, but with Mrs Pritchard, I was under the impression that she had been using antimony for some time. I had nothing to judge from but her appearance.'

'Do you mean she was getting antimony medicinally, or for some other purpose?'

'Of course, I could form no opinion as to how or by what means she was getting antimony.'

'Was the condition you have described one attributed to the medicinal use of antimony?'

'Not exactly medicinal use, but a long-continued use; a judicious practitioner would not carry it to such an extent as to produce debility and prostration.'

'Did you mean to convey to us that she had been taking antimony medicinally, or that antimony was poisoning her?'

'My impression was that antimony was poisoning her.'

'And you formed that conviction by only looking at her?'

'Yes, judging from the signs of disease.'

'Doctor Paterson, as you thought, Mrs Pritchard was suffering in that way from antimony, did you ever go back to see her again?'

'No, I did not, and I believe that I would never have been called back again if I had not met Pritchard accidentally on the street.'

'Why did you not go back?'

'Because she was not my patient. I had nothing to do with her!'

Mr Clark had never come across anyone as arrogant or tenacious as this man; he found it difficult to comprehend the doctor's lack of empathy and compassion for a fellow human being. Weren't doctor's supposed to save lives? He found the ageing doctor's answers amazing.

'Let me get this straight, Doctor Paterson, you are a doctor, and you saw a person suffering from what you believed to be poisoning by antimony, yet you did not think it worth your while to go near her again?'

'It was not my duty. I had no right to interfere in any family without being invited.'

'Doctor Paterson, is it not your duty to look after a fellow human being who, you believe, is being poisoned by antimony. Is it not your duty to preserve the destruction of human life and fulfil your public duty as a citizen?'

Dr Paterson shook his head not liking this rude line of questioning one bit. He felt as if he was the one on trial here. There was no need for these unwarranted and invidious remarks. In his opinion, he had done his duty. If it hadn't been for him, Pritchard would not even be standing trial today. If that gormless registrar had done his job correctly, and read between the lines of his letter, instead of just throwing it away, then it might have been another story. Perhaps, if the clerk had ordered a postmortem for Mrs Taylor, then who knows – Mrs Pritchard may be here today.

What were these people trying to do? Discredit his professionalism? He raised his voice when answering further questions, making sure that they understood his disapproval.

'There was another doctor in the house. I did the best I could by apprising the registrar.'

'Did you tell Doctor Pritchard…?'

'No, I did not. Had I been called in consultation with another medical man, I should certainly have considered it my duty to have stated my medical opinion distinctly.'

'But you stood upon your dignity, and did not go back to see what you believed to be a case of poisoning?'

'I had no right.'

'No right!Not even when you suspected that these two ladies were slowly being poisoned?'

'I had no power to do it.'

'No power?'

'I was under no obligation.'

'You were under no obligation to go back to see a person who you believed was being poisoned?'

'I took what steps I could to prevent any further administration of antimony, and by refusing to certify the death! Had there been a post-mortem examination of Mrs Taylor's body, I believe that probably the drugging with antimony would have gone no further, at least at that time.'

'But still, you could not be sure of that. The way I see it is that it comes down to this, that although you had formed your suspicions, you never went near her again until you were called in by Doctor Pritchard?'

'Yes.'

'Well, did you find her labouring under the same symptoms or similar symptoms to those you observed when you saw her on your first visit?'

'Yes.'

'And, you still believed her to be suffering from poisoning by antimony?'

'I did, and I thought that I had prescribed accordingly.

'Did you see her alone on that occasion?'

'I did.'

'Did you give her any indication of what you thought was wrong with her?'

'I did not mention antimony to her.'

'Did you mention poison to her?'

'I did not.'

'Did you give her any idea that she was labouring under anything other than a natural disease?'

'I did not.'

Mr Clark felt his jaw tighten; he was about to snap with this arrogant, stupid witness. For relief he clenched his fist and banged it against the desk in front of him, then in a loud, high voice said, 'Why ever not!'

'Because the treatment I prescribed ensured that she got nothing else, and was quite sufficient, in my opinion, to have soon brought her round, and I took it for granted that the patient was indeed taking my advice.'

'It was Doctor Pritchard who asked you to visit his wife upon that occasion?'

'Yes.'

'Did you mention to him your opinion as to his wife being poisoned by antimony?'

'No, I did not.'

'Why did you not visit her the next day to ensure that the patient had heeded your advice?'

'I did not consider at all, sir, that she was my patient, and I had no right or title to go back and visit her. I would have considered myself intruding upon the family had I done so.'

'The prisoner himself asked you to visit her on the first of March?'

'I believe that if I had not met him accidentally, he would not have asked me. I understood that visit more in the light of a friendly call of condolence under painful circumstances than as a medical visit.'

'Had you known Mrs Pritchard before?'

'No.'

'Then, why did you call to pay a visit of condolence to a person you never saw before?'

'It was at Pritchard's request that I condole with her?'

'What was the use of calling on a person whom you did not know, to condole with her?'

'I had seen her at her mother's deathbed.'

'Were you not called in as a medical man?'

'No, I understood Pritchard was attending her himself, and that I was only to call during the day, and that when he came back in the evening, I had nothing more to do with the case.'

'But when you saw something so seriously the matter, why did you not call back?'

'Simply because it was none of my business. I did not consider it my duty. Doctor Pritchard was there, himself a medical man.'

'Having been in a house where you thought there was poisoning going on, you did not consider it your duty to go back?'

'I had discharged my duty, so far as I thought.'

'What, by prescribing certain things, and not following it up!'

'Where a consultation is given, the consulting physician has no right to go back to see the patient.'

'Doctor Paterson, are you saying that it was the dignity of your profession that prevented you from going back?'

'Yes, it would be a breach of the etiquette of my profession.'

'You said you wrote to the registrar. Did you write first, or did you get a letter from the registrar before you wrote to him?'

'I got the schedule sent to me in the first place.'

'That was about Mrs Taylor?'

'Yes; I got no notice regarding Mrs Pritchard.'

Re-examined by the Solicitor General

'It was to visit Mrs Taylor, who was thought to be very ill on the twenty-fourth of February, that you were called in?'

'Yes, that was the only occasion I called.'

'You were not consulted about Mrs Pritchard at all?'

'No.'

'Was your meeting with Doctor Pritchard accidental?'

'Yes, purely coincidental.'

'What time of day was it?'

'About eleven o'clock in the morning, he told me that he was going from home, and would be obliged if I would call and see his wife next day.'

'You had no reason to suppose, and do not suppose, that he was coming for you?'

'Certainly not.'

'And it was, therefore, from your accidentally meeting him that day, and his asking you to call at eleven o'clock the next, that you thought it was an accidental invitation?'

'Yes.'

'You said that it might not have been safe for you to communicate your suspicions to Doctor Pritchard himself?'

'It would not have been very natural.'

'You mean that your suspicions concerned himself?'

Dr Paterson was agitated, he knew what they were trying to do, they were trying to blame him for not alerting the authorities sooner. Well, he was not going to have any of it. None of this was his fault. He had done his job. He could feel a flush creeping across his face, damn it. With obvious annoyance, he gave a dismissive wave of his hand.

'I would rather not answer that question.'

Re-cross-examined by Mr Clark

Mr Clark, jumped to his feet, in amazement; he couldn't quite believe what he had just heard.

'Doctor Paterson, are you telling the jury you did not communicate your suspicions to any of Doctor Pritchard's family?'

'No, I didn't.'

'Nor the Taylor family?'

'I never saw any of the Taylor family, apart from Mr Taylor himself, when he came for the certificate.'

'Doctor Paterson, were you the person responsible for the anonymous letter sent to the Fiscal General?'

'I most certainly was not. I have never written an anonymous letter in my life!' He looked straight at Mrs Lattimer when he said it. He was getting the blame for this, but he would put his life on it being her.

The Solicitor General

'You told us that you wrote to the registrar, Mr Struthers?'

'I did. I wrote it very guardedly.'

Mr Clark

'Is there a copy in existence?'

'The original copy was destroyed.'

The Solicitor General
'I have a copy taken from the witness's dictation.'
The Lord Justice Clerk
'You must have the destruction of it proved.'
The Solicitor General
'I shall do so now. Thank you, Doctor Paterson, you are now excused.'

* * *

CHAPTER FIFTY-FOUR
JAMES STRUTHERS-REGISTRAR

Examined by the Solicitor General

'My name is James Struthers. I am registrar of deaths for the Blythswood District in Glasgow.

'The prisoner's house was in that district. I received intimation in the usual way of the death of Mrs Taylor in his home on the twentieth of February, between twelve and half-past twelve in the afternoon, by Mr Taylor, her husband. I asked him who was the medical attendant; he said, Doctor Pritchard and Doctor Paterson. He mentioned that Doctor Paterson had been called in shortly before her death, and I asked him if I might send to Doctor Paterson, as I did not consider him (Doctor Pritchard) as the medical attendant. He said he would prefer I should send to Doctor Paterson for the certificate. I accordingly sent Doctor Paterson the usual printed form of the Registrar General with blanks to be filled in. The certificate was returned empty, with a note. I am sorry to say that the letter has since been destroyed. It recommended me to apply to Doctor Pritchard, which I did, and I afterwards I got the certificate from Doctor Pritchard, which certified that the primary cause of death was paralysis, the duration of which was twelve hours, and the secondary cause was apoplexy, the duration of which was one hour. Doctor Pritchard got a similar schedule when he came to register the death of Mrs Pritchard on Monday, the twentieth of March, at ten o'clock in the morning. At the time, he called he signed the entry in the register and gave me the certificate, which stated that the primary disease and cause of death was gastric fever, the duration of which was two months.'

Dr James Paterson was recalled, examined by the Solicitor General.

'Doctor Paterson, state to us the terms of the letter, as well as your memory serves you, which you sent to the registrar.'

'The letter was headed No. 6 Windsor Place, and dated the fourth of March 1865, and was as follows:

Dear Sir,

I am surprised that I am called on to certify the cause of death in this case. I only saw the person for a few minutes a very short period before her death. She seemed to be under some narcotic, but Dr Pritchard, who was present from the first moment of illness until death occurred, and which happened in his own house, may certify the cause. The death was certainly sudden, unexpected, and to me mysterious.'

Cross-examined by Mr Clark

'Was that was the whole letter?'

'Yes, I believe it is. I sent it off that day through the post-office, directed to James Struthers, the registrar.'

'When I was asking you whether you had taken any means for the protection of Mrs Pritchard, this was the communication to which you referred?'

'Yes.'

'And the only communication you refer to?'

'The only communication and I had three motives for making it.'

'Never mind the reasons, but you say this was the only communication, and Mrs Pritchard was not mentioned in it?'

'No.'

'You did not make any communication whatever to any one of Mrs Pritchard's family?'

'No, I spoke of the matter in my own family, that was all.'

The Lord Justice Clerk

'In answer to a question from the prisoner's counsel, I think you stated that your impression when you first saw Mrs Pritchard, on the twenty-fourth of February, and afterwards when you saw her again, on the second of March, was that antimony was poisoning her?'

Dr Paterson, was sick of this constant ridicule, in complete frustration, he let out a loud sigh, what were these people implying –did they not listen?

'That is what I said!'

The Lord Justice Clerk ignored the distinct sense of annoyance in the witness's voice as he repeated his line of questioning.

'Do you mean that you believed that as a doctor and a professional man that you thought that some person was engaged in administering antimony to Mrs Pritchard to procure her death?'

'Yes, that was my meaning.'

Lord Justice Clerk, could feel the anger rising inside him, already his knuckles were white from clenching his fists together. His eyes narrowed as he stared at the man in front of him. Thank goodness Patterson was not his doctor, but that didn't help those poor women, too late for them now. If this so-called doctor had done his duty as a human being and alerted the authorities then perhaps at least one of them may not have had to endure weeks of endless pain and agony, and maybe she would be alive today. He regained his composure, as much as he would have enjoyed telling this so-called professional precisely what he thought of him, he remembered his position. Still, there was a slight trembling in his voice as he dismissed the witness.

'You are free to go.'

* * *

CHAPTER FIFTY-FIVE
DR JAMES MOFFATT COWAN

Examined by Mr Gifford

'I am James Cowan, a doctor of medicine in Edinburgh. I have not been in practice for very long. I was a relative of the late Mrs Pritchard. We are or rather were, second cousins. I remember getting a letter from the prisoner in February last; I do not have the letter now. Unfortunately, I destroyed it. The letter stated that Mrs Pritchard had been ailing for some time and that Doctor Pritchard was becoming very anxious about her case. He wished to call in another medical man in Glasgow. He wanted me to come through and see her. If I possibly could. I went to Glasgow on the seventh.'

'Did you go to Doctor Pritchard's house?'

'Yes, I got there between four and five o'clock. In the afternoon.'

'Did you see the prisoner before you saw Mrs Pritchard?'

'Yes, he met me in the lobby, and I inquired after Mrs Pritchard, and he said she was very much better that day, and that she would be down to see me in a few minutes.'

'When you saw Mrs Pritchard in the drawing-room, how did you find her?'

'I found her very much better than I expected.'

'Did you put questions to her as to what her symptoms were?'

'Yes, she said she had been troubled with considerable pain in her stomach, that she could not retain food, and had been vomiting for some time.'

'Did you put what questions you required to enable you to judge the situation as a medical man?'

'Well, she is my second cousin, so I did not go exactly like a medical man. I would say that I went more like an old friend, but I did ask one or two questions, and I ordered the application of a mustard poultice to her stomach, and if there was much prostration, I advised small quantities of champagne, with ice.'

'Did you remain overnight?'

'Yes, I did.'

'Did anything occur in the evening with Mrs Pritchard?'

'Yes, it did, while I was sitting in the dining-room with the children, Doctor Pritchard came down from her bedroom and told me that Mrs Pritchard had been vomiting again, and requested me to go with him to the bedroom to see her, which I did.'

'You saw her.'

'Yes, and she told me she had again been vomiting. She complained greatly of feeling hungry, and yet she could not retain it. I proposed to administer beef tea injections to see if that would do any good.'

'Was she in bed when you left her?'

'She was in bed at that time.'

'Did you see her the next morning?'

'I did, in her bedroom first thing in the morning, she was much the same as on the previous night.'

'Did you return to Edinburgh that evening?'

'Yes, I stayed in Glasgow during the day.'

'Did you see her that day again?'

'Yes, I saw her when I left, but nothing particular occurred that made an impression on me.'

Mr Gifford

'Was it you who took the message to Mrs Taylor to go to Glasgow?'

'I did.'

'Who gave you the message?'

'Well, Mrs Pritchard desired that her mother should come through and attend to her. It was my proposal partly, and she acceded to it.'

'You suggested it?'

'Yes, the Pritchard's are a large family, and I thought she required undivided attention. On my return to Edinburgh, I saw Mrs Taylor, and she went to nurse her daughter the next day.'

Cross-examined by Mr Clark

'You knew Doctor and Mrs Pritchard well?'

'Yes, very well.'

'During the whole time of their married life?'

'Yes.'

'Did they live happily together?'

'Exceedingly so to the last moment I saw them together.'

'When was the last time you saw Mrs Pritchard?'

'I saw Mrs Pritchard at the time of Mrs Taylor's death.'

'You never heard of any disagreement whatever between them?'

'Good grief no, the very reverse. I never heard them speak a disrespectful or unkind word to each other. On the contrary, they both talked about each other very kindly. In fact, very much so.'

'How did Doctor Pritchard and Mrs Taylor get along?'

'As far as I'm aware he was Mrs Taylor's, idol she, doted on him.'

'Do you recall Mrs Pritchard's body laid out at her parent's house in Edinburgh?'

'I do. She was taken to her father's house on Lauder Road. I accompanied the body to the house.'

'Did the prisoner attend it also?'

'He did.'

'When in the house, was the coffin opened?'

'It was, at Doctor Pritchard's desire.'

'For what purpose?'

'To gratify the servants. They were very much attached to her, and the doctor thought that they might have a last look at the body.'

'What day was that?'

'It was on Monday, the twentieth of March.'

'Now, Doctor Cowan, just tell us what passed on this occasion?'

'The coffin was in the bedroom at the time it was opened, and the servants and Mr Taylor were present. Doctor Pritchard exhibited a great deal of feeling on this occasion and kissed the body, and after some time we retired.'

Re-examined by Mr Gifford

'Were you well acquainted with Mrs Taylor?'

'Yes, I had known her all my life.'

'You visited her frequently?'

'Very often.'

'Was she a person of temperate habits?'

'Very temperate.'

The Lord Justice Clerk

'Have you seen much of Doctor and Mrs Pritchard during the last two years?'

'A good deal, mainly when they both were in Edinburgh.

'No further questions.'

* * *

CHAPTER FIFTY-SIX
MICHAEL TAYLOR

The last person to be called was Mr Michael Taylor the prisoner's father-in-law and the husband of Jane Taylor. Michael had aged considerably since the death of his wife and daughter. His pure white hair now long and unkept, his once bright blue eyes now bloodshot with the endless tears he'd cried. Deep wrinkles traced the torment on his face that wasn't there before. Michael was broken and unrecognisable from the man he was three months ago.

Tired and nervous, he just wanted to curl up into a ball and go to sleep. And he didn't care if he never woke up. He found it difficult to grasp all that had happened over the last couple of months. To him, it was all one big dream. He craved normality. He wanted his wife fussing around him worrying about their daughter. He missed the letters from Mary Jane chatting about the children's achievements. All this talk of murder has been just surreal. Yes, he'd had doubts about his son-in-law's philandering ways, but murder – no, never! Edward didn't have it in him. He was a kind, gentle man. So Edward had a roving eye, that was normal for a man! Especially one whose wife had been so ill. A man had needs, Michael understood that. He just wanted to get it all over and done with and let Edward get home to his children. They missed and adored him.

Michael Taylor, examined by the Solicitor General

'I am Michael Taylor. The late Mrs Taylor, who died in Glasgow in February last, was my wife. Before she went to visit our daughter, Mrs Pritchard, her health was only middling; she had been complaining a good deal. She had been delicate for years, and subject to violent perspirations and neuralgic headaches.'

'Did she take anything for her headache?'

'Yes, she took the infamous Battley's Solution known as 'Lancaster Black Drops', she had taken it for five or six years; she took it for the perspirations.'

'Excuse me for asking the question, but was she of temperate habits?'

'Perfectly so, in every respect.'

'She did not appear to be the worse for the medicine?'

'I sometimes observed a high inclination in her to sleep after she had taken the medication.'

'She took it in your presence?'

'No, never.'

'You knew she was taking it?'

'Yes, I knew that she was taking medicine, but I did not know what it was until last year. Still, it was a habit, yes, but it's not like my wife was frequenting the opium dens the press is reporting about!'

'Your daughter was with you upon a visit from the end of November until a few days before Christmas?'

'She was. She had been ailing before she came.'

'How was she when she was in your house?'

'Very delicate. Mary Jane took meals with us, but ate very little.'

'Was she confined to bed while in your house at all?'

'Sometimes she lay in bed when she first came.'

The Lord Justice Clerk

'She got somewhat better while she was staying with you, and was more in the way of getting up for breakfast?'

'Yes.'

The Solicitor General

'Did she complain about anything?'

'She complained of sickness.'

'At what time of day did she complain?'

'In the latter end of November, when she first came. She frequently complained of weakness and sickness.'

'Did you ever see her sick?'

'I have heard her being sick; she had been obliged to leave the table on that account two or three times.'

'Was she very much better when she went away from you than before she came?'

'She was a little better.'

'You were telegraphed to from Glasgow that your wife was dangerously ill, and then that she was dead?'

'Yes: I received the two telegrams together. I went through to Glasgow by the first train.'

'You went to Doctor Paterson's house in the morning?'

'Yes, on a Saturday morning, my son-in-law, Doctor Pritchard, asked me if I would go down and register the death.'

'And you went to Doctor Paterson's first?'

'Yes, to ask him to give me a certificate regarding the cause of my wife's death.'

'It was Doctor Pritchard, who sent you to Doctor Paterson?'

'Yes.'

'Did Doctor Pritchard tell you what your wife died of?'

'I think he said it was apoplexy and paralysis.'

'Had your wife ever any fits?'

'Not to my knowledge.'

'Were you present when your wife's body was disinterred in the presence of doctor's Maclagan and Littlejohn?'

'Yes.'

'And Mrs Pritchard's also?'

'Yes.'

Cross-examined by Mr Clark.

'Were you frequently in Glasgow?'

'I may say a week in every month.'

'Were Doctor and Mrs Pritchard living happily together?'

'I never saw anything to the contrary. Although, Edward is a man and has needs. I suspected he liked the company of other women. I understood that.'

'Needs.'

'Yes, sexual needs – every man does.'

Mr Clark raised his eyebrows to the witness's response.

'You understood that!' Astonished at the old man's reply, Mr Clark shook his head. 'Did they appear to be happy and affectionate, and kind to one another?'

'Yes, I would say so.'

'When you went to Glasgow did you always stay at their house?'

'I stopped three days at a hotel, and after finishing business usually spent Saturday, Sunday, and Monday with them.'

'You spent two or three days in their house in each month?'

'Yes.'

'Do you remember when you were in Glasgow you stated something to Mrs Pritchard about a nurse or did she speak to you about a nurse?'

'The prisoner wrote that he was either going to get a nurse or had got one.'

'But did Mrs Pritchard?'

'Never.'

'Do you remember Mrs Pritchard saying to you that she did not want a nurse?'

'She may have said so, but I cannot remember.'

'You told me you knew that Mrs Taylor took Battley's Solution, though you did not know the name of it?'

'I knew she was taking some medicine.'

'Do you have any idea where she got it?'

'She got it at Duncan & Flockhart's in Edinburgh.'

'You did not know the quantity she took?'

'No, only that she did get it and took it.'

The Court adjourned at six o'clock.

* * *

CHAPTER FIFTY-SEVEN
THIRD DAY - WEDNESDAY, 5TH JULY 1865

The Court met at ten o'clock.

Superintendent McCall was a naturally suspicious man; he had not liked Dr Pritchard from the first day he clapped eyes on him. McCall had trained as a lawyer in his early days, and he could tell when someone was lying or fabricating a version of the truth, and to him, Pritchard was that man. 'Shifty' was the word he would use to describe him. Pritchard was the type that thought of himself so smart that nobody could see through his lies and deceit. Well, he may try to fool the women around him, but the manipulating doctor would have to get up very early to catch the superintendent out.

How could he do that to his wife and mother-in-law? The mother of his children. Day by day these ill-fated women suffered in excruciating agony while the doctor pretended to be an attentive husband and son-in-law. Disgusting! As superintendent, he would try his best to ensure that justice prevailed. He had an excellent reputation in the police force and a nose for these things, and in his eyes, Pritchard was a wrong 'un. His gut reaction was his first port of call; he had noted the split-second fear in the doctor's eyes the day he arrested him as he stepped off the train. He hadn't expected capture for his brutal, murderous crimes. No, Pritchard thought he was far too smart for that. Well, not anymore.

The superintendent knew the importance of detective work and substantial hard evidence. Professionalism was his motto. He would have to play it by the book; he wouldn't want to get tripped up by the defence team he would do his utmost to ensure justice was done, and see Pritchard swing from the gallows.

Glancing around the room as he took his place at the bar, he recognised some familiar faces in the public gallery. One of them immediately caught his attention. John Henry Greatrex. At six feet tall he towered above the other spectators. Greatrex was a lay preacher and a photographer. The superintendent had noted Greatrex's name on Prichard's numerous carte de visite cards the doctor had in his possession. Greatrex's studio was on the corner of Sauchiehall Street and West Campbell Street, so not far from Pritchard's house. Pritchard and Greatrex had much in common; they were both from respectable families, they even looked similar with their striking good looks, long beards, well-built physiques, all of which were of great appeal to the opposite sex. The Superintendent caught the man's eye, but Greatrex looked away. McCall decided that something was amiss with that man, the superintendent thought it best to keep his eye on him, once again his gut reaction told him something wasn't quite right – exactly what he wasn't sure, but, he would make it his duty to find out. Making a mental note to figure out the relationship Greatrex had with Pritchard, probably innocent enough, but still, he would keep an eye on him.

Alexander McCall, examined by Mr Crichton.

'I am Superintendent of the Central District of Glasgow Police. I apprehended the prisoner on Monday, the twentieth of March. I immediately searched him, and I found a couple of letters on him. I visited his house in Clarence Place on Tuesday; I found a collection of diaries in the consulting-room. I was also given a bottle from Mary McLeod. She took it out of a chest of drawers which was standing on the stairhead in the passage on the top floor. There was a brownish coloured liquid in the bottle. It was about half-full – up to about the middle of the upper label. I went back the next day, the twenty-second. I took possession of seven paper packets, which I found in the consulting room. I discovered a quart bottle in the same room in a locked press; it contained ginger wine. The key to that press I found in the prisoner's pocket when apprehended. It was the press next to the fire. I found a small phial in the consulting-room with the remains of a label bearing the name 'Timon' found in an open press. There were three phials, two corks, and a glass stopper, again found in the unlocked, press in the same room.'

The superintendent was then shown an exhibit.

'Is this the phial to which you are referring?'

'Yes, I got it from the mantelpiece in the drawing-room. The cork was in it then. On the twenty-third, I went back to the house and took some bed-linen and some trinkets. I handed them all to John Murray and Doctor Penny for examination in the same state I found them. I also found two prescriptions and an envelope in a desk in the consulting-room, together with some letters and a prescription and envelope.'

Cross-examined by Mr Clark.

'Did you take all the bottles from the consulting room?'

'No, I left thirty-five phials or bottles in the open press. In the locked press, there was a bottle of brandy, a bottle of whisky, and some bottles labelled 'chloroform'. The medicines were in the open press. Doctor's McLeod and M'Hattie examined these thirty-five bottles on the spot and found them to contain drugs which were not poisonous. I took all the bottles except the thirty-five. I gave the key to the locked press to the prisoner's brother, Charles Pritchard, on the thirty-first of March. I handed over to the prisoner's agent the medicine bottles which, the doctors did not retain; they were then in the same condition in which I found them.'

Superintendent McCall stepped down from the stand more than aware that John Henry Greatrex had not taken his eyes off him throughout his testimony. McCall had a strong suspicion that the handsome preacher and photographer was up to no good. He made a mental note that once this trial was over, he would make it his business to find out what.

* * *

CHAPTER FIFTY-EIGHT
JOHN CAMPBELL

Examined by Mr Gifford

John Campbell, manager of the Apothecaries Company in Glasgow, gave evidence as to the prisoner had purchased at various dates from November 1864 to February 1865, tincture of aconite, tartarised antimony, tartar emetic, and laudanum. On February 8th, he bought one ounce of tartarised antimony and one ounce of tincture of aconite. On February 9th, he bought another ounce of the same poison together with two ounces of tincture of digitalis. The witness declared that he had never sold an ounce of tartarised antimony to a medical man before. He had a sizeable dispensing trade, and he was struck with the quantity of antimony sold to the prisoner, and with the amount of tincture of aconite. He only sold two ounces of tartarised antimony in a year to the medical profession and the public in Glasgow. The prisoner got more chloroform from him than all his other customers put together. During his twenty-eight years as a dispensing apothecary, he had never furnished so much poison to any other medical man.

The witness was shown an exhibit of phials and asked, 'Are these phials from your establishment?'

'Yes, these are the kind of phials we use for tincture of aconite and other purposes, and these labels are the ones we use. When we sold these phials to the prisoner, they were all carefully labelled. On these phials, the labels are all scraped off, but on one the letters 'act' remains in the handwriting of one of my assistants. His name is Rose.'

* * *

CHAPTER FIFTY-NINE
JOHN CURRIE

Examined by Mr Gifford.

'I am John Currie, a chemist in Glasgow, and my shop is on Sauchiehall Street. I have known the prisoner since he came to Glasgow three years ago. He came to my shop frequently and made purchases. On the eighteenth of February last, I sold the prisoner two ounces solution of morphia and one ounce of Fleming's tincture of aconite. I also sold the prisoner, on the thirteenth of March last, half an ounce of Fleming's tincture of aconite, and three times in March last, quantities of a solution of atropine.'

* * *

Dr Douglas Maclagan, Dr Littlejohn, and Dr Gamgee, Edinburgh, and Dr Penny of Glasgow gave evidence as to the result of the post-mortem examinations of the bodies of the prisoner's wife and mother-in-law, and as to the result of the chemical analysis of the contents of the different organs. They found that there were no morbid appearances in the bodies capable of accounting for death. Concluding, that Mrs Pritchard had taken a large quantity of antimony in the form of tartar emetic in repeated doses which had caused her death and that Mrs Taylor had also taken a considerable amount of antimony in a succession of doses in the form of tartar emetic, which had caused her death.

Dr Maclagan believed that in the case of Mrs Taylor the symptoms described by the witnesses were attributed to opium, aconite, and antimony been administered at the same time.

* * *

CHAPTER SIXTY
POST-MORTEM

The post-mortem report prepared by Messrs Maclagan and Littlejohn on 21st March was the next piece of evidence presented to the jury.

'We, the undersigned, in virtue of a warrant issued by the Sheriff of Lanarkshire, confirm that we examined the body of Mary Jane Pritchard. The deceased's father and her sister-in-law Mary Taylor confirmed the body of the deceased.

The body appeared to be that of a healthy woman, of thirty-nine years of age. Externally, everything was normal except for a yellow stain on the right side of the abdomen, which was most likely the remains of a mustard poultice. The deceased's expression was placid, and her eyes natural. We examined the deceased's principal organs, concluding that despite a small degree of irritation they were all normal and healthy, and did not contain anything that would account for her death!'

The Solicitor General.

'That is an accurate report.'

'It is.'

The jurors found this account interesting – could it be that the doctor was innocent after all?

The witness continued reading his statement.

'Because of our findings, we took a portion of the deceased's heart, kidneys, liver, spleen and a urine sample so they could be sent for chemical analysis. The chemical report conducted by Doctor Maclagan confirmed that the doctor applied both the Reinsch and Marsh process to the deceased's organ samples, which unequivocally detected the presence of antimony in the body of Mrs Pritchard. Doctor Maclagan also confirmed that he is satisfied that Mrs Pritchard digested the poison in a dilution with a tartic emetic, which is used daily as a medicinal agent. Tartic emetic is a colourless solution with no odour which can be absorbed with other substances. Thus, it is not easily detected.

I have no doubt that the antimony found in Mrs Pritchard's body was taken in this form. I next examined the other organs from the deceased, and I found antimony in the whole of them! There were signs of poison in the spleen, kidneys, heart, brain and uterus. Also, I was asked to examine stained clothing belonging to Mrs Pritchard, given to me by John Murray, Sheriff of Glasgow. I found that there were traces of antimony on the chemise and undergarments of the deceased.'

The Solicitor General

'Is this an accurate statement?'

'It is.'

Dr Maclagan continued with his testimony.

'With regards to the exhumed body of Mrs Jane Taylor, I found that the heart, lungs and major organs were all healthy. Consequently, we were unable to discover in the body of Mrs Pritchard any morbid appearance capable of accounting for her death. Therefore, we believe the cause of Mrs Taylor's death cannot be determined without chemical analysis.

Consequently, I examined the organs and tissues from Mrs Taylor's body, in each case using the Reinsch's method. I found that there was antimony present in the heart, spleen, kidneys, the contents of the stomach, rectum, uterus and the brain. I also subjected the contents of the stomach to the process known as Stass, used primarily for the detection of the active principles of vegetable poisons. The result, however, was that no trace of any of these was detected. A particular test was also applied, with the view of discovering in the stomach meconic acid, one of the characteristic constituents of opium, but in this, I was again unsuccessful.

Lastly, as Mrs Taylor's body was exhumed, I thought it my duty to examine some of the earth from its original resting place, although this was superfluous, as the soil from the cemetery was dry and the coffin entire. For this purpose, I boiled eight ounces of the earth with water, filtered and concentrated the decoction, and subjected it to Reinsch's process, but it was found not to contain a trace of soluble antimony and was therefore incapable of impregnating with this metal anybody buried in it.

Finally, we took the precaution of replicating our findings on mice. Mice were given overdoses of Battley's Sedative Solution, and they all survived. Whereby, we administered aconite and Battley's, and the mice died in the same manner as Mrs Taylor.'

Dr Littlejohn was of opinion, after hearing the evidence, that Mrs Pritchard died from repeated doses of antimony, administered in small quantities, and that Mrs Taylor might have died from a dose of antimony administered shortly before her death, or else from some of the sedative narcotic poison. Tartar emetic could be easily added to the egg flip, and a sufficient dose to keep up illness could be given in a lump of sugar.

* * *

CHAPTER SIXTY-ONE
CHAMPAGNE, BRANDY & CHLOROFORM

After some cross-examination of the medical evidence, two declarations, emitted by the prisoner, were then read. In the first, made on the 2nd March, the prisoner said that his wife's last illness was 'gastric fever' and that he gave her no medicine at all himself, except wine, champagne, and brandy to support her strength and to help her sleep. The prisoner said he had given her a small quantity of chloroform, but it entirely disagreed with her, and he discontinued it. To assist and comfort her he sent for her mother to nurse her. He then stated his wife could not get over the loss of her mother, which had upset her tremendously. He went on to say that he had never given his wife antimony, but on one occasion, in October last. He applied it externally to her when she had a swelling of a gland in her back. He also gave his wife a small bottle of antimony for rubbing behind her ear. He used antimony extensively in his practice and kept it in a cupboard in his consulting-room.

In his second declaration, made on the 21st of April, he said that he was in no way an accessory to Mrs Taylor's death, that he never administered poison to her, and that he believed she died from paralysis and apoplexy.

This testimony closed the case for the prosecution, and the Court adjourned at half-past five till next morning at ten o'clock, when the evidence for the defence commenced.

* * *

CHAPTER SIXTY-TWO
THE DEFENCE

The solicitor general addressed the jury for the prosecution and Mr Clark for the prisoner.

In his opening speech for the defence, Mr Rutherfurd Clark urged the jury to consider the enormity of the charges against the prisoner. Emphasising that double-murder was the most serious of crimes and to reach a unanimous guilty verdict the jury must prove by strong, clear, overwhelming evidence and without a doubt the guilt of the prisoner. The defence's argument suggested that while Dr Pritchard had the opportunity to poison his wife and her mother, that this goes a short way – indeed no way at all – in an indication of his guilt.

'What was the doctor's motive? Well, members of the jury there isn't one! It certainly was not for money! There wasn't any! Except for an insurance policy for £2,500 a manifestly insignificant sum to someone of the doctor's standing, and as to the possibility of him killing his wife to marry the servant girl he had long since seduced, is a preposterous proposition.

On the other hand, Mary McLeod had a motive. She wanted to marry her lover. She wanted to be the mistress of the house! If her mistress were to die, then the doctor had said he would marry her? Her standing in life would be significantly improved.

The cook, Catherine Lattimer, had a motive. She had lost her position. In fact, the doctor had written in his diary that she was 'too old' and had previously caught her handing leftover food out to neighbours. Could it be that she held a grudge and wanted to get her own back on the family for the way she had been treated? The case for the prosecution asked Mrs Lattimer if she had added anything to Mrs Pritchard's tapioca – why was the same question not put to Mary McLeod?

The prisoner has stated that leading such a busy life, he was often prone to absent-mindedness and could not swear under oath that he always locked his medicine cupboard. Plenty of people went into that room including Catherine Lattimer and Mary McLeod – they both had ample opportunity either one of them could be guilty.

Gentlemen of the jury, Doctor Pritchard did not murder his mother-in-law. Mrs Taylor was an addict. Addicted to the opium found in Battley's Sedative Solution; she could not live without it! But in the end, this dependency killed her. Doctor Pritchard is a professional man who has dedicated his life to medicine, to saving people; he loved his family and was a reliable provider, father and husband. He did not kill anybody.'

Surprisingly, the defence did not call any expert scientific witnesses to disprove the case for the prosecution's findings. Relying solely on the doctor's standing in the community and suggesting Mary McLeod as the murderer. Dr Michael Taylor, Mrs Pritchard's brother, gave evidence as to the kind and loving relationship his sister had with her husband.

However, at Edward's request, the defence did have one final card up their sleeve, which in their opinion must persuade the jury of their client's innocence. The doctor's eldest children were to take the stand.

The first child to enter the witness box was eleven-year-old Charles Edward Pritchard. Nervously, he entered the court with a half-smile on his face. He avoided looking at his father; he knew that if he did, he would burst into tears. Instead, he looked straight ahead, seeing no one.

The sight of his son had a profound effect on Edward; he had not seen his children since this wretched thing began. He broke down completely, sobbing uncontrollably, tears streamed down his face and dropped onto his long beard. Devastated, Edward buried his face in his hands.

'I am Charles Edward Pritchard, Doctor Pritchard's eldest son I lived with my parents on Sauchiehall Street, Glasgow. I was there when Mama died. My papa and mamma lived happily together. Papa and Mama were fond of one another.'

The prisoner's daughter was brought in next, evidently deeply upset with the awful position in which her father was placed. Like her brother, she never looked at her father.

'I am Jane Frances Pritchard, the daughter of the prisoner, and I am fourteen years of age. I have lived a great deal with my grandparents in Edinburgh. Papa was often there with my grandmother. Grandmama and Papa were very fond of each other. I have often heard her speaking very kindly of him, and he of her.'

As she walked back through the courtroom Jane could feel herself getting weak, her vision became blurred, and she came over all hot, clammy and lightheaded as the blood rushed to her head. Thankfully, she made it out of the side door just as her knees gave way. She fainted into the arms of the shocked court official.

Hearing the obvious anguish in his children's voices Edward was beyond reproach, he turned to the guard at his side and said, 'Oh my God, to think that my children should bear witness against their father.' He hung his head in shame.

After three hours of questioning, this concluded the case for the defence.

* * *

Throughout the trial, Edward's brother Charles Augustus Pritchard had sat beside him in the dock to show family solidarity and to offer support. However, on the last day of the trial, the authorities did not allow this as they were concerned in case Charles furtively handed Edward any form of self-destruction.

* * *

CHAPTER SIXTY-THREE
THE SOLICITOR GENERAL'S
ADDRESS TO THE JURY

The solicitor general began by pointing out the atrocious nature of the crime imputed to a member of an honourable profession, whose function, it was to save a life, not destroy it, and who was now charged with turning his knowledge with a devilish purpose against two defenceless women. These crimes were two acts of wilful murder, committed in his own house, deliberately, and in cold blood, and with such cruelty to his wife and mother-in-law. He argued that the evidence proved that there were only two people who could have committed the murders, namely the prisoner or Mary McLeod either jointly or separately.

Mary McLeod, a servant girl of sixteen, had ample opportunity to carry out these crimes, as did the doctor. However, it was now scientifically proven that Mrs Taylor's death was attributed to aconite poisoning, which had been mixed with Battley's Sedative Solution. Could it be possible that this young servant girl could plan and execute such a heinous crime? The mixture had been carried out by the doctor. Therefore, there could only be two possibilities of guilt; either Doctor Pritchard or Mary McLeod. However, the prosecution did not believe that Mary was guilty of these crimes. And so, the prisoner must be. Therefore, Doctor Pritchard should be found guilty.

Throughout the solicitor general's speech, Edward showed just the right amount of emotion, he remained calm and calculating, raising his eyebrows and quivering his lips at the appropriate moment when something damaging was stated, aware that the jury was watching him closely.

* * *

CHAPTER SIXTY-FOUR
COUNSEL FOR THE DEFENCE

Counsel for the defence, Mr Andrew Rutherfurd Clark, maintained that the prosecution had not traced poison to the prisoner. All that the solicitor general had suggested was that there were only two possible perpetrators: Dr Pritchard and Mary McLeod and that the jury must decide against them. Mr Clark went on to show that all the poison had passed through Mary McLeod's hands, while all the medicines and drugs in the house were in an open press within reach of the whole household. He pointed out the opportunities which Mary McLeod had in her attendance on Mrs Pritchard. Emphasising that 'Mary McLeod told terrible lies' and that the prosecution had not even asked Mary McLeod if she had added anything to Mrs Pritchard's food, but they had asked the cook, Mrs Lattimer. Consequently, the whole evidence was based purely on a probability and so could not possibly justify a guilty verdict against his client.

'Gentlemen of the jury. I have done. I ask for an acquittal for the prisoner. In your hands alone are the issues of life and death. On you, and you alone is the responsibility of the verdict. I ask you to restore the prisoner by your verdict to his orphaned family and sorrowing relatives.'

***

Having heard both sides of the argument Lord Justice Clerk addressed the jury reminding them of their duties.

'To return a verdict of guilty regarding either of the two charges contained in the indictment, then there were three things that they must be satisfied upon the evidence. In the first place, that the deceased died by poison, second that the poison was wilfully administered to destroy life, and in the third place that it was the prisoner at the bar who so administered, or caused it to be administered. If the evidence is defective in any of these, then the prisoner is entitled to an acquittal, but on the other hand, if you are satisfied with these three things, then there remains nothing for you but the stern and painful duty of conviction.'

In a final statement, Lord Inglis could not resist the chance to criticise Dr Paterson, severely stating, 'I care not for professional etiquette or professional rule. There is a rule of life for consideration that is far higher than these – and that it is the duty of every citizen in this country, that every right-minded man owes to his neighbour, to prevent the destruction of human life in this world. A duty I cannot but say that Doctor Paterson failed.'

Edward observed the jury, with a sinking feeling in his stomach, knowing that his life, his children's lives and their future rested in their hands. Oh, what had he done. He felt sick, his whole face crumpled, his shoulders heaved, as he sobbed loudly no longer able to contain his emotions.

At twenty minutes past one, the jury retired to study the case and return a verdict.

* * *

CHAPTER SIXTY-FIVE
THE JURY DELIBERATES

Edward was taken down to a cell below the courtroom. He had no idea how long he would have to wait. The guard brought him a cup of tea laced with sugar. He sipped it slowly; his mind turned to thoughts of freedom and how when he was acquitted, he would indulge his children and his family for putting them all through this terrible ordeal. He would take the family south, well away from Scotland; he would get them all settled then he would go to Italy and join his friend Garibaldi.

***

Dr Paterson was furious; he felt as if he had been tossed into a tempestuous sea without a rudder, how dare Inglis degrade him so publicly. Now he was nervous. If this case was found 'Not Proven' and the prisoner acquitted, then it would mean certain ruin for him and his family. He regretted every single day that he had encountered the wretched Pritchard man and his dysfunctional family. In his opinion, and given the circumstances, he believed that he had done all that he could rationally be expected to do either as a physician or as a good citizen. In his view, he had been mistreated throughout this trial and referred to in the rudest and most disagreeable tone. A person of his position should be protected by the court not subjected to scorn and contempt. He had done his duty by refusing to sign the death certificate for Mrs Taylor. It certainly was not his fault that the imbecile of a clerk did not have the gumption to read between the lines. Perhaps, if the man had done his job properly, then a post-mortem may have been carried out on Mrs Taylor. Furthermore, it wasn't his business as a prominent doctor to go casting accusations and sticking his nose into a fellow doctor's business!

* * *

CHAPTER SIXTY-SIX
PIECING TOGETHER THE EVIDENCE

The chairman of the jury, Mr Sim, and the other gentlemen of the jury followed the judge's instructions and carefully pieced together the evidence as they saw it. Mary McLeod certainly looked pitiful on the stand, she had made bad judgements in her young life and had put a lot of trust in the doctor, but the jury must now decide if she was capable of a double murder? Would she be intelligent enough to know how to mix the exact amount of poison over a period to kill her mistress and her mother? And what of the doctor? Was he the caring, devoted husband and father, he claimed to be, what was his motive for murder, could it be love, lust, money or pure greed. After all, no motive had been given as to why these crimes were committed. After deliberating for only one-hour Mr Sim, and his fellow gentleman jurors had come to a unanimous decision. Judge Inglis was informed, and the court was back in session.

* * *

CHAPTER SIXTY-SEVEN
THE VERDICT

The only sound to be heard in the courtroom as the jury waited in their seats for the prisoner to appear was the creaking of the bar floor as it was raised, the measured tread of the policeman and the prisoner could plainly be heard in the silent court as they marched up the stone stairs. The doctor emerged from the vacant space to a sea of eyes staring directly at him. He stood still for a moment at the top of the steps and gave a hasty glance around. The dock rail having been opened, he entered the enclosure and took his seat flanked by two burly police officers. Edward remained calm and collected, but inside he was petrified, his stomach in knots, his face ashen. He knew by the stern look on the faces of the jurors that it was not going to be good news.

The chairman of the jury, Mr Sim, stood up and with confidence, announced that the jury had agreed upon the following verdict.

'The jury unanimously finds the prisoner guilty of both charges as libelled.'

In shock, Edward clasped his hands to his face; he couldn't believe it. 'This is so wrong,' he muttered. 'I loved my Minnie and Grandmama; you are so very wrong. I am innocent.' Suddenly, he felt faint and fell against the police officer at his side. He sat down and was offered a glass of water; he sipped it and regained his composure. There was nothing else he could do. He looked around the room catching the eye of his brother who, like him, was devastated, shook his head and threw up his hands. His father-in-law, Michael Taylor, was equally as shocked. Edward saw his two eldest children in the crowd; he couldn't face them – it was far too painful for him.

The verdict having been recorded, the solicitor general moved that the court pass sentence. Edward was asked to stand.

'Edward William Pritchard, you have been found guilty by a unanimous verdict of the jury of the two murders charged against you in this libel, there is no unreasonable doubt of your guilt. You are aware that upon such a verdict there is only one sentence that can be pronounced.' In acknowledgement, Edward bowed graciously.

'You must be condemned to suffer the last penalty of the law (Edward bowed again). Let me remind you that you have but a short time left on this earth, and I beseech you to devote that short space of time to make your peace with God. Listen now to the sentence of the court.'

The Lord Justice Clerk put on the black cap.

'Edward William Pritchard, the jury have found you guilty of the charges on all counts. You will be taken back to prison in Edinburgh, then you will then be transported under guard to the prison in Glasgow, where you will be fed on bread and water only, until the twenty-eighth day of July 1865, when between the hours of eight and ten o'clock in the morning you will be taken to a place of execution and be hanged by the neck until you are dead. Then your body will be buried within the precincts of the prison of Glasgow. May almighty God have mercy on your soul.'

Emotionless, Edward bowed to the judge, then turned and bowed to the jury.

* * *

Down in the cell, the enormity of his situation hit him; he started to shake, the guard fetched him a cup of tea. Edward looked at him and said, 'I am innocent of this crime, I didn't murder anyone.'

Edward, shackled to a prison guard, was brought up the stairs from the cells to a waiting prison van where his journey back to Glasgow began. Outside in the July sunshine, he breathed in the fresh air aware that soon this simple act would be denied him. A large crowd had gathered in the High Street, all wanting to catch a glimpse of the handsome convicted murderer. The police had done their best to keep Parliament Square clear, but a considerable number of people managed to get onto the piazza.

Despite his predicament, Edward gave a quick smile as he saw Dr Paterson in the crowd frantically reporting to the broadsheets, and still fuming over the treatment he received in the courtroom.

'The weight of the abhorrence and undisguised rancour, which was so injuriously thrust upon me during this trial was almost too great to bear. Well, their minds soon changed once the autopsy reports revealed my suspicions. No, there was an unjustifiable tirade against me for my innocent part in this double tragedy!'

Safe in the prison van Edward covered his face with his hat; he'd had enough drama for one day. The van stopped at the train station where the prisoner would take the short journey back to Glasgow. At the station, the crowds had already gathered, Edward was the star of the moment, everyone wanted a glimpse of him, women tugged at his clothes and grabbed at his beard hoping for a keepsake.

Reports in the newspapers stated that the Pritchard's home on Sauchiehall Street had been ransacked, even the steps outside had been chipped away into small fragments and sold as relic worship from the doomed house of death. Unbelievable.

Today Edward was in danger of being mobbed. The prison guard ushered him into the station master's office while the police attempted to disperse the crowd. They could not allow the prisoner to board the train until the group moved on. Edward had his fame, at last, he just wished that it was under different circumstances.

Using, his initiative the station master blew the whistle pretending that the train was about to depart, people rushed to get on the train, the savvy station master then locked the doors of the train, allowing Edward to be safely escorted down the platform and into a private waiting carriage.

* * *

CHAPTER SIXTY-EIGHT
FIRST CONFESSION

Since the trial Edward had been restless, sleep was difficult, he longed to be free and move on with his life, knowing he had to act fast and devise a plan. He remembered reading in the papers about Constance Kent and the murder that had occurred at Road Hill House. The young woman had confessed to murdering her infant brother and sentenced to death, but she had been reprieved and had instead received a lengthy jail sentence. That's what he needed to do: confess, then maybe like Miss Kent, Queen Victoria may take pity on him also, and revoke his death sentence.

Edward paced up and down in his cell, grinding his teeth together with his face distorted as he decided what he needed to do. It came to him; he would confess to a member of the cloth and blame Mary McLeod. He summoned the guard and told him that he had something important to say to Revered Oldham.

Edward took the ageing priest by the arm, and drawing close to him, whispered that he would like to pour into his ear a confession of his guilt. Before entering upon the subject, however, he intimated his wish that the confession is kept secret.

Reverend I do not like to drop anyone in it, especially a woman, but Mary McLeod is not what she seems. She is a thoroughly bad woman! She has pursued me ever since she stepped foot in my house; she wanted to be rid of my wife and my mother-in-law so that we could be together and get married. This is all her doing, not mine! I even heard her threaten to kill them both several times. I did mean to get rid of her before she carried out her threats, but it was too late. If you search the house for poison, you will find some in her room.'

Edward was sure that indeed poison would be found in Mary's room, he had planted it there himself, just in case questions were ever asked.

On hearing his verbal confession, the priest was not satisfied. He had heard many confessions in his time in prison and church, and he had become an expert in deciphering truth from fiction, and this transfer of blame onto the poor misguided wretched girl, had to be false. The priest declined to receive any statement from Edward upon these conditions, pointing out that his crime was an offence against society, and concluded that this confession should not be released to the public.

Edward felt squeezed into a corner. For the first time in his life, he didn't know what to do. Depressed, he fell into a deep despair not wanting to talk to anybody at all. He just lay on the bed in his cell. The weight of everything seemed to press down on his shoulders. The image of himself he held so dear was crumbling before him. It was too much. His over-confidence gave way to a prostration of mind and body. For the first time in his life, Edward realised that he wasn't invincible after all.

* * *

CHAPTER SIXTY-NINE
SECOND CONFESSION

Monday 10th July 1865

Edward took to religion in a big way, and he began to have faith in his future and was feeling a little brighter. To his surprise and delight, he had a visit from his younger brother, his sister who had travelled from Dublin and his eldest daughter Jane Francis. They had arrived unannounced and were all very distressed. Edward missed his family so much and was so pleased to see them. After they had all said their greetings, the conversation turned, as delicately as possible to Edward's predicament.

Up to now, they had all believed in his innocence, but a niggling doubt had begun to fester in their minds. The one person who could set their minds at rest was Edward himself, so they thought it best to challenge him openly, hoping he would settle their uncertainties, and for them all to satisfy themselves to either Edward's guilt or his innocence.

The firm determination to believe the best of him, which his relations evinced up to his condemnation, would appear to be more assumed than real. At all events, his conviction had shaken their trust in his innocence. The family repeatedly asked if he had anything to tell them about the mysterious deaths of Mrs Pritchard and his mother-in-law, and he at first hesitatingly reiterated his innocence. Breaking down in sobs, he cried.

'It wasn't me. I loved my Minnie; I would never do anything to hurt her. She was my life. Life is nothing without her!'

Jane Frances could take it no longer. All she could recall was the look of anguish on her mother's face the last time she saw her, and the thought that maybe, just maybe she could have done something to save her. She fell on her knees before her father into a paroxysm of sobbing, imploring him to satisfy them as to his innocence.

'Papa, please, please, just tell the truth. Do it for Mummy, and Granny. Please, Papa, God will know if you are guilty!'

Edward watched his daughter in such obvious pain, and he again broke down, a miserable man. His heart gave way to an agony of grief, during which no precise word could be got from him, and his unhappy family had to bid him farewell, still with a faint hope that he might be guiltless. Before they left, they intimated to him that the Rev. Mr Oldham would visit him the next afternoon, and to this, he gave silent assent.

After this last meeting with his daughter, Edward had time to reflect; perhaps he should tell the truth? Just now he found it difficult to cope and had suffered a nervous fit, and the prison doctor had attended him. He recovered but continued in an exceedingly depressed state of body and mind throughout the night.

The following day, Edward was more composed. The Rev Oldham felt it his duty to convince Edward that the best way forward was to make a full public confession. Edward hesitated, knowing there would be no going back from this. Putting his faith in God, he started reading the Bible and other religious works. After a good deal of deliberation, he ultimately consented to make a full written public confession. This time the authorities took his account of events seriously.

'I, Edward William Pritchard, M.D., M.R.C.S.E., and L.A.S., &c., At this moment make in writing, in the presence of the Rev. R.S. Oldham, M.A., the following confession, for transmission by him to the proper authorities:

It was when my wife was at Edinburgh, in the summer of 1863, that I first became intimate with the girl Mary McLeod, sleeping with her in my house, at No. 22 Royal Crescent. This continued at intervals up to the time of our removal to No. 131 Sauchiehall Street. She became pregnant in May last year and, with her consent, I produced a miscarriage. I have reason to believe that Mrs Pritchard was quite aware of this and rather sought to cover my wickedness and folly. My mother-in-law, Mrs Taylor, came last February to our house, and caught Mary McLeod and myself in a compromising position in the consulting-room; and the day before her death, having watched us, nothing more passed. I declare Mrs Taylor to have died in the manner I have before stated, and I now believe her death to be caused by an overdose of Battley's Solution of opium.

The aconite found in that bottle was put in by me after her death, and designedly left there to prove death by misadventure in case any inquiry should take place. Mrs Pritchard was much better immediately after her mother's death but subsequently became exhausted from want of sleep. I accounted for this by the shock produced by her mother's death; and hardly knowing how to act, at her request, I gave her chloroform. It was about midnight. Mary McLeod was in the room, and in an evil moment, (being, besides, somewhat excited by whisky) I yielded to the temptation to give her sufficient to cause death – which I did.

I, therefore, declare before God, as a dying man, and in the presence of my spiritual adviser, that I am innocent of the crime of murder, as far as Mrs Taylor is concerned, but acknowledge myself guilty of the adultery with Mary McLeod and the murder of my wife.

I feel now as though I had been living in a species of madness since my connection with Mary McLeod, and I declare my solemn repentance of my crime, earnestly praying that I may obtain Divine forgiveness before I suffer the penalty of the law.'

EDWARD W PRITCHARD.
JOHN STIRLING, Governor, witness.
R.S. OLDHAM, witness.
JOHN MUTRIE, witness.

NORTH PRISON, GLASGOW, July 11, 1865.

* * *

After publication of the confession, a couple of prison clergy, including the prison chaplain, the Revered McLeod, visited Edward. The Reverend announced to him that they were concerned for his soul and that nobody including them believed a word of his confession. Edward tutted and lay down on his bed, staring at the ceiling. Annoyed, he turned calmly to the Revered and remarked with contempt, 'Do you know Revered McLeod, after your statement I now understand how Jesus suffered from the unbelievers of men in the world.'

'You wrote your so-called confession without the slightest hint of repentance on your part! Do you feel nothing for the pain and suffering you subjected on the people you are supposed to love so dear? What about your children; they are now orphaned and struggle every day not only grieving over the loss of their mother and grandmother but with the knowledge and shame that their father was the one responsible!'

Edward responded airily. 'I will meet you in heaven.'

'Sir!' retorted the indignant minister. 'I shall meet you at the judgement seat!'

For weeks following the trial and the doctor's conviction

* * *

CHAPTER SEVENTY
THE SCORN OF DR PATERSON

For weeks following the trial and the doctor's conviction, the press continued to run the story. Many filled their columns with the doctor's confessions, some re-ran his life story and the disputable circumstances surrounding Lizzie McGirn's death in the fire at Berkley Square, and other tabloids devoted their pages to Dr Paterson and his lack of duty by not alerting the authorities of his suspicions sooner. Public opinion on the matter differed, one paper reporting:

'A doctor of previous good standing, with a 'real' medical degree, his behaviour in not reporting this case was disgraceful, he did nothing – he just went home!'

The letters pages were filled with letters outraged by Dr Paterson's behaviour.

'What confidence can the public be expected to have in any set of men who value professional etiquette above human life?'

Some people blamed the registrar for not acting on the 'notable language' used by the doctor in his letter when he refused to sign Mrs Taylor's death certificate.'

Overall, the medical profession supported Dr Paterson, but not all. The Lancet wrote a particularly scathing report suggesting that despite Dr Paterson is an uncommonly wise fellow and a martyr to his very sagacity and acuteness, his defence was weak and illogical and in terrible taste from start to finish.

While some medical men took pen to paper vindicating Dr Paterson's role in the case, Dr Paterson himself was outraged and responded to the papers with a full and frank discussion depicting his side of the story.

* * *

CHAPTER SEVENTY-ONE
THIRD CONFESSION-THE ABSOLUTE TRUTH

After, his second confession Edward's demeanour changed. He withdrew altogether, not wanting to talk to anybody, preferring to lie on his bed in a stupor, looking endlessly at the photographs of him and his family, wishing he could turn back time. Reality had dawned on him that the public was no longer the slightest bit sympathetic towards him, reserving their sympathy for the victims who had needlessly lost their lives and the poor orphaned children.

Unlike other convicts, Edward realised that there would be little point in attempting a commutation of his conviction. Instead, he thought about what the Reverend had said to him; perhaps the time had now come to tell the absolute truth and make his peace with God and ask his forgiveness. He read the Bible each day and within a week, seeking atonement, he decided that he needed to withdraw his last confession and tell the truth this time.

Once again, Edward called the Reverend and told him that he knew he could not be spared, but for the sake of his family, he wanted to admit the truth. Yes, he had done it, Mary McLeod had nothing to do with it. He killed them and him alone.

'I am ready to make my statement in writing.'

This time he was believed.

19ᵗʰ July 1865,

I, Edward William Pritchard in full possession of my senses, and understanding of the awful position I find myself in; do make a free and accurate confession that the sentence pronounced on me is just; that I am guilty of the death of my mother-in-law Mrs Taylor and my wife, Mary Jane Pritchard; and that I can assign no motive for the conduct which actuated me beyond a species of 'terrible madness' and the use of 'ardent spirits'. I hereby freely and fully state that the confessions made to the Rev R.S Oldham, on the 11ᵗʰ this month, was not true; and I hereby confess that I alone, not Mary McLeod, poisoned my wife in the way brought out in the evidence at my trial. Mrs Taylor's death was caused, according to the wording of the indictment. I further state to be true the main facts brought out at my trial. I hereby fully acknowledge, and now plead, wholly and solely, 'guilty' thereto, and may God have mercy on my soul. I pray earnestly for 'repentance not to be repented of', and for forgiveness from Almighty God. Fellow creatures pray for me, I am in charity with all men. I have now to record my humble thanks to all that have taken part in any way for my interest – first to their Lordships, the judges, for their great patience, forbearance, and careful consideration of my case, and the gentlemen of the jury, and to all the officials. I wish to thank all the prison officials and all the ministers that have guided me. I particularly want to thank Captain McCall and all the Glasgow police officers. Above all, to Sir Archibald Alison, for his humanity and his gentle treatment while undergoing his legal duties. May each and all accept the thanks of a profoundly penitent sinner, and may Heaven be their reward.

Edward William Pritchard

* * *

CHAPTER SEVENTY-TWO
27ᵀᴴ JULY 1865-10 HOURS
BEFORE THE EXECUTION

The night before the execution, Edward was understandably nervous. Now ready to meet his maker, he just wanted it all over and done with. 'Only ten hours to go and I will be no more,' he remarked to the prison guard. 'I hope it's quick and that they don't make a bungle of it,' he joked.

'Before I forget, would you please be kind enough to pass this list of invoices to my lawyer – unpaid accounts that people owe me for medical visits. I am sure he will know what to do with them. Also, do you think it possible to acquire a small bottle of scented olive oil, for my hair and beard on the big day? I still want to look my best!' The guard said that he would try his best, but that the prisoner was not to expect miracles.

'I think I am far beyond a miracle now, my dear man. It was money that made me a criminal you know, the love of money is the cause of much sin and misery in the world, I curse the day that I ever let the money fever take its hold on me.'

Turning to the Reverend by his side, he asked. 'Will God ever forgive my sins?'

'Yes,' the Reverend replied.

'Good, then I can die in peace, death cannot come too soon.'

Following, a supper of bread, cheese and beer, Edward received a final visit from his brother, sister and his two eldest children. Fanny and Charles were most distressed, knowing that this would be the last time they would see their father, and the last time they would be able to ask him any questions. Charles angrily ran at his father, and with clenched fists, he beat them hard against his father's chest.

'Oh, father, father how could you kill our mother and leave us like this?'

At first, Fanny was unwilling to even speak to her father, but seeing her brother in such pain, Fanny too said her piece.

'You killed our mother; you let her suffer like that, we loved her! But I cannot forget that you are my father, I forgive you and pray that God will forgive you and all your sins.'

Charles avoided his father's eyes and looked away. Unlike his elder sister, he refused to say one word of kindness to his father. Edward was devastated, and couldn't bear to hear the tone of anguish in his children's voices, he crumpled to the floor and sobbed uncontrollably. All he could do was wail; 'Oh my God, oh my God. Had I foreseen all this it might have been different.' Recovering, he knew that he had a duty to his children, he needed their forgiveness.

'Oh, my poor children do not reproach me. I am the unhappiest of men, my remorse and the sight of your reproachful eyes are punishment far greater than that which awaits me in a few hours.'

The family group remained in silence together for a few more minutes, and then they parted. Charles reluctantly murmured to his father that he would forgive him, which raised Edward's spirits immensely. Now he felt cleansed; his thoughts turned to his approaching end.

Earlier in the week, he had asked the governor if he could see Mary McLeod one last time to beg her forgiveness for the wrong he had done to her. Mary understandably refused. Edward made his last confession and declared that. 'Death cannot come too soon.'

* * *

PART FOUR
THE EXECUTION

Edward had retired to bed at around midnight, he had slept reasonably soundly and arose at 5 a.m. to his last breakfast of porridge and a sweet cup of tea. He dressed in his dark morning suit, and his expensive black buttoned leather boots, the same outfit he wore throughout the trial, and on the day that he was first apprehended by the Superintendent (now Captain) McCall as he stepped off the train in Glasgow.

At 7 am the prison chaplain visited him and together they engaged in prayer. Dr McLeod and the Reverend Oldham visited him at 7.30 am, and the religious devotional activities continued until five minutes to eight. Edward had asked the Prison Governor if he would be allowed to address the crowd and give a speech on the gibbet. His request was refused.

Just before 8 a.m. Edward was pinioned by William Calcraft the most notorious executioner of the day. Edward then walked with a firm and steady step accompanied by Reverend Oldham into the concert hall where the Reverend read the first opening sentences of the Church of England Burial service.

Edward was asked by a senior magistrate if he had anything to say, to which he merely replied, 'I beg to acknowledge the justice of my sentence.'

The solemn procession to the gibbet was then formed, headed by the prisoner and the executioner, followed close behind by the magistrates, Captain McCall and several members of the police force.

Outside, people gathered, all wanting to see the convict hang for his wrongdoing. The previous evening people had congregated in groups in every corner of the jail square. A labyrinth of barriers had been erected early in the morning, and a large body of police employed. There was another barricade six or eight feet outside and nearer the Green. Before their arrival, however, a line of police had managed without any other barricade than themselves and their batons to keep the crowd back to the line from the front of the Clothes Market to the Circus. As the crowd increased, it was evident from the way the restless were weaving their way through the barriers that an eruption would soon take place. The commotion grew, and the vast crowd pushed the thin blue line of police before them towards the outside of the two barriers.

As day dawned, the crowd got bigger. Extra trains were put on to transport people from all over the country. People were everywhere, with no space left on the Green people climbed on the roof of the Episcopal church and the roofs of the outhouses on the North Green to ensure they could get a good view of the hanging. Residents rented out bedrooms and attics, especially for the occasion. The atmosphere was jovial with people telling jokes and ridiculing the plight of the hapless doctor.

The crowd was indeed a colourful one with loose women, thieves, pickpockets and people whose nights merged into the morning. Many had watched the scaffold being erected and the coffin being placed beside it.

There were vendors selling pies, drinks and gingerbread. Police had arrested a photographer, for selling pictures of Pritchard and his family at a shilling each.

A general ruckus was inevitable with the police attempting to stem the torrent with free use of their batons. But it was of no use. The police had to creep under both barricades and take refuge, leaving the crowd in possession of the whole exterior space. However, for the most part, people's behaviour was quiet and decorous, though occasionally a suppressed roar seemed to come from the crowd.

At 6 am Mr Harrison Ord, a lay preacher, ascended a pulpit that had been erected close to the northern side of the Circus and began to sing a well-known revival hymn. Lay preacher John Henry Greatrex made a dramatic appearance in front of the scaffold under the watchful eye of Captain McCall.

Edward led the solemn procession with a steady step. As they reached the gibbet, Greatrex pointed directly at the doomed man and exclaimed in a loud voice of thunder, 'Unless you take heel, so also shall you perish.'

Edward ignored Greatrex's ramblings and slowly walked up to the foot of the scaffold. He turned to address the crowd to say, 'My sentence is just.' His eyes settled on a distinguished looking couple with a familiar knowing smirk on their faces. Constance and Edwin Taylor had travelled all the way from Yorkshire to see him hang.

'I would not miss this for the world, Constance, to see that murdering scoundrel swing!' Edwin declared loud enough for Edward to hear.

As he walked slowly up the steps of the gibbet, he saw nothing else, his mind and soul filled with sorrow and regret. Reverend Oldham had accompanied him to the top step where he began reading a prayer for the dying while his hand clutched rosary beads tightly. Great commotion prevailed amongst the crowd, with expressions such as. 'How well he looks' or 'He's rather pale!'

Without assistance, Edward stepped off the gibbet and onto the drop. He stumbled slightly but managed to recover himself and stand firm.

Executioner William Calcraft busied himself adjusting the rope which dangled from a beam above around Pritchard's neck. Calcraft wore a faded pink rose in his lapel, and the seasoned executioner's hands began to shake as he placed the white hood over Pritchard's head, moving aside Pritchard's hair and beard, to allow the rope to be correctly positioned. He then tied the legs. Calcraft had had quite a bit to drink the night before, so he knew that he needed his wits about him that morning. With quick and scrupulous care, he examined the length of the rope and finally fastened it to the cleat on the other side of the gibbet. Once more he turned to the convict and steadied him on the drop. Satisfied, Calcraft moved towards the bolt. A split second later a crash shuddered through the air. The large crowd were silent as they watched the drop fall, for a moment there was no movement in the body, but suddenly violent convulsions ripped through Pritchard's back and neck. He then swung pugnaciously around, his whole frame quivering and his hands jerked up and down with a robust, muscular action. The glove in his right hand, which he had taken off dropped to the ground, symbolically like a white feather of surrender. His whole body, then shook uncontrollably, the crowd shrieked in shock and amazement, women screamed, men applauded, and some turned their heads away, many more in tears. Acting quickly, Calcraft went below and pulled on Pritchard's legs, which eventually brought him to stillness.

At last Dr Edward William Pritchard's body went utterly still.

He was dead.

Pritchard's final struggles were no doubt fierce and painful, but the execution lasted no longer than two minutes. However, just as the crowd thought it was all over and were about to leave, Pritchard's body again started to shake with an involuntary muscular action. The crowd screamed, 'He's not dead, he's not dead,' and 'That's another one Calcraft's botched and butchered.'

* * *

The body was left to hang until a quarter to nine when it was lowered with such force that it knocked the bottom out of the plain, pauper coffin. The coffin was soon repaired, and the body was taken to the vault below the Courthouse where Pritchard's hair and beard were shaved off, to allow Alexander Stewart to take a cast of the convict's head for a Phrenology study.

* * *

The body of Edward William Pritchard was interned in the graveyard of the prison. Scratched upon a stake were marked the letters E.W.P

* * *

AFTERWARD

Edward William Pritchard's grave, together with that of other inmates who had suffered the same fate, was eventually covered over as the High Court was expanded.

In 1985, following renovations, the tunnel leading from the cells to the execution spot was filled in as it was dangerous to the road above. Just inside the tunnel workmen found a pair of Victorian black button boots, in which was found a pile of hair wrapped in newspaper. The boots were allegedly sold in a pub. Pritchard's most precious possession – the hair from his head and his beard, was destroyed.

* * *

The End

Mrs. Pritchard.

Mary Jane Pritchard

Dr Pritchard's Carte de Visite himself and with his family.

Dr. Pritchard

Mrs Taylor

Mary McLeod with one of the Pritchard children

A LAMENT FOR MR MICHAEL TAYLOR

As I was walking one evening of late,
A Reverend old man I chanced to meet;
His name was Michael Taylor; I must let you know
But his fate was overshadowed with great grief and woe.

He said there once I could happiness find.
My wife and my children were loving and kind;
Dr Pritchard, he came with his false word and smile.
And my daughter's heart won by his deluding wiles.

Alas! I ne'er thought that for a few pounds sake,
He would poison my wife, and my daughter's life take,
For we thought he was generous, loving and kind,
To his false heart and conduct alas! We were all blind.

It was woeful to see, my poor wife day by day ebb.
Through effects of poison, her life wore away,
The Doctor hard-heartedly did calmly look on.
And never suspected the cause of her pain.

But, he was not content with taking one life,
For the hard-hearted Doctor next poisoned my wife.
The thoughts of foul play at length flashed on our mind,
They opened the bodies and poison did find.

He was then apprehended and tried in July.
And for these cruel murders condemned for to die
For my wife, and my daughter I am now left to mourn,
For alas! To my heart, they will never return.

* * *

ABOUT THE AUTHOR

Wendy was born in Yorkshire in the late 1950's; She moved to the coastal town of Filey in North Yorkshire with her husband and family in the middle 1990's. She studied English Literature at The Open University where she graduated with a BA (Hons) degree. She later went on to graduate from Teesside University with a Master's degree in Creative Writing.

Wendy has had many jobs from working in a library, a bank, a financial advisor, and former founder member of Norwich Union Direct, to owning a Bar/Restaurant. She now lives in Europe with her husband, rescue dog Lolli and four cats.

* * *

THANK YOU

I do hope that you enjoyed my true Victorian story. The doctor was indeed a nasty piece of work. How his poor victims must have suffered. Hopefully, you found the book interesting and will recommend it to others who enjoy true historical crime-fact-based fiction.

If you enjoyed it, I really would appreciate a review on Amazon and Goodreads.

* * *